SCHOTT'S
QUINTESSENTIAL
MISCELLANY

A good title page ought, methinks, like a bill of fare at a tavern, to contain such a list of the articles dished up by the literary cook for the entertainment of the public, as may enable his reader at once to determine, whether the book contains any thing likely to suit his taste and palate.

– *The London Budget of Wit*, 1817

SCHOTT'S
QUINTESSENTIAL
MISCELLANY

Conceived, written, and designed by

BEN SCHOTT

BLOOMSBURY
NEW YORK · BERLIN · LONDON · SYDNEY

Schott's Quintessential Miscellany™

© BEN SCHOTT 2011 - All rights reserved

Published by Bloomsbury USA, New York
175 Fifth Avenue, New York, NY 10010, USA

First US Edition 2011

www.benschott.com - @benschott (on Twitter)

ı   ıı   ııı   ıı   ıı   ııı   ııı   ıııı   ıııı   ııı   -
                   ıı   ıı   ııı   ııı   ıııı   ıııı   ııı

Also by Ben Schott, and published by Bloomsbury USA
Schott's Original Miscellany (2003)
Schott's Food & Drink Miscellany (2004)
Schott's Sporting, Gaming, & Idling Miscellany (2005)
Schott's Almanac 2007 · Schott's Miscellany 2008, 2009

Cover illustration by Alison Lang. © Ben Schott 2011. All rights reserved.
Proof correction marks on pp.90–91 courtesy of Sir Harold Evans.

ISBN 978-1-60819-021-8
Library of Congress Cataloging-in-Publication Data have been applied for.

All papers used by Bloomsbury USA are natural, recyclable products made from
wood grown in well-managed forests. The manufacturing processes conform
to the environmental regulations of the country of origin.

Designed and typeset by BEN SCHOTT
Printed in the USA by Worzalla, Stevens Point, Wisconsin

A NOTE ON SOURCES: Where no specific source is given, the excerpt is proverbial, widely quoted, constructed from public domain sources, or a combination of these. ❦ A NOTE ON SAUCES: Debate exists as to the difference, if any, between sauce and gravy. Some claim that sauce is that poured *over* a dish whereas gravy is that upon which a dish *rests*. Others claim that while sauce can be poured over anything, gravy can only properly be poured over meat. Perhaps the most convincing distinction is that gravy is a substance made from the juices of meat, whereas sauce can be made from any ingredients. (It is curious that there is a 'gravy train', but not a 'sauce train'.) According to Wilfred Granville's *Dictionary of Theatrical Terms* (1952), actors know 'gravy' as 'easy laughs from a friendly audience', or 'good lines, or business, in a farce or comedy'.

SCHOTT'S
QUINTESSENTIAL
MISCELLANY

A Quaaltagh[1]? A Quab[2]? A Quaedam[3]? A Quaesitum[4]? A Quaestor[5]?
A Quaffer[6]? A Qualimeter[7]? A Quelet[8]? A Quellenforschung[9]?
A Querencia[10]? A Querent[11]? A Quisby[12]? A Quodlibet[13]? A Quoz[14]?

Quite. *Schott's Quintessential Miscellany* aims to be all of these, and more.

In alchemy, the QUINTESSENCE is the fifth element which incorruptibly
and ethereally binds air, earth, fire, and water to form the heavens and,
according to Isaac Newton (1642–1727), 'the condensed spirit of the world'.

Some 350 years ago the German alchemist Johann Glauber (1604–68) gave
these instructions for obtaining the quintessence of all metals and minerals:

> *Dissolve gold, or any other metal (save silver), in the strongest spirit of salt, and
> draw off the water in balneo* [a narrow-necked glass vessel in a water bath]. *To that
> which remains pour on the best rectified spirit of wine, and put it to digesting,
> until the oil be elevated to the top, as red as blood, which is the tincture and
> quintessence of that material, being a most precious treasure in medicine.*

By an odd coincidence – also relying heavily on the spirit of wine – this is
exactly the same method used to select and distil the contents of this book.

On a good day, alchemy and miscellany have a lot in common. Both seek 'a
lower kind of heaven', as the Swiss alchemist Paracelsus (1493–1541) said, 'by
which the sun is separated from the moon, day from night, medicine from
poison, what is useful from what is refuse'. Now and then, they strike gold.
(If readers notice any base metals despoiling these pages, they are invited to email ben@benschott.com)

:: :: ::

[1] The first person one meets on a special occasion (e.g., New Year's Day, or on beginning a journey).
[2] A quagmire of quicksand. [3] A woman who is no better than she ought to be. [4] The solution
to a conundrum. [5] A church official who grants indulgences in exchange for alms. [6] A drink that
is especially pleasant. [7] A machine that measures the power of x-rays. [8] A collection or gathering.
[9] The study of a literary work's sources. [10] The area of the ring in which the bull takes his stance and,
by extension, any place where someone feels comfortable or at home. [11] One who makes inquiries.
[12] One who idles. [13] A fantasia or medley of various themes. [14] A curious, strange, or absurd thing.

Peter Piper's Polite Preface

Peter Piper Puts Pen to Paper, to Produce his Peerless Production, Proudly Presuming it will Please Princes, Peers, and Parliaments, and Procure him the Praise and Plaudits of the Progeny and Posterity, as he can Prove it Positively to be a Paragon, or Playful, Palatable, Proverbial, Panegyrical, Philosophical, Philanthropical, Phaenomenon of Productions.

– ANON, The Bodley Head, 1926

Eight years on from *Schott's Original Miscellany* there are a myriad of people to thank. They know who they are — but in case they've forgotten:

Pavia Rosati · Jonathan, Judith, Geoff, Oscar, Otto Schott · Anette Schrag

Ben Adams, Richard & Jenny Album, Clare Algar,
Stephen Aucutt, Catherine Best, Martin Birchall,
Keith Blackmore, Kim Bost, John Casey, Julia Clark,
Claire Cock-Starkey, James Coleman, Martin Colyer,
Victoria Cook, Aster Crawshaw, Rosemary Davidson,
Jody Davies, Liz Davies, Colin Dickerman, Robert Doak,
David Driver, Mary Duenwald, Jennifer Epworth,
Sir Harold Evans, Alona Fryman, George Gibson,
Tobin Harshaw, Catherine Haughney, Jon Hill,
Mark Hubbard, Gill Hudson, Nick Humphrey,
Honor Jones, Max Jones, Maureen Klier, Snigdha Koirala,
Alison Lang, Annik La Farge, John Lloyd, Ruth Logan,
Mark Lotto, Bess Lovejoy, Chris Lyon, Iona Macdonald,
Carmel McCoubrey, Sharon McCulloch, Jess Manson,
Sara Mercurio, Aviva Michaelov, David Miller, Sarah Miller,
Polly Napper, Nigel Newton, Sarah Norton, Alex O'Connell,
Cally Poplak, Dave Powell, Alexandra Pringle, Brian Rea,
James Sanders, Sarah Sands, Leanne Shapton, David Shipley,
Rachel Simhon, Sarah Spankie, Bill Swainson, Caroline Turner,
Greg Villepique, Rett Wallace, and Lily Weisberg.

Schott's Quintessential Miscellany would not exist were it not for the readers of the previous three *Miscellanies* who – from countries across the globe – have been unstinting in their support, eagle-eyed in their observations, and generous with their suggestions. To date, some 2,500,000 *Miscellanies* have been sold – translated into more than 20 languages, including Braille.

Some of the entries herein first appeared in columns published by the *Daily Telegraph* on Saturdays between 2003–05; a few come from the *Times*, *Condé Nast Traveller*, and *Reader's Digest*; and a smattering were first seen on the Op-Ed page of the *New York Times*. Grateful thanks are extended to the editors and designers of all of these august publications.

ANIMAL HYBRIDS OF NOTE

Animal hybrids are created when two animals of similar species mate; the results are generally sterile and short-lived. Below are some examples:

Bison + cow	BEEFALO†	♀ lion + ♂ tiger	TIGON
♀ llama + ♂ camel	CAMA	Cow + yak	YAKOW
♀ donkey + ♂ horse	HINNY	♀ horse + ♂ zebra	ZORSE
♂ leopard + ♀ lion	LEOPON	♀ donkey + ♂ zebra	ZEDONK
♀ tiger + ♂ lion	LIGER	♀ shetland pony + ♂ zebra	
♀ horse + ♂ donkey	MULE		ZETLAND
Sheep + goat	SHOAT (or GEEP)		
Swan + goose	SWOOSE		

† Usually ⅜ bison + ⅝ domestic cow, the meat is used in the US as a beef alternative.

TIGGERS

After exhausting research, it seems that Tiggers like best *extract of malt*. They dislike *honey*, *haycorns*, *thistles*, and *everything in Kanga's cupboard*. Tiggers also like to *bounce* – an activity that seems to make them bigger.

THE LIFE & DEATH OF A APPLE PIE

A Apple Pie	*J* Join'd it	*S* Stole it
B Bit it	*K* Kept it	*T* Took it
C Cut it	*L* Long'd for it	*U* Upset it
D Dealt it	*M* Mourn'd for it	*V* View'd it
E Eat it	*N* Nodded at it	*W* Wanted it
F Fought for it	*O* Open'd it	*X, Y, Z,* and
G Got it	*P* Peep'd in it	*Ampersand* [see p.13]
H Had it	*Q* Quarter'd it	they all wish'd
I Inspected it	*R* Ran for it	for a piece in hand.

Equity sends questions to Law, Law sends questions back to Equity; Law finds it can't do this, Equity finds it can't do that; neither can so much as say it can't do anything, without this solicitor instructing and this counsel appearing for A, and that solicitor instructing and that counsel appearing for B; and so on through the whole alphabet, like the history of the Apple Pie.
— CHARLES DICKENS, *Bleak House*, 1852–53

KNIGHTLY VIRTUES

The eight virtues expected of a Knight Templar were:
Piety · Chastity · Modesty · Temperance · Truth · Loyalty · Generosity · Valor

---

ON CRUISING

Vessels *cruise* ON a particular coast; OFF a cape or town;
and IN a particular body of water – though they *cross* an ocean.

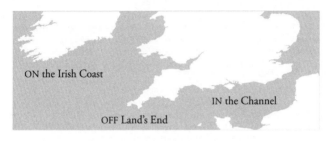

ON the Irish Coast

IN the Channel

OFF Land's End

PRESIDENT HU'S EIGHT DOs & DON'Ts

In 2006, Hu Jintao, China's president, proclaimed the following 'honors
and shames' to revivify the country's values. [Translation via chinaelections.net]

The HONOR of loving the motherland;
the SHAME of endangering the motherland.

The HONOR of serving the people;
the SHAME of turning away from the people.

The HONOR of upholding science;
the SHAME of ignorance and illiteracy.

The HONOR of industrious labor;
the SHAME of indolence.

The HONOR of togetherness and cooperation;
the SHAME of profiting at the expense of others.

The HONOR of honesty and keeping one's word;
the SHAME of abandoning morality for profit.

The HONOR of discipline and obedience;
the SHAME of lawlessness and disorder.

The HONOR of striving arduously;
the SHAME of wallowing in luxury.

WEDDING TRADITION SYMBOLISM

Something ... OLD (*the bride's past and her family*) · NEW (*the future*)
BORROWED (*passing on of good luck*) · BLUE (*purity and innocence*)
& A SILVER SIXPENCE IN HER SHOE (*wealth*)

———— EARLY PHILADELPHIA DIRECTORIES ————

The American Bibliopolist for June–July 1871 informs us that the first Philadelphia Directories were published in the year 1785, and notes that one – McPherson's – 'contains some things worth making a note of' – viz:

Some persons do not seem to have comprehended the object of the inquiries made of the inhabitants as to their names and occupations; supposing, perhaps, that they had some connection with taxation. The answers given by such are put down in the Directory as the names of the respondents. Thus – :

'I won't tell you,' 3 Maiden's Lane
'I won't tell it,' 15 Sugar Alley
'I won't tell you my name,' 160 New Market Street
'I won't have it numbered,' 478 Greene Street
'I won't tell my name,' 185 St John Street
'I shall not give you my name,' 43 Stamper's Alley
'What you please,' 49 Market Street

———— MARITIME DECLARATION OF HEALTH ————

Under maritime law, masters of vessels are obliged to answer the following questions (and provide relevant details) when they arrive at foreign ports:

1. Has any person died on board during the voyage otherwise than as a result of accident?
2. Is there on board or has there been during the international voyage any case of disease which you suspect to be of an infectious nature?
3. Has the total number of ill passengers during the voyage been greater than normal/expected?
4. Is there any ill person on board now?
5. Was a medical practitioner consulted?
6. Are you aware of any condition on board which may lead to infection or spread of disease?
7. Has any sanitary measure (e.g., quarantine, isolation, disinfection or decontamination) been applied on board?
8. Have any stowaways been found on board?
9. Is there a sick animal or pet on board?

'Note: In the absence of a surgeon, the Master should regard the following symptoms as grounds for suspecting the existence of a disease of an infectious nature: (a) fever, persisting for several days or accompanied by (i) prostration; (ii) decreased consciousness; (iii) glandular swelling; (iv) jaundice; (v) cough or shortness of breath; (vi) unusual bleeding; or (vii) paralysis (b) with or without fever: (i) any acute skin rash or eruption; (ii) severe vomiting (other than sea sickness); (iii) severe diarrhea; or (iv) recurrent convulsions.'

—THE ONE WITH ALL THE 'FRIENDS' EPISODES—

The One ... Where Monica Gets a Roommate (*aka* Pilot) · With the Sonogram at the End · With the Thumb · With George Stephanopoulos · With the East German Laundry Detergent · With the Butt · With the Blackout · Where Nana Dies Twice · Where Underdog Gets Away · With the Monkey · With Mrs Bing · With the Dozen Lasagnas · With the Boobies · With the Candy Hearts · With the Stoned Guy · With Two Parts (1) · With Two Parts (2) · With All the Poker · Where the Monkey Gets Away · With the Evil Orthodontist · With the Fake Monica · With the Ick Factor · With the Birth · Where Rachel Finds Out ❤ With Ross's New Girlfriend · With the Breast Milk · Where Heckles Dies · With Phoebe's Husband · With Five Steaks and an Eggplant · With the Baby on the Bus · Where Ross Finds Out · With the List · With Phoebe's Dad · With Russ · With the Lesbian Wedding · After the Super Bowl (1) · After the Super Bowl (2) · With the Prom Video · Where Ross and Rachel ... You Know · Where Joey Moves Out · Where Eddie Moves In · Where Dr Ramoray Dies · Where Eddie Won't Go · Where Old Yeller Dies · With the Bullies · With the Two Parties · With the Chicken Pox · With Barry and Mindy's Wedding ❤ With the Princess Leia Fantasy · Where No One's Ready · With the Jam · With the Metaphorical Tunnel · With Frank Jr · With the Flashback · With the Race Car Bed · With the Giant Poking Device · With the Football · Where Rachel Quits · Where Chandler Can't Remember Which Sister · With All the Jealousy · Where Monica and Richard Are Just Friends · With Phoebe's Ex-Partner · Where Ross and Rachel Take a Break (1) · With the Morning After (2) · Without the Ski Trip · With the Hypnosis Tape · With the Tiny T-Shirt · With the Dollhouse · With the Chick and the Duck · With the Screamer · With Ross's Thing · With the Ultimate Fighting Champion · At the Beach ❤ With the Jellyfish · With the Cat · With the 'Cuffs · With the Ballroom Dancing · With Joey's New Girlfriend · With the Dirty Girl · Where Chandler Crosses the Line · With Chandler in a Box · Where They're Going to Party! · With the Girl from Poughkeepsie · With Phoebe's Uterus · With the Embryos · With Rachel's Crush · With Joey's Dirty Day · With All the Rugby · With the Fake Party · With the Free Porn · With Rachel's New Dress · With All the Haste · With All the Wedding Dresses · With the Invitation · With the Worst Best Man Ever · With Ross's Wedding (1) · With Ross's Wedding (2) ❤ After Ross Says Rachel · With All the Kissing · Hundredth · Where Phoebe Hates PBS · With the Kips · With the Yeti · Where Ross Moves In · With the Thanksgiving Flashbacks · With Ross's Sandwich · With the Inappropriate Sister · With All the Resolutions · With Chandler's Work Laugh · With Joey's Bag · Where Everybody Finds Out · With the Girl Who Hits Joey · With the Cop · With Rachel's Inadvertent Kiss · Where Rachel Smokes · Where Ross Can't Flirt · With the Ride Along · With the Ball · With Joey's Big Break · In Vegas (1) · In Vegas (2) ❤ After Vegas · Where Ross Hugs Rachel · With Ross's Denial · Where Joey Loses His Insurance · With Joey's Porsche · On the Last Night · Where Phoebe Runs · With Ross's Teeth · Where Ross Got High · With the Routine · With the Apothecary Table · With the Joke · With Rachel's Sister · Where Chandler Can't Cry · That Could Have Been (1) · That Could Have Been (2) · With Unagi · Where Ross Dates a Student · With Joey's Fridge · With Mac and C.H.E.E.S.E. · Where Ross Meets Elizabeth's Dad · Where Paul's the Man · With the Ring · With the Proposal (1) · With the Proposal (2) ❤ With Monica's Thunder · With Rachel's Book · With Phoebe's Cookies · With Rachel's Assistant · With the Engagement Picture · With the Nap Partners · With Ross's Library Book · Where Chandler Doesn't Like Dogs · With All the Candy · With the Holiday Armadillo · With All the Cheesecakes · Where They're Up All Night · Where Rosita Dies · Where They All Turn Thirty · {Friends: The Stuff You've Never Seen} · With Joey's New Brain · With the Truth About London · With the Cheap Wedding Dress · With Joey's Award · With Ross and Monica's Cousin · With Rachel's Big Kiss · With the Vows · With Chandler's Dad · With Monica and Chandler's Wedding (1) · With Monica and Chandler's Wedding (2) ❤ After 'I Do' · With the Red Sweater · Where Rachel Tells Ross ... With the Videotape · With Rachel's Date · With the Halloween Party · With the Stain · With the Stripper · With the Rumor · With Monica's Boots · With Ross's Step Forward · Where Joey Dates Rachel · Where Chandler Takes a Bath · With the Secret Closet · With the Birthing Video · Where Joey Tells Rachel · With the Tea Leaves · In Massapequa · With Joey's Interview · With the Baby Shower · With the Cooking Class · Where Rachel Is Late · Where Rachel Has a Baby (1) · Where Rachel Has a Baby (2) ❤ Where No One Proposes · Where Emma Cries · With the Pediatrician · With the Sharks · With Phoebe's Birthday Dinner · With the Male Nanny · With Ross's Inappropriate Song · With Rachel's Other Sister · With Rachel's Phone Number · With Christmas in Tulsa · Where Rachel Goes Back to Work · With Phoebe's Rats · Where Monica Sings · With the Blind Dates · With the Mugging · With the Boob Job · With the Memorial Service · With the Lottery · With Rachel's Dream · With the Soap Opera Party · With the Fertility Test · With the Donor · In Barbados (1) · In Barbados (2) ❤ After Joey and Rachel Kiss · Where Ross Is Fine · With Ross's Tan · With the Cake · Where Rachel's Sister Babysits · With Ross's Grant · With the Home Study · With the Late Thanksgiving · With the Birth Mother · Where Chandler Gets Caught · Where the Stripper Cries · With Phoebe's Wedding · Where Joey Speaks French · With Princess Consuela · Where Estelle Dies · With Rachel's Going-Away Party · {With All the Other Ones (1) · With All the Other Ones (2)} · The Last One (1) · The Last One (2) [❤ Indicates a new season]

—— DELTA TAU CHI & OMEGA THETA PI ALUMNI ——

ΔTX *alumni*   *later became*

Robert Hoover, '63 .... Public Defender, Baltimore, Maryland
Larry 'Pinto' Kroger, '66 .... Editor, *National Lampoon* magazine
Eric 'Otter' Stratton, '63 .... gynecologist, Beverly Hills, California
Kent 'Flounder' Dorfman, '66 .... sensitivity trainer, Cleveland
Daniel 'D-Day' Simpson Day, '63 .... whereabouts unknown
John 'Bluto' Blutarsky .... US Senator, married Mandy Pepperidge
Donald 'Boon' Schoenstein .... married Katy (1964); divorced (1969)

ΩΘΠ *alumni*

Gregory Marmalard, '63 .... Nixon White House aide (raped in prison, 1974)
Douglas C. Neidermeyer, '63 .... killed in Vietnam by his own troops

———— THE CIRCLE OF THE MORAL WORLD ————

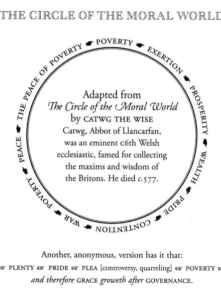

Adapted from
The Circle of the Moral World
by CATWG THE WISE
Catwg, Abbot of Llancarfan,
was an eminent c6th Welsh
ecclesiastic, famed for collecting
the maxims and wisdom of
the Britons. He died *c.*577.

[Circle labels, clockwise from top:] POVERTY ☛ EXERTION ☛ PROSPERITY ☛ WEALTH ☛ PRIDE ☛ CONTENTION ☛ WAR ☛ POVERTY ☛ PEACE ☛ THE PEACE OF POVERTY ☛ POVERTY

Another, anonymous, version has it that:

PEACE ☞ PLENTY ☞ PRIDE ☞ PLEA [controversy, quarreling] ☞ POVERTY ☞ PEACE
and therefore GRACE *groweth after* GOVERNANCE.

———————— ON LIFE ————————

The *Bread* of life is LOVE; the *Salt* of life is WORK;
The *Sweetness* of life, POESY; the *Water* of life, FAITH.

— ANNA JAMESON, *A Commonplace Book of Thoughts, Memories, & Fancies,* 1854

—— ON THE VARIOUS TYPES OF CHESS MATES ——

The QUEENE'S MATE	a *Gracious* mate
The BISHOP'S MATE	a *Gentle* mate
The KNIGHT'S MATE	a *Gallant* mate
The ROOKE'S MATE	a *Forcible* mate
The PAWNE'S MATE	a *Disgraceful* mate
The MATE BY DISCOVERY	the most *Industrious* mate of all
The MATE IN A CORNER OF THE FIELD	*Alexander's* mate
The MATE IN THE MIDDEST OF THE FIELD	an *Unfortunate* mate
The MATE ON THE SIDE OF THE FIELD	a *Coward's* mate
The BLINDE MATE	a *Shameful* mate
The STALE	a *Dishonorable* mate
The MATE AT TWO DRAUGHTES [moves]	a *Foole's* mate

– quoted by GEORGE H. SELKIRK, *The Book of Chess*, 1868

—— HOT-WEATHER VOCABULARY ——

HORSES *Sweat* ☞ MEN *Perspire* ☞ LADIES *Glow*

—— 'FAWLTY TOWERS' EPISODE GUIDE ——

Episode	*hotel sign reads*	*first aired*
A Touch of Class	FAWLTY TOWER*S*	19 ix 1975
The Builders	FAW*L*TY TOWER	26 ix 1975
The Wedding Party	FAW TY TO*W*ER	3 x 1975
The Hotel Inspectors	FAW TY TO ER	10 x 1975
Gourmet Night	WA RTY TOWELS	17 x 1975
The Germans	[no sign; episode opens on a hospital]	24 x 1975
Communication Problems	FAW*L*TY TOWER	19 ii 1979
The Psychiatrist	WATERY FOWLS	26 ii 1979
Waldorf Salad	FLAY OTTERS	5 iii 1979
The Kipper and the Corpse	FATTY OWLS	12 iii 1979
The Anniversary	FLOWERY TWATS	26 iii 1979
Basil the Rat	FARTY TOWELS	25 x 1979

—— AMPERSAND ——

& Some claim the ampersand symbol was devised in 63 BC by Marcus Tiro for his shorthand system, others that it is a ligature formed from the Latin 'et'. The word is said to be a conflation of 'and *per se*, and'.

M · A · S · H

MANSION · APARTMENT · SHACK · HOUSE

· SPOUSE ·	· HONEYMOON LOCATION ·
1 _____	1 _____
2 _____	2 _____
3 _____	3 _____
4 _____	4 _____
☠ _____	☠ _____

· CAR ·	· NUMBER OF KIDS ·
1 _____	1 _____
2 _____	2 _____
3 _____	3 _____
4 _____	4 _____
☠ _____	☠ _____

· DRESS COLOR / TUXEDO ·	· JOB ·
1 _____	1 _____
2 _____	2 _____
3 _____	3 _____
4 _____	4 _____
☠ _____	☠ _____

INSTRUCTIONS: PLAYER 1 completes the first four options in each category. PLAYER 2 picks the final option – typically an undesirable one (e.g., the *Shack* in the list of *Mansion, Apartment, Shack, House*). PLAYER 2 then draws hash marks until PLAYER 1 yells 'Stop'. The number of hash marks is the game standard. PLAYER 2 ticks off the options, crossing off the option at the standard number. PLAYER 2 continues counting and crossing off until there is only one option left in each category. The remaining options *foretell the future*.

ON THE SPELLING OF 'SCISSORS'

In January 1829, T. T. Barrow published the following list of 480 ways to spell the word 'scissors', noting: 'I am aware of many others but most of them are objectionable; you may probably be inclined to think those more than sufficient, and be led to inquire their use, which I must acknowledge is not an easy task to assign, but however, if any person should feel a longing desire to be an author; instead of lighting the fire of contention, and abusing his neighbors to his own detriment, let him try his hand at Scissars. If engaged in writing for the amusement of the public and cannot refrain from introducing subjects which may be prejudicial to the morals of the rising generation, had he not much better write nothing but Scissers.'

Scis-sars	Scyss-zors	Sys-sars	Ciss-zors	Scis-sarz	Scyss-zorz	Sys-sarz	Ciss-zorz
Scis-sers	Scyss-zurs	Sys-sers	Ciss-zurs	Scis-serz	Scyss-zurz	Sys-serz	Ciss-zurz
Scis-sirs	Scyss-zyrs	Sys-sirs	Ciss-zyrs	Scis-sirz	Scyss-zyrz	Sys-sirz	Ciss-zyrz
Scis-sors	Scyz-sars	Sys-sors	Ciz-sars	Scis-sorz	Scyz-sarz	Sys-sorz	Ciz-sarz
Scis-Surs	Scyz-sers	Sys-surs	Ciz-sers	Scis-Surz	Scyz-serz	Sys-surz	Ciz-serz
Scis-Syrs	Scyz-sirs	Sys-syrs	Ciz-sirs	Scis-Syrz	Scyz-sirz	Sys-syrz	Ciz-sirz
Scis-ars	Scyz-sors	Sys-ars	Ciz-sors	Scis-arz	Scyz-sorz	Sys-arz	Ciz-sorz
Scis-ers	Scyz-surs	Sys-ers	Ciz-surs	Scis-erz	Scyz-surz	Sys-erz	Ciz-surz
Scis-irs	Scyz-syrs	Sys-irs	Ciz-syrs	Scis-irz	Scyz-syrz	Sys-irz	Ciz-syrz
Scis-ors	Scyz-ars	Sys-ors	Ciz-ars	Scis-orz	Scyz-arz	Sys-orz	Ciz-arz
Scis-urs	Scyz-ers	Sys-urs	Ciz-ers	Scis-urz	Scyz-erz	Sys-urz	Ciz-erz
Scis-zars	Scyz-irs	Sys-zars	Ciz-irs	Scis-zarz	Scyz-irz	Sys-zarz	Ciz-irz
Scis-zers	Scyz-ors	Sys-zers	Ciz-ors	Scis-zerz	Scyz-orz	Sys-zerz	Ciz-orz
Scis-zirs	Scyz-urs	Sys-zirs	Ciz-urs	Scis-zirz	Scyz-urz	Sys-zirz	Ciz-urz
Scis-zors	Scyz-zars	Sys-zors	Ciz-zars	Scis-zorz	Scyz-zarz	Sys-zorz	Ciz-zarz
Scis-zurs	Scyz-zers	Sys-zurs	Ciz-zers	Scis-zurz	Scyz-zerz	Sys-zurz	Ciz-zerz
Scis-zyrs	Scyz-zirs	Sys-zyrs	Ciz-zirs	Scis-zyrz	Scyz-zirz	Sys-zyrz	Ciz-zirz
Sciss-zars	Scyz-zors	Syss-zars	Ciz-zors	Sciss-zarz	Scyz-zorz	Syss-zarz	Ciz-zorz
Sciss-zers	Scyz-zurs	Syss-zers	Ciz-zurs	Sciss-zerz	Scyz-zurz	Syss-zerz	Ciz-zurz
Sciss-zirs	Scyz-zyrs	Syss-zirs	Ciz-zyrs	Sciss-zirz	Scyz-zyrz	Syss-zirz	Ciz-zyrz
Sciss-zors	Sis-sars	Syss-zors	Cys-sars	Sciss-zorz	Sis-sarz	Syss-zorz	Cys-sarz
Sciss-zurs	Sis-sers	Syss-zurs	Cys-sers	Sciss-zurz	Sis-serz	Syss-zurz	Cys-serz
Sciss-zyrs	Sis-sirs	Syss-zyrs	Cys-sirs	Sciss-zyrz	Sis-sirz	Syss-zyrz	Cys-sirz
Sciz-sars	Sis-sors	Syz-sars	Cys-sors	Sciz-sarz	Sis-sorz	Syz-sarz	Cys-sorz
Sciz-sers	Sis-surs	Syz-sers	Cys-surs	Sciz-serz	Sis-surz	Syz-serz	Cys-surz
Sciz-sirs	Sis-syrs	Syz-sirs	Cys-syrs	Sciz-sirz	Sis-syrz	Syz-sirz	Cys-syrz
Sciz-sors	Sis-ars	Syz-sors	Cys-ars	Sciz-sorz	Sis-arz	Syz-sorz	Cys-arz
Sciz-surs	Sis-ers	Syz-surs	Cys-ers	Sciz-surz	Sis-erz	Syz-surz	Cys-erz
Sciz-syrs	Sis-irs	Syz-syrs	Cys-irs	Sciz-syrz	Sis-irz	Syz-syrz	Cys-irz
Sciz-ars	Sis-ors	Syz-ars	Cys-ors	Sciz-arz	Sis-orz	Syz-arz	Cys-orz
Sciz-ers	Sis-urs	Syz-ers	Cys-urs	Sciz-erz	Sis-urz	Syz-erz	Cys-urz
Sciz-irs	Sis-zars	Syz-irs	Cys-zars	Sciz-irz	Sis-zarz	Syz-irz	Cys-zarz
Sciz-ors	Sis-zers	Syz-ors	Cys-zers	Sciz-orz	Sis-zerz	Syz-orz	Cys-zerz
Sciz-urs	Sis-zirs	Syz-urs	Cys-zirs	Sciz-urz	Sis-zirz	Syz-urz	Cys-zirz
Sciz-zars	Sis-zors	Syz-zars	Cys-zors	Sciz-zarz	Sis-zorz	Syz-zarz	Cys-zorz
Sciz-zers	Sis-zurs	Syz-zers	Cys-zurs	Sciz-zerz	Sis-zurz	Syz-zerz	Cys-zurz
Sciz-zirs	Sis-zyrs	Syz-zirs	Cys-zyrs	Sciz-zirz	Sis-zyrz	Syz-zirz	Cys-zyrz
Sciz-zors	Siss-zars	Syz-zors	Cyss-zar	Sciz-zorz	Siss-zarz	Syz-zorz	Cyss-zarz
Sciz-zurs	Siss-zers	Syz-zurs	Cyss-zers	Sciz-zurz	Siss-zerz	Syz-zurz	Cyss-zerz
Sciz-zyrs	Siss-zirs	Syz-zyrs	Cyss-zirs	Sciz-zyrz	Siss-zirz	Syz-zyrz	Cyss-zirz
Scys-sars	Siss-zors	Cis-sars	Cyss-zors	Scys-sarz	Siss-zorz	Cis-sarz	Cyss-zorz
Scys-sers	Siss-zurs	Cis-sers	Cyss-zurs	Scys-serz	Siss-zurz	Cis-serz	Cyss-zurz
Scys-sirs	Siss-zyrs	Cis-sirs	Cyss-zyrs	Scys-sirz	Siss-zyrz	Cis-sirz	Cyss-zyrz
Scys-sors	Siz-sars	Cis-sors	Cyz-sars	Scys-sorz	Siz-sarz	Cis-sorz	Cyz-sarz
Scys-surs	Siz-sers	Cis-surs	Cyz-sers	Scys-surz	Siz-serz	Cis-surz	Cyz-serz
Scys-syrs	Siz-sirs	Cis-syrs	Cyz-sirs	Scys-syrz	Siz-sirz	Cis-syrz	Cyz-sirz
Scys-ars	Siz-sors	Cis-ars	Cyz-sors	Scys-arz	Siz-sorz	Cis-arz	Cyz-sorz
Scys-ers	Siz-surs	Cis-ers	Cyz-surs	Scys-erz	Siz-surz	Cis-erz	Cyz-surz
Scys-irs	Siz-syrs	Cis-irs	Cyz-syrs	Scys-irz	Siz-syrz	Cis-irz	Cyz-syrz
Scys-ors	Siz-ars	Cis-ors	Cyz-ars	Scys-orz	Siz-arz	Cis-orz	Cyz-arz
Scys-urs	Siz-ers	Cis-urs	Cyz-ers	Scys-urz	Siz-erz	Cis-urz	Cyz-erz
Scys-zars	Siz-irs	Cis-zars	Cyz-irs	Scys-zarz	Siz-irz	Cis-zarz	Cyz-irz
Scys-zers	Siz-ors	Cis-zers	Cyz-ors	Scys-zerz	Siz-orz	Cis-zerz	Cyz-orz
Scys-zirs	Siz-urs	Cis-zirs	Cyz-urs	Scys-zirz	Siz-urz	Cis-zirz	Cyz-urz
Scys-zors	Siz-zars	Cis-zors	Cyz-zars	Scys-zorz	Siz-zarz	Cis-zorz	Cyz-zarz
Scys-zurs	Siz-zers	Cis-zurs	Cyz-zers	Scys-zurz	Siz-zerz	Cis-zurz	Cyz-zerz
Scys-zyrs	Siz-zirs	Cis-zyrs	Cyz-zirs	Scys-zyrz	Siz-zirz	Cis-zyrz	Cyz-zirz
Scyss-zars	Siz-zors	Ciss-zars	Cyz-zors	Scyss-zarz	Siz-zorz	Ciss-zarz	Cyz-zorz
Scyss-zers	Siz-zurs	Ciss-zers	Cyz-zurs	Scyss-zerz	Siz-zurz	Ciss-zerz	Cyz-zurz
Scyss-zirs	Siz-zyrs	Ciss-zirs	Cyz-zyrs	Scyss-zirz	Siz-zyrz	Ciss-zirz	Cyz-zyrz

NUMERICAL MORALITY

KEEP 10 [Commandments] ☞ FLEE 7 [sins] ☞ USE WELL 5 [senses] ☞ WIN HEAVEN

ON SMOKING CIGARS & READING THE NEWS

GRAMMATICAL SMOKING · As smoking is an innocent indulgence, and as it is customary with people of all classes to relate the news of the day with cigars in their mouths; and as the generality of smokers make an awkward appearance, in consequence of their ignorance of the theory of punctuation in smoking, the following system is recommended:

A *simple puff* serves for a COMMA; *'Puff, puff,* a SEMICOLON; *'Puff, puff, puff,* a COLON; *Six puffs,* a PERIOD. *A pause,* with a cigar kept in the mouth, represents a DASH, longer or shorter in continuance. With the *under lip raise the cigar almost against the nose,* for an EXCLAMATION. And to express GREAT EMOTION, even to the SHEDDING OF TEARS, only raise, as before, the cigar to the *end of the nose.* For an INTERROGATION, it is only necessary to open the lips and draw the cigar round the *corner of the mouth.* Taking the cigar *from the mouth,* and *shaking the ashes from the end,* is the conclusion of a PARAGRAPH. And *throwing it in the fire* is a FINAL AND STYLISH PAUSE. Never begin a story with a half-smoked cigar; for to light another while conversing, is not only a breach of politeness, but interferes with the above system of punctuation, and destroys all harmony of expression.

– 'From a New York Paper' quoted in *The Portfolio of Entertaining & Instructive Varieties in History, Literature, Fine Arts, &c.,* 1829

SOFTWARE TYPES OF NOTE

Abandonware ..... *'old' software seemingly no longer supported by its creator*
Adware .... *obliges you to view ads before or while using*
Beggarware, Guiltware, Nagware...
　　　　　　　　　　 asks, pesters, or shames you to send payment or a donation
Demoware, Crippleware.................*time- or function-limited software*
Freeware... *distributed for free, but often with a catch (like those in this list)*
Malware .... *designed to harm a computer (e.g., a virus)*
Postcardware ....*requests you to send the author a thank-you postcard*
Rogueware .... *malware masquerading as anti-spyware*
Shareware ....*asks for (or later requires) registration or payment*
Spyware .... *maliciously designed to monitor or control a computer*
Vaporware.... *hyped software (often a 'new version') that fails to materialize*

1, 2, 3, 4, &c.

Single	Simplex	Monad	Solo	Primary	Monometer
Double	Duplex	Dyad	Duo	Secondary	Dimeter
Triple	Triplex	Triad	Trio	Tertiary	Trimeter
Quadruple	Quadruplex	Tetrad	Quartet	Quaternary	Tetrameter
Quintuple	*Quintuplex*	Pentad	Quintet	Quinary	Pentameter
Sextuple	Sextuplex	Hexad	Sextet	Senary	Hexameter
Septuple	*Septuplex*	Heptad	*Septet*	Septenary	Heptameter
Octuple	Octuplex	Octad	Octet	Octonary	Octameter
Nonuple	*Nonuplex*	Ennead†	Nonet	Nonary	*Nonameter*
Decuple	*Decuplex*	Decad	Dectet	Denary	Decameter

† In Egyptian mythology the Ennead referred to the nine gods worshipped at Yunu (Heliopolis). These gods were Ra the Sun (or Atum) and four descendant pairs of male and female twins: Shu & Tefnut, Geb & Nut, Isis & Osiris, and Set & Nebthet. [Italics signify a word is not in the *Oxford English Dictionary*.]

BROTHERS OF NOTE

Brother ... a fellow ...	Bung . . . . *tapster or brewer*	Gusset . . . . *pimp*	Shuttle . . . . *weaver*
Angle . . . *angler or fisherman*	Buskin . . . . *comedian or actor*	Jonathan . . . . *American*	Smut . . . . *friend*
Benedict . . . . *married man*	Chip . . . . *carpenter*	Mason . . . . *Freemason*	Starling . . . *who shares a woman*
Birch . . . . *schoolmaster*	Clergyman . . . . . . *clergyman*	Quill . . . . . . *author or writer*	Stitch . . . . *tailor*
Blade . . . . *soldier*	Coif . . . . *sergeant at law*	Robe . . . . *judge*	String . . . . *violinist*
Brush . . . . *painter*	Crispin . . . . *shoemaker*	Salt (or Tar) . . *seaman or sailor*	Whip . . . . *coachman*

——————— THE VARIOUS FORMS OF LAUGHTER ———————

[1] The *wide-mouthed* or *indecent*. [2] The *gracious* laugh, or the *smile*. [3] The laugh of *dignity* or *protection*. [4] The *silly* or *simple* laugh, which must be distinguished from the naturally ingenuous. [5] The *self-approving* laugh, or that of *sheer vanity*. [6] The laugh of *courtesy, civilized compact*, or *fashionable usage*. [7] The laugh of *affectation* or *disdain*. [8] The laugh of *sincerity, openness, invitation*, and *serenity*, that in a pleasing manner diffuses itself over the whole countenance. [9] The laugh of *hypocrisy* or *dissimulation*, or (according to the vulgar phrase) *in one's sleeve*; which must be distinguished from, [10] the laugh of *determined* and *absolute malice*. [11] The laugh *constrained*, is that observable when we make effort to repress an unseasonable impulse. [12] The laugh *extorted*, or *machinal*, is brought on by EXCESSIVE TICKLING, or by WOUNDS OF THE DIAPHRAGM, or by certain NOXIOUS BEVERAGES. [13] The laugh caused by a *sourness of the mind*, despite, resentfulness, desire of revenge, mixed with a certain pleasure that is in near alliance with pride. And, lastly, [14] The laugh *inextinguishable*, as Homer calls it in Greek, but that, in our vulgar phrase, may be expressed by the *outrageous* or *horselaugh*, whose explosive bursts we cannot stop. They so violently agitate our sides and breasts, as to throw the whole body into a kind of CONVULSIVE AGONY.

– ANON, 1769, quoted in *The Gentleman's Magazine*, 1837

In his handbook, *Voice Culture and Elocution* (1890), William T. Ross explored various forms of laughter and gave the following technical advice:

Laughter employs the abrupt stresses. It is as capable of development and culture as the other means of expression. Not only may individual laughter be encouraged and improved, but through practice different kinds may be learned for purposes of personation. Laughter – earnest, hearty laughter – is a health-promoting exercise, and one of the best means for strengthening the lungs. A tabulated arrangement of the different kinds of laughter is given below, and may be practiced as follows: First, simply as a vocal drill, then with full expression of hearty laughter. The long vowel, representing the drawl or vocal rest in hearty laughter, should be prolonged obscurely, and the syllable repeated six or more times in quick succession:

1	ē	hĭ	hĭ	hĭ	hĭ	hĭ	hĭ	THE GIGGLE
2	ā	hĕ	hĕ	hĕ	hĕ	hĕ	hĕ	
3	â	hă	hă	hă	hă	hă	hă	
4	ä	ha	ha	ha	ha	ha	ha	OPEN AND HEARTY
5	a	hŏ	hŏ	hŏ	hŏ	hŏ	hŏ	COARSE, UNCULTURED, HORSE, BOORISH
6	ō	hŭ	hŭ	hŭ	hŭ	hŭ	hŭ	
7	o	họ	họ	họ	họ	họ	họ	THE LAUGH OF THE MISER

——— INSTRUMENTS IN PETER & THE WOLF ———

Character	*instrument*		
Bird	flute	Grandfather	bassoon
Duck	oboe	Wolf	French horn
Cat	clarinet	Hunter	timpani & bass drum
		Peter	strings

——— HIGH ROAD TO SUICIDE ———

Foppery begat a spruce shop-boy ☞ A spruce shop-boy begat a pair of half boots ☞ A pair of half boots begat a little stick ☞ A little stick and the half boots begat ambition ☞ Ambition begat credit ☞ Credit begat a shop ☞ A shop begat a horse ☞ A horse begat a chaise ☞ A chaise begat a curricle† ☞ A curricle begat expenses ☞ Expenses begat a hazard table ☞ A hazard table begat losses ☞ Losses begat a bankruptcy ☞ A bankruptcy begat a gaol ☞ A gaol begat want and misery ☞ Want and misery begat a disregard for life ☞ And disregard for life begat suicide ☞ *Sic transit gloria mundi!*

– *Rural Repository*, published by W. B. Stoddard, 1833 [† A light two-horse carriage]

——— SAVOY OPERAS ———

The 'Savoy Operas' are the thirteen operettas (excluding *Thespis*) written by Arthur Sullivan and W. S. Gilbert. Although the first five were premiered elsewhere, the series is named after the Savoy Theatre in London.

Operetta	*first performed*		
Trial by Jury	1875	*Princess Ida*	1884
The Sorcerer	1877	*The Mikado*	1885
HMS Pinafore	1878	*Ruddigore*	1887
The Pirates of Penzance	1879	*The Yeomen of the Guard*	1888
Patience	1881	*The Gondoliers*	1889
Iolanthe	1882	*Utopia Limited*	1893
		The Grand Duke	1896

——— RELIGIOUS ENIGMA ———

It is said that the letters below were inscribed above the Ten Commandments in a chapel in Wales, where they remained an enigma for a hundred years before it was realized that the addition of a vowel revealed their truth.

P R S V R Y P R F C T M N   V R K P T H S P R C P T S T N

BY ADDING THE LETTER 'E' – PERSEVERE YE PERFECT MEN   EVER KEEP THESE PRECEPTS TEN

—————— BOONTLING ——————

Boontling is a curious dialect that emerged in Boonville – a town in Mendocino County, California. A 1969 article for *Time* traced the language back to one day in 1892, when 'Reg and Tom Burger and the Duff brothers started putting some of their old Scotch-Irish dialect words together with some on-the-spot code words into a language that the enemies – be they womenfolk, their rivals, their elders, their children – could not possibly understand. It caught on, rapidly losing its value as a code; soon "Boontlingers" and their friends were eagerly trying to *shark* [con] each other with new inventions.' Boontling neologisms derived from a range of sources, including Spanish, French, and Native American terms, and words adapted from scripture. However, many of the most curious inventions were allusions to local life. Thus, coffee was *zeese*, in honor of the hunter 'Z.C.', whose brew was legendarily strong; and a roaring fire was a *jeffer* after Jeff Vestal, whose grate was never dark. (Sexual intercourse was *ricky chow*, after the noise of the creaking bedsprings in the local hotel's honeymoon suite.) Boontling's heyday lasted until the 1920s, according to the linguist Charles C. Adams, who studied the language in the 1960s and wrote *Boontling: An American Lingo*. In 2001, Adams told the *San Francisco Chronicle* that Boontling was 'virtually obsolete', noting 'it really was a creature of a unique time and place'. Below is a very brief lexicon of Boontling terminology.

Ab	to push into a line	*Ink stands*	hemorrhoids
Airtight	a sawmill	*Jimheady*	confused
Apple-head	young girl(friend)	*Kilokety*	to travel by train
Bahl	good (quality)	*Lockin'*	a wedding
Barl	to fire a gun	*Moosty*	a mustache
Barney man	a cowboy	*Netty*	to dress fancy
Belhoon	a dollar	*Nickelonk*	to play cards
Blood 'n' hair	a car accident	*Ose-draggy*	extremely tired
Briney glimmer	a lighthouse	*Ot*	to work hard
Buzz chick	baseball	*Plenty white*	snow
Chipmunk	to hoard/collect	*Pusseek*	a cat
Cock a fister on	to get in a fight	*Roopey harpin'*	empty talk
Doolsey	candy	*Spat*	22 rifle
Dreef	to jump about nervously	*Scratcher*	a chain saw
Eelstig	an old man	*Shoveltooth*	a medical doctor
Ex	to vote	*Tune a fiddle*	to sharpen a saw
Fourth of Jeel	the Fourth of July	*Upper-cuttin*	a fistfight
Fuzzy tail	a horse	*Visalia*	a roping saddle
Glimmers	reading glasses	*Walter Levi*	a telephone
Grizz	an old bachelor	*Wess*	to fib
Haines-crispin	a feud	*Yebbelow*	to talk
High git	to become drunk	[Source: Mendocino Unified School Dist]	

————————— 'A SERIES' PAPER SIZES —————————

mm	A SIZE	*inches*
1,189×841	A0	46·8×33·1
841×594	A1	33·1×23·4
594×420	A2	23·4×16·5
420×297	A3	16·5×11·7
297×210	A4	11·7×8·3
210×148	A5	8·3×5·8
148×105	A6	5·8×4·1

105×74	A7	4·1×2·9
74×52	A8	2·9×2·0
52×37	A9	2·0×1·5
37×26	A10	1·5×1·0

US PAPER SIZES

216×279	letter	8·5×11
216×356	legal	8·5×14

————————— THREE TYPES OF MEN TO AVOID —————————

With three sorts of men enter into no serious friendship – the UNGRATEFUL man, the MULTILOQUIOUS man, or the COWARD; the 1st *cannot prize thy favors*; the 2nd *cannot keep thy counsel*; the 3rd *dare not vindicate thy honor.*

HAILSTONE SIZE EQUIVALENCE

Description	diameter (inches)
Pea	0·25
Marble or mothball	0·50
Penny or dime	0·75
Nickel	0·88
Quarter	1·00
Half dollar	1·25
Walnut or Ping-Pong ball	1·50
Golf ball	1·75
Hen's egg	2·00
Tennis ball	2·50
Baseball	2·75
Teacup	3·00
Grapefruit	4·00
Softball	4·50

[Source: NOAA]

CHIEF WEAPONS OF THE SPANISH INQUISITION

Fear · Surprise · Ruthless efficiency · An almost fanatical
devotion to the Pope · Nice red uniforms – MONTY PYTHON

LEGAL ANIMUS

with the intention of …	
Animus cancellandi	canceling
Animus defamandi	defaming
Animus derelinquendi	disowning
Animus furandi	stealing
Animus injuriandi	causing injury
Animus lucrandi	gaining
Animus manendi	remaining
Animus possidendi	possessing
Animus recuperandi	recovering
Animus republicandi	republishing
Animus residendi	residing
Animus revocandi	revoking
Animus testandi	making a will

ADVICE

Go not for every *grief* to the PHYSICIAN,
for every *quarrel* to the LAWYER, nor for every *thirst* to the POT.

– attributed to GEORGE HERBERT. It has also been said, 'There are three persons whom you
should NEVER DECEIVE: your PHYSICIAN, your CONFESSOR, and your LAWYER.' And, 'the
wisest man will never thoroughly UNDERSTAND: HIMSELF, his WIFE, and his BEST FRIEND.'

SEASONAL GODS

Spring	MERCURY
Summer	APOLLO
Autumn	BACCHUS
Winter	HERCULES

FAT TRAVELERS

If fat men ride, they tire the horse,
and if they walk themselves that's
worse: Travel at all, they are at best,
Either OPPRESSORS or OPPRESSED.

AIRPORT RUNWAY MARKINGS

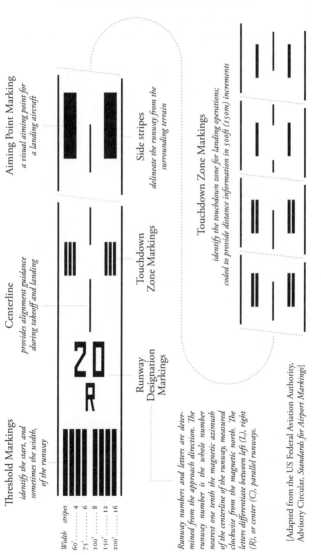

Aiming Point Marking
a visual aiming point for a landing aircraft

Side stripes
delineate the runway from the surrounding terrain

Centreline
provides alignment guidance during takeoff and landing

Touchdown Zone Markings

Touchdown Zone Markings
identify the touchdown zone for landing operations; coded to provide distance information in 500ft (150m) increments

Threshold Markings
identify the start, and sometimes the width, of the runway

Width	stripes
60'	4
75'	6
100'	8
150'	12
200'	16

Runway Designation Markings

Runway numbers and letters are determined from the approach direction. The runway number is the whole number nearest one tenth the magnetic azimuth of the centreline of the runway, measured clockwise from the magnetic north. The letters differentiate between left (L), right (R), or center (C), parallel runways.

[Adapted from the US Federal Aviation Authority, *Advisory Circular, Standards for Airport Markings*]

TIMEPIECE OF COURTING

Below is an anonymous c18th 'timepiece' to guide a gentleman's courtship. Curiously, in giving advice for every hour, it leaves no time for sleep.

WINDCHILL

Windchill – the cooling effect of air as it passes across the skin – can be critical in extreme cold, because frostbite forms more quickly in windy conditions. One of the earliest windchill indexes was devised by Antarctic explorers Siple and Passel, who, in 1940, calculated heat loss from water as it froze in a plastic container suspended from a pole. The formula now most widely used – created by Osczevski and Bluestein – is reproduced below; at its most simple, a 10 mph wind will make 32°F feel like 24°F.

$$\text{Windchill (°F)} = 35.74 + 0.6215T - 35.75(V^{0.16}) + 0.4275T(V^{0.16})$$
$$\text{where } T = \text{air temperature (°F) and } V = \text{wind speed (mph)}$$

—— MYSTERY INC. ——

❤ { Frederick Herman Jones }
  { Daphne Ann(e) Blake } ❤
Velma (Dace/Eugenia) Dinkley
Norville 'Shaggy' Rogers
and
Scooby-Doo (a Great Dane)

—— ON TEARS ——

There are 6 sorts of tears
~ 3 good and 3 bad ~
Those caused by *smoke*, *grief*,
or *constipation* are BAD; and those
caused by *fragrant spices*, *laughter*,
and *aromatic herbs* are GOOD.

– HEBRAIC FOLKLORE

—— TYPES OF SNEAK ——

MORNING SNEAK
*One who pilfers early in the
morning, before it is light.*

EVENING SNEAK
A late-night pilferer.

UPRIGHT SNEAK
*One who steals pewter
pots from the alehouse boys
employed to collect them.*

SNEAKING BUDGE
One that robs alone.
(A STANDING BUDGE is a thief's spy.)

TO GO UPON THE SNEAK
*To steal into houses whose
doors are carelessly left open.*

– *Lexicon Balatronicum*, 1811, &c.

—— NOT TRIFLING ——

A Burmese proverb maintains
that a wise man should not
despise as trifling: a NOBLEMAN,
a SNAKE, FIRE, or a PRIEST.

- NINE POINTS OF LAW -

To him that goes to law
NINE THINGS *are needed:*

In the first place
a good deal of money,
Secondly, *a good deal
of patience,*
Thirdly, *a good cause,*
Fourthly, *a good attorney,*
Fifthly, *good counsel,*
Sixthly, *good evidence,*
Seventhly, *a good jury,*
Eighthly, *a good judge,*
And ninthly, *good luck*!

—— 3 TYPES OF MEN ——

There are but three classes of men:

THE RETROGRADE

THE STATIONARY

THE PROGRESSIVE

– JOHANN KASPAR LAVATER (1741–1801)

—— MONOCULAR MAN ——

A SEVEN-SIDED ANIMAL was a slang
term for a ONE-EYED MAN, with an:
*inside, outside, left side, right side,
foreside, backside,* and a *blind side.*

─── TINTIN & THE FOREIGN TRANSLATORS ───

French	Tintin	Milou	Capitaine Haddock	Dupont et Dupond
Afrikaans	Kuifie	Spokie	Kaptein Sardijn	Uys en Buys
Arabic	Tin Tin	Milou	Captain Haddock	Tik-Tak
Bengali	Tin Tin	Kuttush	Captain Haddock	Jonson & Ronson
Catalan	Tintin	Milu	Capità Haddock	Dupont i Dupond
Danish	Tintin	Terry	Kaptajn Haddock	Dupont og Dupond
Dutch	Kuifie	Bobbie	Kapitein Haddock	Jansen en Janssen
English	Tintin	Snowy	Captain Haddock†	Thomson & Thompson
Finnish	Tintti	Milou	Kapteeni Haddock	Dupont ja Dupond
German	Tim	Struppi	Kapitän Haddock	Schultze und Schulze
Greek	Ten-Ten	Milou	Kapetanié Xantok	O Ntupon O Ntupont
Icelandic	Tinni	Tobbi	Kolbeinn Kapteinn	Skapti og Skafti
Iranian	Tainetaine	Milou	Capitane Hàdock	Douponte & Doupon(t)e
Italian	Tintin	Milù	Capitano Haddock	Dupont e Dupond
Japanese	Tan Tan	Snowy	Hadock	Dupont-Duvont
Polish	Tintin	Miluś	Kapitan Barylka	Tajniak i Jawniak
Portuguese	Tintim	Milu	Capião Haddock	Dupont e Dupond
Spanish	Tintín	Milú	Capitán Haddock	Hernández y Fernández
Syldavian	Ťîñţįñ	Šżpłùǧ	Ķâpıţäär̈ Háđđöčk	Țhømsôň ð Țhómpsôň
Turkish	Tenten	Milu	Kaptan Haddok	Düpont ve Düpond

† Tirades include: *Billions of blue blistering barnacles! · Wretch! Ignoramus! Abominable snowman! · You miserable iconoclast! · Get going, filibusters! Buzz off, you weevils! Be off with you, slubberdegullions! · Patagonians! Bashi-bazouks! Carpet-sellers! Kleptomaniacs! · Stand back, anachronisms! Keep off, you imitation Incas, you! · You dunderheaded Ethelreds! · You moth-eaten marmot! · Swine! Jellyfish! Tramps! Troglodytes! Toffee-noses! · Ten thousand thundering typhoons!*

─── PAUL SIMON'S ZOOLOGICAL ANALYSIS ───

Animal	*characteristic*		
Monkeys	honest	Zookeepers	predilection for rum
Giraffes	insincere	Zebras	reactionary
Elephants	kindly, dumb	Antelopes	missionary
Orangutans	skeptical of change	Pigeons	secret plotters
		Hamsters	frequently 'turn on'

─── ON THE BEST THINGS ───

There is nothing *purer* than HONESTY; nothing *sweeter* than CHARITY; nothing *warmer* than LOVE; nothing *brighter* than VIRTUE; and nothing more *steadfast* than FAITH. These, united in one mind, form the *purest*, the *sweetest*, the *richest*, the *brightest*, and most *steadfast* HAPPINESS.   – ANON

─────────── ON DRESS CODES ───────────

BLACK TIE (or TUXEDO, SMOKING JACKET, DINNER JACKET, DJ, CRAVATE NOIRE) consists of a single- or double-breasted black (or midnight blue) dinner jacket, worn with matching trousers with a single row of braid down the leg, a soft white dress shirt, and a black bow tie. (Wing collars, cummerbunds, white jackets, and showy bow ties are to be avoided.) WHITE TIE consists of a black tailcoat worn with matching trousers with a double row of braid down the leg, a white stiff-fronted wing-collar shirt, a white waistcoat, and a white bow tie. MORNING COAT *or* DRESS consists of a morning coat, waistcoat, striped gray trousers, and (often) a top hat. Below are some of the more unusual dress codes to be found on formal invitations:

Bush shirt . . . *long- or short-sleeved (embroidered) shirt worn outside trousers*
Evening dress . . . . *white tie*
Informal . . . . *business suit or jacket with or without tie (not jeans)*
Island casual . . . .*Hawaiian shirt and casual (usually khaki) trousers*
Lounge suit . . . .*business suit and tie*
National dress . . . . *self-explanatory; if one has no national dress, a lounge suit*
Planters . . . .*long-sleeved white shirt with a tie and dark trousers*
Red Sea rig *or* Gulf rig . . . .*black tie (or lounge suit) without the jacket*
Tenue de Ville . . . . *business suit (sometimes national dress)*
Tenue Decontractée; Tenue de Détente . . . .*smart-casual*
Tenue de Gala . . . .*black tie*
Tenue de Sport/Voyage . . . .*sporting/traveling attire*
Tenue de Cérémonie . . . .*white tie*
Windsor Uniform . . . .*see below*

Dispute exists between sources, and different rules apply in military, academic, and ecclesiastical settings. This list follows the tradition of giving the requirements for male attire, on the understanding that women have an intuitive grasp of such things. ❦ Windsor Uniform consists of a dark blue evening tailcoat with scarlet at the collar and cuffs, worn with a white single-breasted waistcoat and plain black evening trousers. The buttons are gilt with a Garter Star within a Garter, surmounted by the Imperial Crown. Introduced by George III in 1779, the Uniform was discontinued by William IV, and revived by Queen Victoria. According to the Palace, the Uniform is worn by male members of the Royal Family and certain Royal Household staff, when approved by the Queen. ❦ The dress code for the wedding of Prince William and Catherine Middleton was: 'Uniform, Morning Coat, or Lounge Suit.'

─────────── ANON ON EATING OYSTERS ───────────

Oysters are a CRUEL MEAT, because *we eat them alive,*
An UNCHARITABLE MEAT, for *we leave nothing to the poor,*
And an UNGODLY MEAT, because *we never say grace.*

———— BEE CUSTOMS & SUPERSTITIONS ————

Many consider it unlucky to sell bees – insisting instead on barter. Others maintain that if bees are to be purchased, gold and wheat are the only lucky currencies.

It is generally held that bees must be informed of the death of their owner, or any death in the owner's family by 'telling the bees'.

In *The Apiary* (1878), Alfred Neighbour stated that French bee-keepers would place their bees in mourning in the event of a family death by draping their hives with black crêpe; red cloth would be used to mark family celebrations such as weddings and christenings.

'The sound of an echo is thought to drive away bees, therefore their hives ought to be placed where the echo or voice does not sound against.' [EDWARD SOMERSET, *A Thousand Notable Things*, 1822]

'Bees must also be treated politely.' One old writer said: "No creature is more wreakful, nor more fervent to take wreak, than is the Bee when he is wroth!" and so all news must be politely given in a whisper; if harshly spoken they will desert. Bees abhor all bad language, as a Northumbrian once remarked: "It wouldn't do to swear before the bees. They'd pretty soon leave the place."' [HILDA M. RANSOME, *The Sacred Bee in Ancient Times and Folklore*, 1937]

A bee flying into the house signals the arrival of a stranger. [Various]

'If thou wilt have the favour of thy Bees that they sting thee not, thou must avoid such things as offend them: thou must not be unchaste or uncleanly: for impurity and sluttishness (themselves being most chaste and neat) they utterly abhor … in a word, thou must be chaste, cleanly, sweete, sober, quiet, and familiar: so will they love thee, and know thee from all others.' [CHARLES BUTLER, *The Feminine Monarchie*, 1609]

'"News bees" buzzing near your head signifies good news; near your feet, bad news.' [FLETCHER DRESSLAR *Superstition and Education*, 1907]

The ashes of dead bees will cure flat feet, if placed in the shoe. [Various]

In Brittany, if a person who kept bees had his hive robbed, he gave them up immediately because they could never succeed afterwards. This idea rises from an old Breton proverb, which says, 'no luck after the robber'. [*Credulities Past & Present*]

'These bee-superstitions are living and flourishing. I believe it would be difficult to meet with any cottage bee-keeper who did not honestly think that his insects were endued with knowledge and sagacity beyond that of the rest of the brute creation, and sometimes beyond that of mankind.' [GEORGINA FREDERICA JACKSON, *Shropshire Folk-lore*, 1883]

It was believed by some that bees predicted war by becoming idle – hence the paucity of honey in 1939.

——— WWI TRENCH WARFARE SCHEMATIC ———

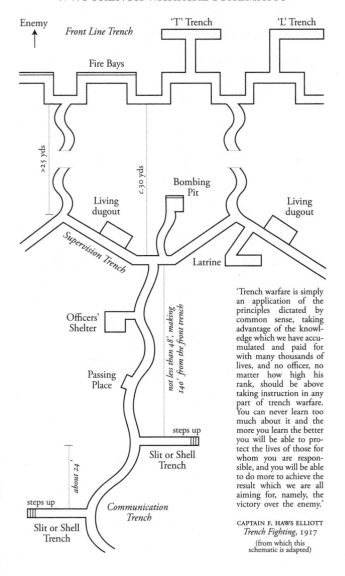

Enemy

Front Line Trench

'T' Trench

'L' Trench

Fire Bays

>25 yds

c.30 yds

Bombing Pit

Living dugout

Living dugout

Supervision Trench

Latrine

Officers' Shelter

not less than 48', making 140' from the front trench

Passing Place

steps up

Slit or Shell Trench

about 24'

steps up

Slit or Shell Trench

Communication Trench

'Trench warfare is simply an application of the principles dictated by common sense, taking advantage of the knowledge which we have accumulated and paid for with many thousands of lives, and no officer, no matter how high his rank, should be above taking instruction in any part of trench warfare. You can never learn too much about it and the more you learn the better you will be able to protect the lives of those for whom you are responsible, and you will be able to do more to achieve the result which we are all aiming for, namely, the victory over the enemy.'

CAPTAIN F. HAWS ELLIOTT
Trench Fighting, 1917
(from which this
schematic is adapted)

ELLIS ISLAND IMMIGRANT CHALK MARKS

Below are the chalk marks used to identify suspected medical conditions of immigrants seeking to enter the United States at Ellis Island, New York:

✗	suspected mental illness	K	hernia
⊗	definite signs of mental illness	L	lameness
B	back	N	neck
C	conjunctivitis	Pg	pregnancy
CT	trachoma[1]	P	physical & lungs
E	eyes	Sc	scalp (favus[3])
F	face	S	senility
FT	feet		
G	goiter[2]		
H	heart		

[1] An infectious eye disease. [2] A swelling of the thyroid gland. [3] A scalp infection.

FOOTWEAR LABELING SYMBOLS

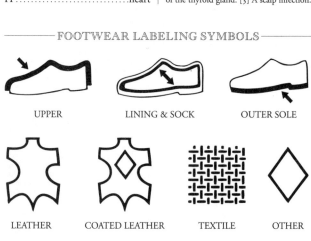

UPPER   LINING & SOCK   OUTER SOLE

LEATHER   COATED LEATHER   TEXTILE   OTHER

ON BELIEVING & COMMUNICATING NEWS

Let the greatest part of the news thou hearest, be the least part of what thou believest, lest the greatest part of what thou believest, be the least part of what is true; and report nothing for truth, in earnest or in jest, unless thou know it, or at least confidently believe it to be so; neither is it expedient at all times, or in all companies, to report what thou knowest to be true; sometimes it may avail thee, if thou seem not to know, that which thou knowest. Hast thou any secret, commit it not to many, nor to any, unless well known unto thee. – ? JOHN HALL, Bishop of Norwich (1574–*c.*1659)

──────── ANNUAL QUEEN BEE COLOR CODING ────────

Around the world, apiculturists (beekeepers) employ a series of color codes to identify queen bees and indicate their age. A smudge of harmless, quick-drying paint is applied to the thorax of the queen so that she stands out within the hive's population. It seems that the origin of this color coding derives from the work of the Nobel Laureate Austrian zoologist Karl von Frisch (1886–1982), who researched the language, orientation, and direction-finding of bees, as well as their senses of hearing, smell, and taste. A number of beekeeping journals change their jacket color annually to match the queen bee color coding system, which is as follows:

Color	last digit of year	example	mnemonic
WHITE	1 *or* 6	2011 / 2016	*Will*
YELLOW	2 *or* 7	2012 / 2017	*You*
RED	3 *or* 8	2013 / 2018	*Raise*
GREEN	4 *or* 9	2014 / 2019	*Good*
BLUE	5 *or* 0	2015 / 2020	*Bees?*

──────── THE CREW OF 'THE ITALIAN JOB' ────────

Below is the crew that helped Charlie Croker pull off *The Italian Job* (1969):

Bill Bailey[1] .... *Croker's No. 2; just done three years in Parkhurst*
Chris, Tony, Dominic................ *getaway drivers and 'chinless wonders'*
William........ *coach driver, known as 'Big William' for very obvious reasons*
Prof. Simon Peach[2] .. *in charge of all matters relating to the Turin computer*
Arthur, Frank, Rozza, Coco, Yellow, Camp Freddie[3] ..... *lads doing the job*
Roger, Dave, Lorna ....*in reserve with three fast cars*

1. *As honest as the day is long.* 2. *A man of reading with some 'very funny habits'.* 3. *You all know.*

──────── MUGGLETONIANS ────────

The Muggletonians were a curious English sect (*c.*1652) founded by Lodowick Muggleton and his cousin John Reeve, both second-rate London tailors. The founders claimed (and their followers believed) that they were the 'two last witnesses' foretold in Revelation 11:3–6. They preached that God had human form; that the Trinity was one; that the sun circled the earth; that Elijah was God's representative in heaven; and that Satan was incarnate in Eve. Reeve died in 1658, and Muggleton in 1698 – both had been jailed for blasphemy. Muggletonian belief struggled on for years, petering out during the 1860s, though the 'last Muggletonian' died in 1979.

AN ABECEDARY OF LOVE

A begins *Amor*, the
Latin for love,

B begins *Beauty*, which that
passion does move.

C stands for *Cupid*, that
wounder of hearts,

D for, with which he does
mischief, his *Darts*.

E begins *Eyes*, which lovers
oft name,

F what they raise in their
heart, a fierce *Flame*.

G lovers do use to set
forth their *Grief*,

H directs you to *Hope*,
the poor lover's relief.

I tells you great   J*oy*
blessed lovers   do find.

K in *Kissing* their charmers,
when once they grow kind.

L stands for *Languish*
and *Lover*, *Love-letter*;

M if you're too *Modest*, you'll
be lik'd ne'er the better.

N tells you that *Nothing's*
oft true love's reward,

O *Oaths*, to which lovers
have little regard.

P stands for *Pity*, *Pangs*,
Passion, and *Pain*,

Q *Quiet*, which lovers
do hope for in vain.

R begins *Rapture*, and
Raging, and *Rove*,

S *Sighs*, words much us'd
in making of love.

T tells us that ladies
Torment us and *Tease*,

V tells us *Variety*
always will please.

W for *Woman*, *Wounds*,
Wonder, and *Woe*.

X I think is like love,
it *crosses* me so.

Y ends the love-letter
in writing of *Your*,

Z Z—*ds* cries the lover,
who pain can't endure.

– ANON, c.1738

WILLs, WON'Ts, & CAN'Ts

There are three kinds of men: the WILLS, the WON'TS, and the CAN'TS:
The first *effect* all, the second *oppose* all, and the third *fail* in all.

——————— UNLIKELY 'CURES' FOR HICCUPS ———————

Take a small piece of lump sugar into the mouth, and let it dissolve very slowly, or drink any liquid very slowly, and the hiccups will cease. [*The Universal Household Assistant*, 1884]

Hiccup, sniccup, look up, right up.

A common hiccup may frequently be removed by holding the breath; or, if this should not succeed, a draught of cold water may be tried, or thirty drops of hartshorn in a little water. Should these fail, fifteen or twenty drops of laudanum may be taken in a little mint-water. Pure air, exercise, and cold bathing, are essentially necessary; the bowels being regulated by the occasional use of mild purgatives. A little vinegar is sometimes an effectual remedy for asthmatic hiccup. It is necessary that attention be paid to diet and regimen. [*The Book of Health*, 1828]

Wet the forefinger of the right hand with spittle, and cross the front of the left shoe or boot three times, repeating the Lord's Prayer backwards. [Various]

Sit erect and inflate the lungs fully; then, retaining the breath, bend forward slowly until the chest meets the knees, and after gradually rising again to an erect position, slowly exhale your breath. Repeat this process a second time, and the nerves will be found to have received an excess of energy that enables them to perform their natural functions. [*Detroit Journal Year Book*, 1888]

Stop up both ears with a finger of each hand and drink slowly some water from a cup held by some one else. If this is not effective, try making yourself sneeze by scattering a few grains of pepper in the air. … Pushing the tongue out firmly and holding it for a minute or two has often proved successful. Taking a spoonful of dry sugar into the mouth or chewing a crust or a cracker will often stop them. [LUTHER H. GULICK, *Emergencies*, 1909]

Put the thumb up against the lower lip, with the fingers under the chin, and say, 'hiccup, hiccup, over my thumb', nine times. [*Memoirs of the American Folklore Society*, 1896]

The magnet promises to be of great service in obstinate cases of hiccup. It is used by applying two strongly magnetized steel plates, a twelfth of an inch in thickness, of an oval shape, and bent so as to fit the part, one to the pit of the stomach, and the other opposite to the spine, so that the magnetic current shall traverse the affected part. A French physician (Laennec), of acknowledged judgment and high authority, says, 'By means of these plates I stopped, at once, a hiccup which had lasted three years. At the end of six months, the patient having one morning neglected to put on the plates, the hiccup returned, but was removed upon their being replaced'. [THOMAS JOHN GRAHAM, *Modern Domestic Medicine*, 1835]

[A doctor writes: Ignore all of this 'advice'.]

EBENEZER SCROOGE'S ABECEDARY

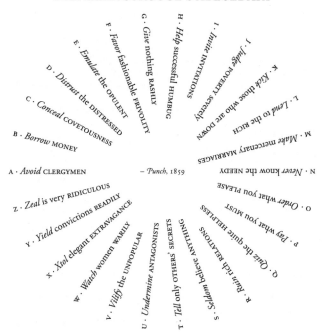

A · *Avoid* CLERGYMEN   – *Punch*, 1859

B · *Borrow* MONEY
C · *Conceal* COVETOUSNESS
D · *Distrust the* DISTRESSED
E · *Emulate the* OPULENT
F · *Favor fashionable* FRIVOLITY
G · *Give nothing* RASHLY
H · *Help successful* HUMBUG
I · *Incite* LITIGATIONS
J · *Judge poverty severely*
K · *Kick those who are* DOWN
L · *Lend to the* RICH
M · *Make mercenary* MARRIAGES
N · *Never know the* NEEDY
O · *Order what you* PLEASE
P · *Pay what you* MUST
Q · *Quiz the quite* HELPLESS
R · *Ruin rich* RELATIONS
S · *Seldom believe* ANYTHING
T · *Tell only* OTHERS' SECRETS
U · *Undermine* ANTAGONISTS
V · *Vilify the* UNPOPULAR
W · *Watch women* WARILY
X · *Xtol elegant* EXTRAVAGANCE
Y · *Yield* convictions READILY
Z · *Zeal is very* RIDICULOUS

COMPOSITION OF CREMATED HUMAN REMAINS

Phosphate	47·5%	Barium	0·0066
Calcium	25·3	Antimony	0·0035
Sulfate	11·0	Chromium	0·0018
Potassium	3·69	Copper	0·0017
Sodium	1·12	Manganese	0·0013
Chloride	1·00	Lead	0·0008
Silica	0·90	Tin	0·0005
Aluminium oxide	0·72	Vanadium	0·0002
Zinc	0·342	Beryllium	0·0001
Titanium oxide	0·026	Mercury	0·00001

Source: *The Journal* of the British Institute of Funeral Directors, Vol. 16, No. 4, Dec. 2002. (According to Michael George Mulhall's 1884 *Dictionary of Statistics*, graves were dug to the following depths: England 5′ 0″; France 5′ 6″; Austria 6′ 0″; Germany 6′ 3″; Russia 6′ 10″.)

— PHRASES OF SUPEREROGATION & STUPIDITY —

Carrying coals to Newcastle · Buttering bacon · Gilding pure gold
Porter de l'eau à la rivière (taking water to the river)
Gilding the lily · Pushing an open door · Putting lipstick on a pig
Noctuas Athenas ferre (taking owls to Athens[1])
Pepper to Hindustan [Arabic] · Enchantments to Egypt [Jewish]
Alcinoo poma dare (giving apples to Alcinous[2])
Sidera caelo addere (adding stars to the sky)
Painting legs on snakes · Giving snow to the Eskimos
Aquam mari infundere (pouring water into the sea)
In sylvam lignum ferre (taking timber to the forest)
Yekhat' v Tulu so svoim samovarom (taking your samovar to Tula[3])
Crocum in Ciliciam ferre (taking saffron to Cilicia[4])

[1] Owls abounded in Athens and many Athenian coins featured an owl's head. [2] Alcinous was the king of Phaeacia, famed for the fecundity of his garden. [3] Tula was the undisputed capital of samovar manufacture in C19th Russia. [4] In *Secrets of Saffron*, Pat Willard states, '[during] the years that span the dawn and dimming of Greece and Rome – the best saffron for perfumes and ointments was gathered in the town of Soli on the coast of Cilicia'.

Below are *Proverbial Phrases Adopted from the Greeks, Applicable to Human Follies, Absurdities, or Pursuits* – collected by Henry George Bohn, 1855:

He opens the door with an ax ❦ He seeks water in the sea
He demands tribute of the dead ❦ He holds the serpent by the tail
He takes the bull by the horns ❦ He is making clothes for fishes
He teaches an old woman to dance ❦ He draws water with a sieve
He is teaching a pig to play on a flute ❦ He chastises the dead
He catches the wind with a net ❦ He changes a fly into an elephant
He takes the spring from the year ❦ He is making ropes of sand
He sprinkles incense on a dunghill ❦ He is ploughing a rock
He is sowing on the sand ❦ He takes oil to extinguish the fire
He puts a rope to the eye of a needle ❦ He is washing the crow
He gives straw to his dog, and bones to his ass ❦ He paints the dead
He numbers the waves ❦ He takes a spear to kill a fly
He seeks wool on an ass ❦ He digs the well at the river
He puts a hat on a hen ❦ He runs against the point of a spear
He is erecting broken ports ❦ He fans with a feather
He strikes with a straw ❦ He cleaves the clouds
He brings his machines after the war is over ❦ He measures a twig
He speaks of things more ancient than chaos ❦ He ploughs the air
He roasts snow in a furnace ❦ He holds a looking glass to a mole
He is teaching iron to swim ❦ He is building a bridge over the sea
He washes his sheep with scalding water ❦ He paves the meadow

———————— DECADE NAMES ————————

Both journalists and the general public struggled to agree on a name for the first decade of the C21st. By 2009, the still-slightly-awkward 'noughties' seemed to be the preferred British term – perhaps helped by the fact that it proved pleasing to say out loud. ❦ Decades that do not herald a new century seem to have had an easier time. Tabulated below are some of the nicknames for other decades, and their salient cultural features:

1890s	Naughty Nineties	*lightheartedness & laxity as Victorian mores faded*
1920s	Roaring Twenties†	*cultural and technological explosions of jazz, film, Art Deco, flappers, &c.*
1930s	Threadbare Thirties‡	*the poverty and shabbiness of the Great Depression (said to have been coined by Groucho Marx)*
1950s	Fabulous Fifties	*ascendancy of 'cool' culture & rock 'n' roll*
1960s	Swinging Sixties	*optimistic, psychedelic, youth-oriented fashion, music, and popular culture, centered in London*
1970s	Me Decade	*individualism, materialism, &c. – coined by Tom Wolfe. (In Britain it describes the 1980s.)*
1990s	We Decade	*shift to communal values, focus on thrift, &c.*

Other phrases used to describe recent decades around the world are below:

1890s	Gay Nineties, US	*same as the Naughty Nineties*
1890s	Mauve Decade, US	*after the popularity of a synthetic dye*
1927–37	Nanjing Decade, China	*semi-dictatorship of Chiang Kai-shek, with Nanjing as capital; also 'Strenuous Decade'*
1930s	Década Infame, Argentina	*depression & discontent after 1930 coup*
1940s	Flying Forties, US	*the growth of aviation*
1950s	Haunting Decade, Romania	*repression under Gheorghiu-Dej*
1950s	Bland Decade, US	*stifling conformity (also 'Plastic Decade', &c.)*
1973–82	Oil Decade, Middle East	*wealth & power after 1973 price hike*
1980s	NGO Decade, Global	*rise of nongovernmental organizations*
1990s	Lost Decade, Japan	*end to expansion after asset price bubble burst*
1990s	Black Decade, Algeria	*civil war that killed c.200,000*

In May 2008, Bank of England Governor Mervyn King called the early 2000s 'the N.I.C.E. decade'. King was primarily referring to 'Non-Inflationary Consistent Expansion', but the phrase captured a sense that the early 2000s had seen an overall rise in prosperity. Some called these years 'the nasty decade'. † In France, the interwar years are called the *années folles* ('mad years'), because of their exuberance. ‡ Other terms for the 1930s include the Devil's Decade, the Hungry Thirties, and the Red (or Pink) Decade – the latter because of the spread of socialism. ❦ The large number of sporting events to be hosted by the UK in the 2010s (including the 2012 Olympics, 2014 Commonwealth Games, and 2015 Rugby World Cup) has led some to predict (hope?) that the 2010s will be a 'Golden Decade' for British sport.

ON WITCH COLOR

White or Good Witches ....do only good and cannot do evil
Black or Bad Witches ....do only evil and cannot do good
Gray Witches .... are capable of both good and evil

---

ON DRINKING CUPS OF WINE

Three cups of wine a prudent man may take,
The FIRST of these *for constitution's sake*;
The SECOND *to the girl he loves the best*,
The THIRD and last *to lull him to his rest*,
Then home to bed: but, if a FOURTH he pours,
That is THE CUP OF FOLLY, and not ours.
Loud noisy talking on the FIFTH attends:
The SIXTH breeds *feuds*, and *falling out of friends*;
SEVEN begets *blows* and *faces stain'd with gore*;
EIGHT, and the watch-patrol *breaks open the door*;
Mad with the NINTH, another cup goes round,
And the swill'd sot *drops senseless on the ground*!

– attributed to EUBULUS (*c.*405–*c.*335 BC)

THE PERILS OF PIPE SMOKING

Smoking ☞ *Drinking* ☞ *Intoxication* ☞ *Bile* ☞ *Jaundice* ☞ *Dropsy* ☞ *Death*

MONDAY BORN

Born on MONDAY, *fair of face*,
Born on TUESDAY, *full of grace*,
Born on WEDNESDAY, *sour and sad*,
Born on THURSDAY, *merry and glad*,
Born on FRIDAY, *worthily given*,
Born on SATURDAY, *work hard for your living*,
Born on SUNDAY, *you'll never know want*.

ON YOUNGER LOVERS

Urban legend has it that the youngest partner a man or woman can take
(assuming they are above the legal age) is half the elder's age, plus 7 years.

ON HOBOES

'If the Depression has done nothing else, it has made the country tramp conscious. ... Bread-lines may come and go, but hoboes go on forever.' In a 1932 article for *American Speech*, Robert T. Oliver identified the three classes of Depression-era hobo: 'The TRAMP stays clear of trains, as a general rule. His living consists of "handouts" from back doors, and most of his traveling is afoot. ... The second grade consists of the HOBOES who work now and then, as the spirit moves them ... and are regular habitués of the railway companies. ... Last, and lowest, of the divisions, is the STETSON, who is usually found in mining regions.' Oliver goes on to identify a range of subdivisions of KLINKITY-KLINK men, including: MUSH-FAKERS, who repaired umbrellas ('mushrooms'); QUALLEY WORKERS, who used wire to make coat hangers, bottle cleaners, &c.; CRIP-FAKERS or THROW-OUTS, who were skilled at faking injuries; STEW BUMS, who begged for the price of a meal; BOODLERS, who welcomed being imprisoned during the colder months; and KID TRAMPS or GA-ZOONEYS, who were under 18 or 19. The professional chroniclers or finks who went house to house, BACKDOOR BUMMING for food and scrawling signs for their comrades, were 'heartily despised' by the hobo 'Brotherhood.'

According to the *OED*, HOBOISM is the realm or world of the hobo, and the correct term for a female hobo is HOBOETTE.

PLANTING PATTERNS

Square Planting

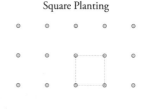

Quincunx Planting

Triangular/Hexagonal Planting

Hedgerow Planting

--- ABBREVS ---

Dictionaries of abbreviations are curious things and – in the face of the information revolution – something of an endangered species. The world is too complex to collect every specialist abbreviation in one volume, and the internet has meant that even the most baffling conglomeration of letters can easily be deciphered. However, hiding within these often dry and dusty volumes is the occasional gem, some of which are below [see p.93]:

A.A.O.	awake, alert, oriented
A.B.C.D.	above and beyond the call of duty
AFFL.	affluent
A.K.	ass-kisser
B.B.I.A.B.	be back in a bit
BEH.	beheaded
B.I.B.A.	brought in by ambulance
B.I.D.	brought in dead
B.S.E.	blame someone else
D.A.	duck's arse (1950s men's hairstyle)
D.O.M.	*Deo optimo maximo* to God, the best and greatest (*also*, dirty old man)
D.V.	*Deo volente* (God willing)
E.U.V.N.V.U.E	*ede ut vivas, ne vive ut edas* eat to live, do not live to eat
F.H.B.	family hold back [at a dinner party]
F.L.K.	funny-looking kid [medical]
G.M.B.	good merchantable brand(s)
I.H.M.	*Jesus Hominum Mundi* Jesus, Savior of the World
I.H.S.	*Jesus, Hominum Salvator* Jesus, Savior of Men
J.I.T.	just in time
KISS	keep it simple, stupid
L.G.B.T.	lesbian, gay, bisexual, transsexual
L.G.B.T.Q.Q.I.	lesbian, gay, bisexual, transsexual queer question(ing), intersex
L.M.F.	lacking/low moral fiber
L.W.E.	long white envelope (e.g., bearing news of a competition win)
N.Q.O.C./S./T.	not quite our class/sort/type
N.S.F.	not sufficient funds
N.S.I.T.	not safe in taxis [said of certain men]
O.B.G.	old but good
P.P.D.	*propria peania dedicavet* with his own money he dedicated it
P.L.W.A.	person living with AIDS
REQID	request if desired
REQTAT	requested that
R.H.I.P.	rank has its privileges
R.H.I.R.	rank has its responsibilities
R.R.R.	risk-reward ratio
R.S.P.	rain stops play
SAL GAL	saloon girl
SANKA	*sans kaffeine* (without caffeine)
S-A-N MAN	stop-at-nothing man (a criminal)
S.A.N.R.	subject to approval, no risk
S.A.S.	so and so
S.B.W.	stolen base wins
S.C.B.	strictly confined to bed
SESQUILIN	sesquilingual (the ability to speak one-and-a-half languages)
S.F.C.W.	search for critical wisdom
S.L.H.	severe legislative hypocrisy
S.M.A.P.	surprised middle-aged person
S:M::M:B	soybean is to milk as margarine is to butter
SNAG	sensitive new age guy
S.N.L.R.	services no longer required
S.O.O.B.	sitting out of bed
S.V.V.	*sit venia verbo* (forgive the expression)
SWLOLAK	sealed with lots of love and kisses
S.W.M.B.O.	she who must be obeyed
SWOT	strengths, weaknesses, opportunities, threats
S.W.Y.M.M.D.	see what you made me do
T.B.W.	thrown by wave
T.J.S.	tight-jean syndrome (impotence, sterility)
TOE	theory of everything
T.O.M.	the old man
U.G.M.I.T.	you got me into this
U.M.O.C.	ugly man on campus
V. & M.M.	vandalism and malicious mischief
V.V.C.	*vidi vivam cultam* I have seen a living cultivated specimen
V.V.S.	*vidi vivam spontaneam* I have seen a living wild specimen
W.T.C.	winning telephone call
X.L.S.	extreme long shot

SHIPPING CONTAINER SIZES

		8'	10'	20'	30'	40'
External ·	Length	8'	10'	20'	30'	40'
	Width	7'1"	8'	8'	8'	8'
	Height · *standard*	7'5"	8'6"	8'6"	8'6"	8'6"
	high cube	—	9'6"	9'6"	9'6"	9'6"
Internal ·	Length	7'6"	9'2"	19'3"	29'4"	39'4"
	Width	6'11"	7'7"	7'7"	7'7"	7'7"
	Height · *standard*	6'8"	7'9"	7'9"	7'9"	7'9"
	high cube	—	8'9"	8'9"	8'9"	8'9"
Floor area (square feet)		51	72	150	227	305
Capacity: *standard* (cubic feet)		348	560	1,160	1,760	2,360
	high cube	—	630	1,310	1,985	2,660
Weight (tons) [approx.; *specs vary*]		0·94	1·5	2·2	2·8	3·3

FACEBOOK RELATIONSHIP STATUS OPTIONS

Single · In a relationship · Engaged · Married
It's complicated · In an open relationship · Widowed
Separated · Divorced · In a civil union · In a domestic partnership

MARKING UNDERGROUND UTILITIES

The American Public Works Association promotes a color code for marking underground utilities (e.g., pipes and cables) to 'prevent accidents and damage or service interruption by contractors, excavators, utility companies, municipalities or any others working on or near underground facilities':

Red .... electric power lines, cables, conduit, and lighting cables
Yellow .... gas, oil, steam, petroleum, or gaseous materials
Orange .... communication, alarm, or signal lines, cables or conduit
Blue..potable water
Green..sewers and drain lines
Purple ....reclaimed water, irrigation, and slurry lines
Pink ....temporary survey marking
White.. proposed excavation

ON PLEASURE & AGE

At 20 we KILL PLEASURE, At 30 we TASTE it, At 40 we are
SPARING of it, At 50 we SEEK it, And at 60 we REGRET it.
– widely quoted, including in *La Belle Assemblée*, 1807 [see also pp.144–153]

———————— WATCHING YOUR MANNERS ————————

In PRIVATE watch your *thoughts*. ❦ In your FAMILY watch your *temper*.
In your BUSINESS watch your *avarice*. ❦ In SOCIETY watch your *tongue*.

———————— MYSTERIOUS TRIANGLES ————————

The US military returned control of Iraq's 'Triangle of Death' to Iraqi forces in October 2008. Located in central Iraq, with Mahmudiyah to the north, Yusufiyah to the west, and Iskandariyah to the south, the triangle was home to a violent Sunni insurgency from 2004 to 2007. Strangely, this area is not the only triangle to contain more than its fair share of danger:

The *Bermuda Triangle*, bounded by Florida, Puerto Rico, and Bermuda, is said to have claimed at least 50 ships and 20 planes. [For the mystery of Flight 19, see p.77.] Marine experts note the frequent storms and strong currents that batter the region, while occultists claim the triangle lies near the lost city of Atlantis, where powerful 'fire crystals' wreak havoc with technical equipment. ❦ The *Bridgewater Triangle*, in Massachusetts, is the location of countless reports of UFOs, prehistoric beasts, and Bigfoot. ❦ The *Golden Triangle* includes parts of Myanmar, Laos, and Thailand, and is one of Asia's primary centers of opium production. ❦ The *Michigan Triangle*, located in central Lake Michigan, is famous for sightings of sea monsters and ghost ships. ❦ The *Dragon's Triangle* of the Pacific, including parts of Japan, Guam, and Taiwan, is said to contain lost vessels and ghost ships – and to explain the 1937 disappearance of Amelia Earhart [see p.77].

———————— A GOOD HORSE ————————

Wynkyn de Worde (*d.*1535) enumerated 'fifteen points of a good horse', viz:

A GOOD HORSE sholde have three propyrtees of a MAN,
three of a WOMAN, three of a FOXE, three of a HAARE, and three of an ASSE.

Of a MAN . . . . Bolde, prowde, and hardye
Of a WOMAN . . . . Fayre-breasted, faire of heere, and easy to move
Of a FOXE . . . . A fair taylle, short eers, with a good trotte
Of a HAARE . . . . A grate eye, a dry head, and well rennynge
Of an ASSE . . . . A bygge chynn, a flat legge, and a good hoof

Wynkyn de Worde was an Alsatian-born pioneer of printing. He was employed at William Caxton's London press, and took control of the business when Caxton died in 1491.

———————— ON GENIUS AND LONGEVITY ————————

In his curious 1833 text, *The Infirmities of Genius*, Richard Robert Madden recorded the age at death of twenty great men in twelve classes of activity, averaged their life spans, and created the following ranking of longevity:

Total years	Class	Average age
1,504	NATURAL PHILOSOPHERS (e.g., Copernicus; Davy; Galileo; Linnaeus; Newton)	75
1,417	MORAL PHILOSOPHERS (e.g., Bacon; Berkeley; Descartes; Hobbes; Kant)	70
1,412	SCULPTORS AND PAINTERS (e.g., Bernini; Michael Angelo; Titian; Canova; Raphael)	70
1,394	AUTHORS ON LAW AND JURISPRUDENCE (e.g., Bentham; Hale; Grotius; Montesquieu; Vatel)	69
1,368	MEDICAL AUTHORS (e.g., Darwin; Gall; Harvey; Jenner; Heberden)	68
1,350	AUTHORS ON REVEALED RELIGION (e.g., Bellarmine; Calvin; Luther; Paley; Wesley)	67
1,323	PHILOLOGISTS (e.g., Bentley; Nurton; Lipsius; Porson; Vossius)	66
1,284	MUSICAL COMPOSERS (e.g., Bach; Beethoven; Gluck; Mozart; Scarlatti)	64
1,257	NOVELISTS AND MISCELLANEOUS AUTHORS (e.g., Cervantes; Rabelais; Fielding; Montaigne; Hazlitt)	62½
1,249	DRAMATISTS (e.g., Marlow; Racine; Schiller; Shakespeare; Voltaire)	62
1,245	AUTHORS ON NATURAL RELIGION (e.g., Bolingbroke; Gibbon; Paine; Rousseau; Spinoza)	62
1,144	POETS (e.g., Byron; Dante; Dryden; Milton; Petrarch)	57

'From these tables,' Richard Robert Madden asserted, 'it would appear, that those pursuits in which imagination is largely exerted is unfavorable to longevity. We find the difference between the united ages of twenty natural philosophers, and that of the same number of poets, to be no less than three hundred and sixty years; or in other words, the average of life to be about seventy-five in the one, and fifty-seven in the other.'

———————— TRADITIONAL HAY MEASURES ————————

36 pounds STRAW		
56 pounds OLD HAY	1 TRUSS ⤐ 36 TRUSSES .... 1 LOAD	
60 pounds NEW HAY		

— BILLINGSLEY'S STORK CLUB HAND SIGNALS —

From the late 1930s to the mid-1950s, the Stork Club was one of the hottest nightclubs in America and – to quote gossip columnist Walter Winchel – 'New York's New Yorkiest place'. The club's founder and owner was Sherman Billingsley, a bootlegger and hustler who by sheer force of personality enticed a heady mix of socialites, politicians, singers, writers, and movie stars with his golden rope to drink, dance, see, and be seen. In 1944, the photographer Alfred Eisenstaedt shot a photo essay for *Life* magazine, in which Billingsley demonstrated the secret hand signals with which he communicated to his waiters messages about the patrons:

Hand on tie . . . . *no bill for this table*
Hand resting on table, palm upward . . . . *bring a bottle of Champagne*
Tugging at pocket handkerchief . . . . *bring a bottle of perfume*†
Hand touching nose . . . . *unimportant people, don't cash their checks*
All five fingers spread on left hand . . . . *the music is too loud*
Hands interlocked, thumbs raised . . . *get them out & don't let them in again*
Pulling the ear . . . . *summon me to a phone call*
Downward-pointing finger . . . . *a round of free drinks*

† Eschewing traditional advertising, Billingsley habitually bestowed gifts on favored customers, ranging from orchids, ashtrays, and club perfume to fine wine and even cars.

—— DISTINGUISHING POVERTY & PAUPERISM ——

POVERTY	PAUPERISM
A sound vessel empty	An empty vessel cracked
A natural want of food	Insatiable ravenousness
Strives to cure itself	Contaminates others
Stimulates to exertion	Paralyzes exertion
Is sincere	Is an arch-hypocrite
Has a naturally proud spirit	Has a base spirit
Is silent & retiring	Is clamorous & imposing

– adapted from THOMAS WALKER, *The Original*, 1835

—————— ANTISCII & PERISCII ——————

The *antiscii* are those who live on the same meridian but on the opposite side of the equator, so that at noon their shadows fall in opposite directions. The *periscii* are those who live in the polar circles, whose shadows revolve like a wheel around them as the sun moves around the heavens on its orbit.

——————— ARCHAIC GEMSTONE LORE ———————

Gems of the Hours

MORNING · AFTERNOON

12 · Diamond · Jacinth · 13 · Emerald · 14 · 11 · Garnet · 10 · Sapphire · 9 · Kunzite · 8 · Amethyst · 7 · Chrysolite · 6 · Tourmaline · 5 · Turquoise · 4 · Lapis lazuli · 3 · Malachite · 2 · Hematite · 1 · Morion · Onyx · 24 · Loadstone · 23 · Jasper · 22 · Jade · 21 · Chalcedony · 20 · Sardonyz · 19 · Opal · 18 · Ruby · 17 · Topaz · 16 · Beryl · 15

F............. fire opal	H ....hyacinth	C............. cat's-eye
A.......... alexandrite	O .... opal	H ....hyacinth
I................iolite	P................pearl	A......... aquamarine
T.......... tourmaline	E............ emerald	R.................ruby
H ....hyacinth		I................iolite
	F.....flèches d'amour	T......... tourmaline
G .... golden beryl	R.................ruby	Y..... yellow sapphire
O .... opal	I................indicolite	
O ....olivine	E............ emerald	L...........lapis lazuli
D .... diamond	N.............nephrite	O .... opal
˘	D .... diamond	V.............vermeil
L...........lapis lazuli	S.............sapphire	E............ emerald
U .... uralian emerald	H ....hyacinth	˘
C............. cat's-eye	I................iolite	M........moonstone
K............. kunsite	P................pearl	E............ essonite

———— ARCHAIC GEMSTONE LORE cont. ————

Symbolic Gems of the Months

January .... jacinth or hyacinth
February................. amethyst
March .... jasper
April............sapphire, diamond
May.............................agate
June......................... emerald
July ....carnelian, onyx
August..............sardonyx, onyx
September...............chrysolite
October .. aquamarine, opal, beryl
November.................... topaz
December .... turquoise, ruby

Gem Emblems of the 12 Apostles

Andrew.................... sapphire
Bartholomew............. carnelian
James .... chalcedony
James the Less............... topaz
John .... emerald
Matthew................. amethyst
Matthias (after Judas)....chrysolite
Peter.........................jasper
Philip..................... sardonyx
Simeon ....hyacinth
Thaddeus.............. chrysoprase
Thomas......................beryl

The Traditional Gem Alphabet

Opaque	*Transparent*
Agate	Amethyst
Basalt	Beryl
Cacholong	Chrysoberyl
Diaspore	Diamond
Egyptian pebble	Emerald
Firestone	Felspar
Granite	Garnet
Heliotrope	Hyacinth
Jasper	Idocrase
Krokidolite	Kyanite
Lapis lazuli	Lynx sapphire
Malachite	Milk opal
Nephrite	Natrolite
Onyx	Opal
Porphyry	Pyrope
Quartz agate	Quartz
Rose quartz	Ruby
Sardonyx	Sapphire
Turquoise	Topaz
Ultramarine	Unanite
Verd antique	Vesuvianite
Wood opal	Water sapphire
Xylotile	Xanthite
Zurlite	Zirco

(A number of different versions exist.)

⁂ ⁂ ⁂

The stones worn by Chinese mandarins as a designation of their rank were undoubtedly determined originally by religious or ceremonial considerations. They are as follows; it will be noticed that red stones [a color that is traditionally considered lucky in China] are given the preference:

Red or pink tourmaline, ruby (and rubelite)	1st rank
Coral or an inferior red stone (garnet)	2nd rank
Blue stone (beryl or lapis lazuli)	3rd rank
Rock crystal	4th rank
Other white stones	5th rank

– adapted from GEORGE FREDERICK KUNZ, *The Curious Lore of Precious Stones*, 1913

ON KISSES AND KISSING

A variety of wags have created a lexicon of 'kissology' – including:

BUS............................*to kiss*
BLUNDERBUSS.....*to kiss by mistake*
BUSKIN.............. *to kiss a cousin*
BUSTER........ *to kiss another's beau*
E-PLURI-BUS-UNUM..... *1,000 kisses*
OMNIBUS............ *to kiss everyone*
REBUS.................. *to kiss again*
SYLLA[Y]BUSS .... *to kiss a teacher*

♡ ♡ ♡

In the c19th, the London magazine *Tit-Bits* offered a two-guinea prize for the finest definition of a kiss. Some of the best are given below:

An insipid and tasteless morsel, which becomes delicious and delectable in proportion as it is flavored with love. [winner] ❦ A thing of use to no one, but much prized by two. ❦ The baby's right, the lover's privilege, the parent's benison, and the hypocrite's mask. ❦ That which you cannot give without taking and cannot take without giving. ❦ Nothing, divided by two. ❦ The only really agreeable two-faced action under the sun, or the moon either. ❦ The thunderclap of the lips, which inevitably follows the lightning glance of the eyes. ❦ What the child receives free, what the young man steals, and what the old man buys. ❦ Contraction of the mouth due to enlargement of the heart. ❦ Cupid's sealing wax. ❦ The soul's ambassador. ❦ A game for two, always in fashion.

– E. L. C. WARD, *The Scrap-Book*, 1899

In *The Kiss & Its History* (1901), Kristoffer Nyrop attributed this PowerPoint-esque taxonomy of kisses to an c18th German jurist:

LAWFUL KISSES
A. Spiritual kisses.
B. Kisses of reconciliation & peace.
C. As customary kisses; partly,
      a. By way of salutation.
        1. At meeting.
        2. On arrival.
        3. At departure; partly,
      b. As mark of courtesy.
      c. In jest.
D. As kisses of respect.
E. As kisses on festive occasions.
F. As kisses of love, between:
      i. Married people.
      ii. Those engaged.
      iii. Parents & children.
      iv. Relations.
      v. Intimate friends; or,
UNLAWFUL, when they are given:
A. Out of treachery or malice.
B. Out of lust.

♡ ♡ ♡

The Romans distinguished between three types of kisses, though there appears to be some disagreement as to what different kisses signified:

OSCULUM
a kiss of duty and respect

BASIUM
*kisses between family members,
or kisses thrown to a crowd*

SAVIUM
*a romantic or erotic kiss,
or kisses of greeting and farewell*

———————— ON KISSES AND KISSING cont. ————————

THE GRAMMAR OF THE KISS has not yet been written. True; a young lady being once asked whether the kiss, being a substantive, was proper or common, archly replied that it was *both* proper and common; but a more enlarged view may be taken of the subject. We find there are only three *regular* kisses (properly so called), and these may be denominated: (1) *the kiss negative*; (2) *the kiss positive*; and, (3) *the kiss superlative*. The first, or *negative*, consists in kissing a lady's hand; the second, or *positive*, consists in kissing her cheek; and the third, or *superlative*, consists in kissing her *lips*. There are, besides, two *auxiliary kisses* – viz., the kiss *passive*, such as is inflicted by old maiden aunts, nurses, and grandmothers; and the *kiss active*, in use (principally) on the Gretna Green Road, *per gli amanti, e novelli sposi*. The first (the kiss *passive*) is generally declined by the *kissee*, whilst the latter (the kiss *active*) governs both *kisser* and *kissee* (or, as it is more analytically written, *kiss-her* and *kiss-he*), in *number* as well as in *gender*. Independent of the preceding *regular* and *auxiliary* kisses, there are, for the convenience of society, a few *supernumerary* or *irregular* ones, such as the *incidental*, or *stage kiss*; the *cooing*, or *à la tourterelle* kiss; the *echo*, or *percussion kiss*; and the *barley sugar kiss*, or kiss *en papillote*.

– ANON, quoted in
The Treasury of Wit & Anecdote,
printed for Thomas Tegg, 1842

Dutch poet Johannes Secundus (1511–36) is credited with observing that Scripture has 8 types of kiss:

SALUTATION	Sam. xx. 41
VALEDICTION	Ruth ii. 9
RECONCILIATION	2 Sam. xiv. 33
SUBJECTION	Psalms ii. 12
APPROBATION	Proverbs ii. 4
ADORATION	1 Kings xix. 18
TREACHERY	Matt. xxvi. 49
AFFECTION	Gen. xlv. 15

♡ ♡ ♡

The *Kama Sutra* also notes 8 kisses: *Nominal kiss* · when a girl only touches the mouth of her lover with her own, but does not do anything. ❦ *Throbbing kiss* · when a girl, setting aside her bashfulness a little, wishes to touch the lip that is pressed into her mouth, and with that object moves her lower lip, but not the upper one. ❦ *Touching kiss* · when a girl touches her lover's lip with her tongue, and having shut her eyes, places her hands on those of her lover. ❦ *Straight kiss* · when the lips of two lovers are brought into direct contact. ❦ *Bent kiss* · when the heads of two lovers are bent toward each other, and when so bent, kissing takes place. ❦ *Turned kiss* · when one of them turns up the face of the other by holding the head and chin, and then kissing. ❦ *Pressed kiss* · when the lower lip is pressed with much force. ❦ *Greatly pressed kiss* · effected by taking hold of the lower lip between two fingers, and then, after touching it with the tongue, pressing it with great force with the lip.

— KEYBOARD LAYOUTS: SHOLES vs DVORAK, &c. —

SHOLES *or* QWERTY *or* UNIVERSAL

Patented in 1868 by the typewriter developer Christopher Latham Sholes, the QWERTY keyboard now dominates the Western market. The precise thinking behind Sholes's arrangement remains a mystery – although the fact that one can produce the word 'type-writer' using just the top row of keys was, some claim, a not accidental benefit to type-writer salesmen. While it seems likely that Sholes did adjust letter placement to avoid certain common letterpairs jamming, it seems unlikely that the entire layout was designed deliberately to slow typists down – as is commonly stated. (One reason for this is that 'touch typing' was some twenty years off when QWERTY was introduced into a 'hunt-and-peck' world.) The name QWERTY, of course, simply refers to the first six upper-left letters.

DVORAK *or* DVORAK SIMPLIFIED KEYBOARD (DSK) *or* DVORAK-DEALEY

August Dvorak patented his Dvorak Simplified Keyboard in 1936 – promising improve-ments in speed, accuracy, and comfort over QWERTY. This assertion of superiority catalyzed the DVORAK-QWERTY debate, which has never fully died – leading some to claim that the 'wrong' design achieved global success (just as VHS bested the superior Betamax video format). Dvorak was keen to even the ergonomic load by promoting 'contralateral' move-ments (where alternate hands strike alternate keys) and ensuring that the stronger fingers are given the most work (a more pressing issue with mechanical machines than with computer keyboards). Although there is still argument as to whether DVORAK is faster than QWERTY, the ubiquity of QWERTY makes it of little more than academic interest – speaking of which:

The FITCH keyboard (1886) grouped all the vowels in the center of the layout, banishing to the periphery the rarer letters.	The DHIATENSOR or SCIENTIFIC keyboard (1893) placed on the bottom row the 10 letters used in >70% of English words.

——— WORD FREQUENCY IN BEATLES' HITS———

Below is the word frequency in The Beatles' 27 US and UK No. 1 singles†:

Word frequency			
You 260	So 37	Was 19	Day 13
I 178	Your 36	Writer 19	Days 13
To 149	Her 35	Help 18	Hard 13
Me 137	Of 35	I'll 18	Ride 13
Love 125	She's 32	I'm 18	Right 13
A 121	He 30	If 18	See 13
The 118	It's 29	Think 18	There's 13
It 107	Na‡ 29	Where 18	Want 13
And 102	But 27	Will 18	Week 13
Be 98	Can't 26	Buy 17	Easy 12
Know 74	No 26	Make 17	People 12
In 70	We 26	One 17	Should 12
She 70	Goodbye ... 25	From 16	Something .. 12
Say 60	Now 24	Go 16	Time 12
That 59	Submarine .. 24	His 16	At 11
Yeah 58	Way 24	How 16	Been 11
All 57	Yellow 24	Said 16	Better 11
Let 53	For 23	Care 15	Eight 11
Can 49	Why 23	Come 15	Glad 11
Get 48	On 22	Just 15	Home 11
Is 46	With 22	Night 15	Once 11
Back 45	Feel 21	Please 15	Work 11
Don't 45	Hold 21	There 15	Yesterday ... 11
Do 41	When 21	They 15	By 10
Hello 41	Like 20	Things 15	Hand 10
Got 40	Out 20	Ticket 15	Lonely 10
My 39	Long 19	Going 14	
Need 37	Oh 19	Loves 14	† Including song titles
	Paperback .. 19	Money 14	‡ Repeated in *Hey Jude*

————— WAYS TO A WOMAN'S HEART———

To find the shortest way to a female heart under any given circumstances:

If she is married, but not a mother .... *praise her* HUSBAND
If she is married, and also a mother .... *praise her* CHILDREN
If she is unmarried, and engaged .... *praise her* LOVER
If she is unmarried, and disengaged .... *praise* HERSELF

– ANON, quoted in *Punch*, 1866

──────── PRECIPITATION LEXICON ────────

While it is often (and erroneously) asserted that Eskimos have hundreds of words for snow, the English language is replete with terms relating to rain. Below are some of the pluvial terms in the great *Oxford English Dictionary*:

ABLAQUEATE · *clearing the soil around the roots of a plant to expose them to rain and sun.* ✝ ACID RAIN · *that contaminated by pollution.* ✝ AFTER DROPS · *rain that falls even after a cloud has passed.* ✝ APRIL SHOWER · *the brief rainfall of spring.* ✝ BANGLE · *rainfall that beats down crops.* ✝ BEDRABBLE · *to make wet and dirty with rain &c.* ✝ BERAIN · *to rain upon; to sprinkle as rain.* ✝ BICKER · *the pattering of rain.* ✝ BIG WET · *an especially rainy period.* ✝ BLASH · *when rain falls in sheets* [blow + splash]. ✝ BLIRT, BLIRTY, BLIRTIE · *a gust of wind and rain.* ✝ BLOOD RAIN · *that which has acquired a red hue.* ✝ BLOUT · *a sudden inundation of rain.* ✝ BRACK · *a sudden inundation of rain.* ✝ BRASH · *a burst of rain.* ✝ BRASHY · *showery.* ✝ BUCK RAIN · *heavy and soaking.* ✝ BUCKET · *to pour down heavily.* ✝ BURST · *a sudden heavy outpouring.* ✝ BUSH WATER · *rainwater that collects in the low-lying parts of tropical forests.* ✝ CATS & DOGS · *to rain heavily.* (In 1738, Jonathan Swift was the first writer to record rain as falling like CATS & DOGS – prior to that, certainly in 1652, the phrase was DOGS & POLECATS.) ✝ CLASH · *the sound of heavy rain.* ✝ CLASHY · *heavy dashes of rain.* ✝ DAG · *a thin and gentle rain or mist.* ✝ DAGGED · *wet with dew or light rain.* ✝ DANK · *drizzling rain.* ✝ DASH · *a sudden fall of rain.* ✝ DELUGE · *an inundation of rain.* ✝ DERAIN · *to rain.* ✝ DOWNFALL · *a heavy fall of rain.* ✝ DOWNPOUR · *a heavy, continuous fall of rain.* ✝ DRIFFLE · *to rain in sparse drops* (e.g., at the end of a shower). ✝ DRIFT · *a shower driven by the wind.* ✝ DRIVING RAIN · *accelerated by a strong wind.* ✝ DRIZZLE, DRIZZLING, &c. · *fine, spray-like rain.* ✝ DROUK · *to drench with heavy rain.* ✝ DROW · *a cold misty rain; a drizzling shower.* ✝ EAVESDRIP, -DROP · *the dripping of water from the eaves of a house.* ✝ ELEPHANT · *a violent rainstorm associated with the Monsoon* [Portuguese]. ✝ EVENDOWN · *rain that falls vertically.* ✝ FALL · *an episode of rain.* ✝ FLASH · *a sudden burst of rain.* ✝ FLAUGHT · *a sudden burst of wind and rain.* ✝ FLAW · *rain with gusty winds.* ✝ FLOOD · *a violent downpour.* ✝ FRET · *a wet fog or drizzle.* ✝ GLEAM · *a bright warm interval between showers.* ✝ GLUT · *an excessive influx of rain.* ✝ GOURDER · *a flooding rain.* ✝ HARD RAIN · *that falls fiercely.* ✝ HEAT-DROP · *a few drops of rain ushering in a hot day.* ✝ HOT GLEAM · *a bright, warm spell between showers.* ✝ HYETAL · *pertaining to rain.* ✝ HYOMETER · *a rain gauge.* ✝ ICE STORM · *freezing rain that leaves a deposit of ice on trees &c.* ✝ IMBRIFEROUS · *showery.* ✝ IMPEARL · *rain that leaves pearlescent drops.* ✝ IMPLUVIOUS · *wet with rain.* ✝ JUPITER PLUVIUS · *Jupiter is the dispenser of rain; thus used in reference to a fall or storm of rain.* ✝ LAVISH · *to pour along in torrents.* ✝ LINE-SQUALL · *a violent straight blast of cold air with snow or rain.* ✝ LONG RAINS · *the rainy season.* ✝ MIZZLE, MIZZLING, &c. · *very fine misty rain.* ✝ MONKEY'S WEDDING · *alternating or simultaneous sunshine and*

─────── PRECIPITATION LEXICON cont. ───────

rain [S African]. ✝ MONSOON · *a season, or description of, heavy and continuous rain.* ✝ MUG · *a mist or drizzle.* ✝ MULL · *to rain lightly.* ✝ MULL-RAIN · *fine rain.* ✝ NUBBIN STRETCHER · *heavy rain that causes ears of maize to develop fully* [US; jocular]. ✝ ONCOME · *a heavy fall of rain.* ✝ ON-DING · *a heavy, persistent fall of rain.* ✝ ONDING · *to rain heavily.* ✝ ONION RAIN · *that which falls unexpectedly in late spring, after the onions have been planted* [US]. ✝ PASH · *a heavy rainfall.* ✝ PEAL, PEALING · *driving rain.* ✝ PELT, PELTER, PELTING, &c.· *of driving rain.* ✝ PEPPER · *to rain heavily.* ✝ PETRICHOR · *the smell accompanying the first rain after a long period of warm, dry weather.* ✝ PINCHING RAIN · *that which is harsh or biting.* ✝ PISS, PISSING, &c. · *to rain heavily.* ✝ Rain PITCHFORKS · *to rain very hard* [US]. ✝ PITTER-PATTER · *the beating of light rain.* ✝ To rain by PLANETS · *localized showers.* ✝ PLASH · *a downpour.* ✝ PLATCH · *to rain in heavy drops.* ✝ PLOUT · *heavy rain.* ✝ PLUMP, PLUMPING · *heavy rainfall.* ✝ PLUNGE · *a downpour of rain.* ✝ PLUNGY · *rainy, stormy.* ✝ PLUVIAL · *characterized by rain.* ✝ PLUVIATILE · *pertaining to rain.* ✝ PLUVIOSE, PLUVIOSITY, &c. · *rainy.* ✝ POUR, POURING · *a heavy fall of rain.* ✝ PRECIPITATE · *(to) rain.* ✝ PRECIPITATION · *rain.* ✝ PUSH · *a large puddle left by a downpour of rain.* ✝ RAINBRED · *producing rain.* ✝ RASH · *a heavy or sudden shower; to pour down torrentially.* ✝ RHEUM · *light mist.* ✝ ROKE · *very light rain.* ✝ ROPING · *when rain falls so heavily it resembles continuous strands.* ✝ RUG · *drizzling rain.* ✝ SAD RAIN · *heavy rain.* ✝ SCAT · *a sudden or passing shower.* ✝ SCUD · *a driving shower.* ✝ SCUFF · *a puff of rain.* ✝ SEREIN · *fine rain falling from a cloudless sky.* ✝ SERENE · *a light fall of moisture or fine rain after sunset.* ✝ SHATTER · *a shower.* ✝ SHEER-POINT · [?] *the rain needed to reach the roots of a crop.* ✝ SHEET, SHEETING · *a wall of rain.* ✝ SHOWER · *a short, usually light spell of rain.* ✝ SHOWERY · *frequent light rain.* ✝ SILE · *to pour down.* ✝ SKEW · *a drizzling rain.* ✝ SKIFF · *a slight shower.* ✝ SKIT · *a slight shower.* ✝ SLASHING · *a heavy downpour.* ✝ SLEET · *partially thawed snow, often falling with rain.* ✝ SLOBBER · *sleety rain.* ✝ SLUICY · *rain that pours copiously.* ✝ SMUR · *fine drizzle.* ✝ SOAK, SOAKING, SOAKER · *saturating rain.* ✝ SPATE · *a sudden heavy downpour.* ✝ SPIT, SPITTING · *a slight sprinkle of rain.* ✝ SPOT · *rain falling in large scattered drops.* ✝ SPOUT · *a heavy downpour.* ✝ SPRINKLE · *to rain in fine or infrequent drops.* ✝ SQUALL · *heavy wind and rain.* ✝ STEEPER · *a soaking rain.* ✝ STILL RAIN · *gentle with no wind.* ✝ STILLICIDE · *rainwater that falls from the eaves of a house upon another's property.* ✝ TEEM, TEEMING · *to pour.* ✝ TEMPEST · *a violent storm.* ✝ THIGHT · *dense rain.* ✝ TIPPLE · *to rain heavily.* ✝ TIRL · *the sound of rain on a roof.* ✝ TOAD-STRANGLER · *a heavy downpour* [US]. ✝ TORRENT, TORRENTIAL · *a violent downpour.* ✝ TRAVADO · *a sudden violent storm.* ✝ VOLLEY · *shower.* ✝ WASHY · *weather that brings rain.* ✝ WHISP · *a sprinkle of rain.* ✝

Douglas Adams predicted such a list in *So Long and Thanks for All the Fish*, in which the truck driver Rob McKenna has 231 descriptions of rain – befitting his status as a rain god.

FLAG, SEMAPHORE, & MORSE SIGNALS

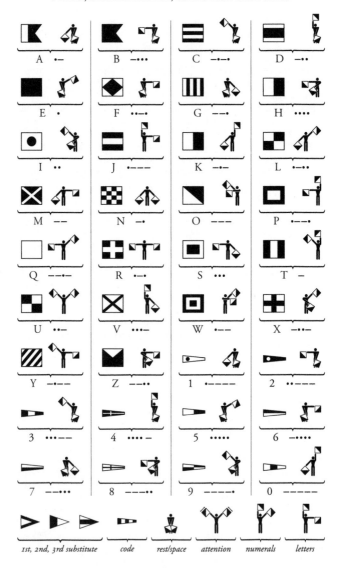

A •—	B —•••
C —•—•	D —••
E •	F ••—•
G ——•	H ••••
I ••	J •———
K —•—	L •—••
M ——	N —•
O ———	P •——•
Q ——•—	R •—•
S •••	T —
U ••—	V •••—
W •——	X —••—
Y —•——	Z ——••
1 •————	2 ••———
3 •••——	4 ••••—
5 •••••	6 —••••
7 ——•••	8 ———••
9 ————•	0 —————

1st, 2nd, 3rd substitute *code* *rest/space* *attention* *numerals* *letters*

─── STATIONS OF THE CROSS ───

─── ON WALKING IN A WINTER WONDERLAND ───

Walk fast in SNOW, in FROST *walk slow*,
And still as you go tread on your TOE;
When FROST and SNOW are both together,
Sit by the fire, and spare SHOE LEATHER.

─── TRAVELING PIQUET ───

Just as some people play 'pub cricket' on long, tedious car journeys – scoring runs by the number of legs (human and animal) depicted on public house signs passed on the way – so C19th coach passengers would play 'traveling piquet', scoring the sights they passed according to the following scale:

A parson riding a gray horse, with blue furniture .... GAME
An old woman under a hedge .... GAME
A cat looking out a window 60
A man, woman, and child in a buggy 40
A man with a woman behind him 30
A flock of sheep 20
A flock of geese 10
A post chaise 5
A horseman 2
A man or woman walking 1

– FRANCIS GROSE, *Lexicon Balatronicum*, 1811

POSTMAN'S PARK

Postman's Park, situated in the City of London near St Paul's, is formed by the churchyard of St Leonard's, Foster Lane, St Botolph's, Aldgate, and the graveyard of Christchurch, Newgate. Inside this small parcel of land, a curious memorial to the heroism of 'ordinary' men and women was erected, conceived in 1887 by the artist G. F. Watts. Recounted on a series of elegant plaques are the exploits of those who sacrificed their lives while attempting to save the lives of others. A few of the inscriptions are reproduced below:

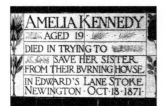

FREDERICK ALFRED CROFT
Inspector Aged 31 · *Saved a lunatic woman from suicide at Woolwich Arsenal Station, but was himself run over by the train* · January 11 1878

HARRY SISLEY OF KILBURN · Aged 10
Drowned in attempting to save his brother after he himself had just been rescued · May 24 1878

JAMES HEWERS · On September 24 1878 · *Was killed by a train at Richmond in the endeavour to save another man*

GEORGE BLENCOWE · Aged 16
When a friend bathing in the Lee cried for help, went to his rescue and was drowned · September 6 1880

PC HAROLD FRANK RICKETTS
Metropolitan Police · *Drowned at Teignmouth whilst trying to rescue a boy bathing and seen to be in difficulty* 11 September 1916

ALEXANDER STEWART BROWN
of Brockley · Fellow of the Royal College of Surgeons · *Though suffering from severe spinal injury, the result of a recent accident, died from his brave efforts to rescue a drowning man and to restore his life* · October 9 1900

EDMUND EMERY of 272 King's Road
Chelsea · Passenger · *Leapt from a Thames steamboat to rescue a child and was drowned* · July 31 1874

ERNEST BENNING
Compositor · Aged 22
Upset from a boat one dark night off Pimlico Pier grasped an oar with one hand supporting a woman with the other, but sank as she was rescued
August 25 1883

WILLIAM FREER LUCAS · MRCS LLD
at Middlesex Hospital · *Risked poison for himself rather than lessen any chance of saving a child's life and died*
October 8 1893

———— POSTMAN'S PARK cont. ————

SAMUEL RABBETH · Medical Officer of the Royal Free Hospital · *Who tried to save a child suffering from diphtheria at the cost of his own life* October 26 1884

MRS YARMAN · Wife of George Yarman · *Labourer at Bermondsey Refusing to be deterred from making three attempts to climb a burning staircase to save her aged mother, died of the effects* · March 26 1900

PC PERCY EDWIN COOK Metropolitan Police *Voluntarily descended high tension chamber at Kensington to rescue two workmen overcome by poisonous gas* 7 October 1927

FREDERICK MILLS, A. RUTTER, ROBERT DURRANT & F.D. JONES *Who lost their lives bravely striving to save a comrade at the sewage pumping works East Ham* · July 1 1895

WILLIAM GOODRAM · Signalman Aged 60 · *Lost his life at Kingsland Road Bridge in saving a workman from death under the approaching train from Kew* February 28 1880

PC EDWARD GEORGE BROWN GREENOFF · Metropolitan Police *Many lives were saved by his devotion to duty at the terrible explosion in Silvertown* · 19 January 1917

WILLIAM DONALD of Bayswater Aged 19 · Railway Clerk · *Was drowned in the Lea trying to save a lad from a dangerous entanglement of weed* July 16 1876

SOLOMAN GALAMAN · Aged 11 Died of injuries · September 6 1901 *After saving his little brother from being run over in Commercial Street. 'Mother I Saved him but I could not save myself'*

MARY ROGERS Stewardess of the *Stella* · March 30 1899 · *Self sacrificed by giving up her life belt and voluntarily going down in the sinking ship*

GEORGE LEE · Fireman · *At a fire in Clerkenwell carried an unconscious girl to the escape falling six times and died of his injuries* · July 26 1876

DAVID SELVES · Aged 12 *Off Woolwich supported his drowning playfellow and sank with him clasped in his arms* · September 12 1886

WILLIAM DRAKE *Lost his life in averting a serious accident to a Lady in Hyde Park whose horses were unmanageable through the breaking of the carriage pole* · April 2 1869

THOMAS SIMPSON · *Died of exhaustion after saving many lives from the breaking ice at Highgate Ponds* · January 25 1885

SARAH SMITH · Pantomime Artiste at Prince's Theatre · *Died of terrible injuries received when attempting in her inflammable dress to extinguish the flames which had enveloped her companion* · January 24 1863

GEORGE FREDERICK SIMONDS of Islington · *Rushed into a burning house to save an aged widow and died of his injuries* · December 1 1886

ASTROLOGICAL SCHEMATIC

	Aries	Taurus	Gemini	Cancer	Leo	Virgo	Libra	Scorpio	Sagittarius	Capricorn	Aquarius	Pisces
Northern	♈	♉	♊	♋	♌	♍	·	·	·	·	·	·
Southern	·	·	·	·	·	·	♎	♏	♐	♑	♒	♓
Fiery trigon	♈	·	·	·	♌	·	·	·	♐	·	·	·
Airy trigon	·	·	♊	·	·	·	♎	·	·	·	♒	·
Earthy trigon	·	♉	·	·	·	♍	·	·	·	♑	·	·
Watery trigon	·	·	·	♋	·	·	·	♏	·	·	·	♓
Movable	♈	·	·	♋	·	·	♎	·	·	♑	·	·
Fixed	·	♉	·	·	♌	·	·	♏	·	·	♒	·
Common	·	·	♊	·	·	♍	·	·	♐	·	·	♓
Masculine	♈	·	♊	·	♌	·	♎	·	♐	·	♒	·
Feminine	·	♉	·	♋	·	♍	·	♏	·	♑	·	♓
Cardinal	♈	·	·	♋	·	·	♎	·	·	♑	·	·
Tropical	·	·	·	♋	·	·	·	·	·	♑	·	·
Equinoctial	♈	·	·	·	·	·	♎	·	·	·	·	·
Right ascension	·	·	·	♋	♌	♍	♎	♏	♐	·	·	·
Oblique ascension	♈	♉	♊	·	·	·	·	·	·	♑	♒	♓
Bicorporeal	·	·	♊	·	·	·	·	·	♐	·	·	♓
Fruitful	·	·	·	♋	·	·	·	♏	·	·	·	♓
Barren	·	·	♊	·	♌	♍	·	·	·	·	·	·
Vernal	♈	♉	♊	·	·	·	·	·	·	·	·	·
Æstial	·	·	·	♋	♌	♍	·	·	·	·	·	·
Autumnal	·	·	·	·	·	·	♎	♏	♐	·	·	·
Hyemal	·	·	·	·	·	·	·	·	·	♑	♒	♓
Mute	·	·	·	♋	·	·	·	♏	·	·	·	♓
Humane	·	·	♊	·	·	♍	♎	·	·	·	♒	·
Bestial	·	♉	·	·	·	·	·	·	·	♑	·	·
Feral	·	·	·	·	♌	·	·	·	♐	·	·	·
Quadrupedian	♈	♉	·	·	♌	·	·	·	·	♑	·	·
Constellations	66	141	85	83	95	110	51	44	69	51	108	113

TRADITIONAL COLORS OF THE ZODIAC SIGNS

♈ … Aries … pure red		♎ … Libra … pure green
♉ … Taurus … red-orange		♏ … Scorpio … green-blue
♊ … Gemini … pure orange		♐ … Sagittarius … pure blue
♋ … Cancer … orange-yellow		♑ … Capricorn … blue-violet
♌ … Leo … pure yellow		♒ … Aquarius … pure violet
♍ … Virgo … yellow-green		♓ … Pisces … violet-red

– RAPHAEL (ROBERT C. SMITH), *A Manual of Astrology*, 1828, and MANLY P. HALL,
The Secret Teachings of All Ages, 1928 [Variations exist between sources; see also p.145.]

LODGMENT & DISLODGMENT

The following terms, from *The Art of Hunting* (?1327) by William Twici, huntsman to King Edward II, were used for the lodgment and dislodgment of animals. (So, a badger would *eartheth* into its set, and then *dig* or *find* out.)

Harboureth	*Hart & Hind*	Unharbour
Seateth; Formeth	HARE	*Start; Move*
Crocheth	BOAR	*Rear*
Traineth	WOLF	*Raise*
Lodgeth	BUCK & DOE	*Dislodge; Rouse*
Kenneleth	FOX	*Find; Unkennel*
Treeth	MARTEN	*Bay*
Beddeth	ROEBUCK & ROE	*Find*
Watcheth	OTTER	*Vent*
Eartheth	BADGER	*Dig; Find*
Burroweth	CONEY	*Bolt*

COUNTING RHYME

1, 2	buckle my shoe	11, 12	who will delve?
3, 4	shut the door	13, 14	maids a-courtin'
5, 6	pick up sticks	15, 16	maids a-kissin'
7, 8	lay them straight	17, 18	maids a-waitin'
9, 10	a good fat hen	19, 20	my stomach's empty

SNORING

A c19th euphemism for snoring — DRIVING ONE'S PIGS TO MARKET.

CELEBRITY BODY PARTS AT AUCTION

Celebrity	*auctioned*	item	*price*
Justin Bieber	2011	*hair, given to Ellen DeGeneres*	$40,688
Michael Jackson	2009	*a dozen strands of singed head hair*	£1,140
Elvis Presley	2009	*hair trimmed when the King enlisted*	$15,000
Lord Nelson	2009	*hair cut from his head after Trafalgar*	£2,500
John Lennon	2007	*hair collected by band's hairdresser*	£24,000
William Shatner	2006	*a kidney stone*	$25,000
Jack Nicholson	2001	*baby teeth; provenance unknown*	unsold
Judy Garland	1979	*a pair of false eyelashes*	$125
Napoleon	1977	*penis, preserved after autopsy*	$3,000

CHARMS FOR CRAMP

Samuel Taylor Coleridge (1772–1834) recounted that as a child at Christ's Hospital these 'charms' were used to counter cramp in the feet and legs:

Foot! foot! foot! is fast asleep!	*The devil is tying a knot in my leg!*
Thumb! thumb! thumb!	*Mark, Luke, and John,*
in spittle we steep:	*unloose it I beg!*
Crosses three we make to ease us,	*Crosses three we make to ease us,*
Two for the thieves,	*Two for the thieves,*
and one for Christ Jesus!	*and one for Christ Jesus!*

'And really upon getting out of bed, where the cramp most frequently occurred, pressing the sole of the foot on the cold floor, and then repeating this charm with the acts configurative thereupon prescribed, I can safely affirm that I do not remember an instance in which the cramp did not go away in a few seconds. I should not wonder if it were equally good for a stitch in the side; but I cannot say I ever tried it for that.'

THE CLASSES OF INTELLECTUAL PLEASURE

FIRST . . . . The pleasures arising from the beauty of the natural world
SECOND . . . . Those from the works of art
THIRD . . . . From the liberal arts of music, painting, and poetry
FOURTH . . . . From the sciences
FIFTH . . . . From the beauty of the person
SIXTH . . . . From wit and humor

– DAVID HARTLEY, *Observations on Man, His Frame, His Duty, & His Expectations*, 1834

APPLE SEEDS & LOVE

'To ascertain one's standing with a sweetheart, select at random an apple and quarter it, carefully gathering the seeds from the core.' The seeds mean:

Pips	meaning		
1	I love	8	They both love
2	I love	9	He comes
3	I love, I say	10	He tarries
4	I love with all my heart	11	He courts
5	I cast away	12	He marries
6	He loves	13	Honor
7	She loves	14	Riches
		– *Encyclopedia of Superstitions, &c.*, 1903	

———————————— FOOL'S ERRANDS ————————————

Fool's errands are absurd tasks set for apprentices, newcomers, and other greenhorns. (They are also known as *sleeveless* or *bootless errands*, or *snipe* or *gowk* [cuckoo] *hunts*.) The objects of such assignments are imaginary and impossible – for example, a junior mechanic might be asked to get some ELBOW GREASE, or a runner on a film set might be sent to collect a LONG STAND. Below are the objects of other fool's errands, ancient and modern:

Bag of sparks	Golden rivets	Population tool
Bag of steam	Grid squares	Portable hole
Blackboard sharpener	Half-round square	Powdered water
Blinker fluid	Hand extender	Prop wash
Bluetooth paste	Hen's teeth	Rainbow ink
Bodge tape	Horsefeather pillow	Rust polish
Bottled vacuum	Yard of flight line	Sky hook
Box of pixels	Horseshoe grease	Sleeve board
Brass-faced file	Iced steam	Soft-pointed chisel
Bushel of air	Inch creeper	Stone stretcher
Chopped flour	Keyboard fluid	Straight hook
Crescent saw	Left-handed hammer	Strap oil
Crocodile quills	Long stand	Tartan paint
Curve straightener	Long weight	10' of shoreline
Dehydrated water	Medicinal compound	Threadless screws
Diet Guinness	Moral compass	Tulip powder
Eel's feet	Mousetrap porridge	Universal solvent
Electric anvil	One-ended stick	WiFi ducting
Error bars	Pigeon's milk	Wild haggis
Ethernet tape	Pig's eggs	Worsted bellows
Glass nails	Plinth ladder	Yard-wide pack thread

Various books have served as fool's errands, including *The Life & Adventures of Eve's Mother*; *The History of Adam's Grandfather*; and *The Life of the Wife of the Unknown Soldier*.

———————————— ON KILLING CATS ————————————

Cats are said to have nine lives, according to John Badcock in his 1823 dictionary of slang, because there is a nonad of ways to dispose of them:

1 . . . . giving her away		5 . . . . submersion in a tub
2 . . . . .carrying her afar off		6 . . . . .shooting
3 . . . . .throwing out at window		7 . . . . starvation
4 . . . . drowning in a river		8 . . . . burning
(in the above cases 'she comes home safe')		9 . . (the one 'effective' method) hanging

— BUILDERS' ADVICE —

Never build after you are FIVE AND
FORTY; have FIVE years' *income*
in hand before you lay a brick;
and always calculate the EXPENSE
at *double the estimate*.

– ANON, *c.*1831

— MARRIAGE LADDER —

. ADMIRATION .
. FLIRTATION .
. APPROBATION .
. DECLARATION .
. HESITATION .
. AGITATION .
. ACCEPTATION .
. SOLEMNIZATION .
. POSSESSION .
. RUMINATION .
. ALTERATION .
. IRRITATION .
. DISPUTATION .
. DESPERATION .
. DETESTATION .
. SEPARATION .

– adapted from an
ANONYMOUS C19th poem

— FOUR OLD THINGS —

Alphonso, King of Arragon, said
there were only four things worth
living for: OLD WINE *to drink*, OLD
WOOD *to burn*, OLD BOOKS *to read*,
and OLD FRIENDS *to converse with*.

— TRUTH'S TRILOGY —

There are three parts in truth:
FIRST, the *inquiry*,
which is the wooing of it;
SECONDLY, the *knowledge* of it,
which is the presence of it;
and THIRDLY, the *belief*,
which is the enjoyment of it.

– FRANCIS BACON (1561–1626)

— ON EMINENCE —

Aristotle defined three
prerequisites for eminence:
NATURE, STUDY, & EXERCISE.

— DIABOLICAL TRIO —

If you want ENEMIES, *excel others*.
If you want FRIENDS,
let others excel you.

There is a diabolical trio, existing
in the natural man, implacable,
inextinguishable, cooperative,
and consentaneous:

PRIDE · ENVY · HATE

PRIDE, that makes us fancy we
deserve all the goods
that others possess;
ENVY, that some should
be admired, while we are
overlooked; and
HATE, because all that is
bestowed on others, diminishes
the sum that we think due
to ourselves.

– C.C. COLTON, 1821

A TAXONOMY OF SMILES

FIRST SPECIES · *Simulated Smiles*

1 .... The condescending or patronizing smile 1
2 .... The insidious smile 2
3 .... The sardonic sneer or furtive leer 3
4 .... The beseeching or persuading smile 4
5 .... The ironical or don't-you-wish-you-may-get-it? smile 5
6 .... The cajoling smirk or wheedling grin 6

SECOND SPECIES · *Vulgar or Unintellectual Smiles*

1 .... The credulous simper or gullible smile 1
2 .... The chuckle or exulting smile 2
3 .... The vague persistent smile or vacant simper 3

THIRD SPECIES · *Refined, Intellectual, & Amiable Smiles*

1 .... The entreating smile of infancy 1
2 .... The confiding smile of childhood 2
3 .... The maternal sympathetic smile 3
4 .... The infant's smile of delight 4
5 .... The grandmother's affectionate smile 5
6 .... The grandchild's grateful smile 6
7 .... The joyous smile of friendly recognition 7
8 .... The supremely affectionate smile 8
9 .... The pensive smile 9
10 .... The self-conceited smile or smile of self-esteem 10

FOURTH SPECIES · *The Creature-Comfort Smiles*

1 .... Sawney's snuff-tickling smile 1
2 ... Jack Tar's joyful smile over 'the cup that cheers but not inebriates' ... 2

– GEORGE VASEY, *The Philosophy of Laughter & Smiling*, 1875

'Oh! What a sight there is in that word "smile" for it changes color like a chameleon. There's a *vacant smile*, a *cold smile*, a *satiric smile*, a *smile of hate*, an *affected smile*, a *smile of approbation*, a *friendly smile*; but above all, a *smile of love*. A woman has two smiles that an angel might envy – the smile that *accepts the lover* before words are uttered, and the smile that *lights on the first-born baby*, and assures him of a mother's love.' – THOMAS HALIBURTON (1796–1865)

JOHN LE CARRÉ'S CIRCUS CODE

Code name	Circus suspect		
Tinker	Percy Alleline	Soldier	Roy Bland
Tailor	Bill Haydon	Poorman	Toby Esterhase
		Beggarman	George Smiley

———— UNUSUAL APRIL FOOL'S DAY HOAXES ————

On April 2, 1803, the *Times* of London bemoaned the previous day's paucity of hoaxes: 'Yesterday is supposed to have been the very dullest and most barren of jests for the last fifty years. No messenger came from Bonaparte. Mr Addington was not diminished, nor did Mr Pitt come in to make war. Even the Bulls and Bears in the Alley were unable to make a hoax or to take in Duck or Gall. With the exception of a few schoolboys who went to buy pigeons' milk [see p.59], as usual, half-a-dozen miserable Frenchmen who were sent to see the lions washed in the Tower, and a fashionable or two who lost their dinners, owing to forged invitations, there was not a joke stirring all over the metropolis, and wit was as much below par as stocks.'

P. T. Barnum submitted his employees and family to a curious hoax on April 1, 1851. Having obtained a swatch of blank telegraph forms, Barnum had delivered a series of 'astounding intelligences', including informing one man that he had become the father of twins, and telling another that his hometown had been razed to the ground along with his house.

Royal lions were housed in the Tower of London from Henry III's reign until 1834, when they were moved to Regent's Park. As noted above, one of the most famous April Fool's hoaxes involved sending innocents to watch the 'annual ceremony of the washing of the lions'. In 1860, thousands were given invitations that read 'Admit the Bearer and Friend to view the Annual Ceremony of washing the White Lions on Sunday April 1st, 1860. Admitted at the White Gate. It is particularly requested that no gratuity be given to the warders or their assistants'.

On April 2, 1857, the *New York Times* reported: 'April Fool Day is going out of remembrance. There was less fooling yesterday than usual – *thanks to advancing civilization.*'

In 1915, the French trench paper *Rigolboche* printed this April Fool's Day jest: 'A telegram dated April 1 announces that England, terrified by the German blockade, has left its ordinary position between the North Sea and the Atlantic and is being towed by its Fleet towards an unknown destination. Admiral Tirpitz wires, "Am in pursuit"'.

Also on April 1, 1915, the *Times* of London reported that 'an airman flying over the Lille aerodrome dropped a football. It fell slowly through the air and the Germans could be seen hurrying from all directions to take cover from what they evidently thought was a bomb. That it bounced to an enormous height before exploding was probably taken to be due to a "delay action" fuse, for it was not till the ball fully came to rest that they emerged from their shelters to examine it. On it was written *April Fool – Gott strafe England*'.

—— UNUSUAL APRIL FOOL'S DAY HOAXES cont. ——

Speculators on the Detroit Stock Exchange were keen to trade in a new stock chalked up for the first time on April 1, 1922. According to the *Times*, trading in American Fire Protection (AFP) was 'spirited' – the stock opened at 6, rose to 12, fell back to 2, and rallied to 8 before the Michigan Securities Commission reported that AFP stood for April Fool Preferred.

According to the *Times* of London's man in Constantinople, in 1924 the Turkish newspaper *Yenigün* perpetrated a *poisson d'Avril* hoax on its readers by printing that a vast fish weighing 500 okes (*c.* 1,400 lbs) had been caught. Not only did great numbers flock to the spot where the monster had been landed, but also the rival newspaper *Tanin* faithfully reproduced the story. When *Yenigün* admitted its deception, *Tanin* did not take the joke well, complaining that 'although such a custom may be perhaps tolerated in the West, it is not understood here and is unsuitable to Turkey'.

On April 2, 1952, the British Home Secretary was questioned in the Commons about top-secret papers from the Harwell atomic research station that had been found in the street and handed in to the police. It soon transpired, however, that these papers were an April Fool's hoax played by a schoolboy, who admitted to 'writing a lot of gibberish on foolscap sheets' using old Norwegian letterheading and a blueprint of a nut and bolt.

In 1982, Athens was thrown into panic when the city's radio station broadcast a hoax news flash that pollution had reached lethal levels. Given the dense yellow-green fog that shrouded the city, this warning seemed all too plausible, and schools and hospitals began evacuation planning. So serious was the hoax that three journalists were charged and tried for deliberately alarming the public. Only after politicians and journalists spoke in their defense were they acquitted.

In 1985, the *Times* of London Diary reported that 'hundreds of phone calls to Mr C. Lion and A. Bear have taken their toll on London Zoo. An answering machine told callers that if they genuinely wished to get in touch with the zoo they should do so through the operator'. The operator said, 'London Zoo would accept no calls at all until the fateful day had passed'.

The Iraqi newspaper *Babel*, run by Saddam Hussein's son Uday, became notorious for running April Fool's Day 'jokes' taunting its readers. In 1998, the paper quoted Bill Clinton as saying that sanctions were soon to be lifted; in 1999, the paper said that rations would soon include bananas, chocolate and soft drinks; and in 2001, the paper claimed that all students would pass their end-of-year exams and that a consignment of BMWs ordered in the 1980s would soon be delivered.

[See also p.119]

———————— TIMETABLES FOR HAPPINESS &c. ————————

If you wish to be happy for a day, GET WELL SHAVED;
If for a week, GET INVITED TO A WEDDING;
If for a month, BUY A GOOD NAG;
If for half a year, BUY A HANDSOME HOUSE;
If for a year, MARRY A HANDSOME WIFE;
If for two years, TAKE HOLY ORDERS;
But, if you would be always gay and cheerful, PRACTICE TEMPERANCE.

❦

If you would be happy for a day, GET DRUNK;
For two days, GET A PIG;
For a month, GET MARRIED;
And for life, PLANT A GARDEN.

❦

Let him who would be happy for a day, GO TO A BARBER;
For a week, MARRY A WIFE;
For a month, BUY HIM A NEW HORSE;
For a year, BUILD HIM A NEW HOUSE;
For all his life, BE AN HONEST MAN.

❦

If you would be happy for a day, GO TO THE BATH;
If a week, HAVE BLOOD LET;
If a month, KILL A SOW;
If, however, a year, TAKE A WIFE.

❦

If you wish a good day, SHAVE YOURSELF;
A good month, KILL A PIG;
A good year, MARRY;
And one always good, BECOME A CLERGYMAN.

❦

For a DAY OF JOY, you count a MONTH OF GRIEF,
For a MONTH OF PLEASURE, you reckon a YEAR OF PAIN.
There is no strength except in ALLAH.
– quoted by CHARLES DICKENS in *All the Year Round*, 1865[†]

❦

If you plan for a year, PLANT A SEED;
If for ten years, PLANT A TREE;
If for a hundred years, TEACH THE PEOPLE.
– attributed to many, including KUAN CHUNG (*d.*645 BC)

[†] Before this 'Arab Thought', Dickens noted the observation: 'Repentance for a day, is to
start on a journey, without knowing where to find shelter for the night. Repentance for a
year, is to sow seed in your fields out of season. Repentance for a whole lifetime, is to marry
a woman without being properly edified respecting her family, her temper, and her beauty.'

A CHRONOLOGY OF CRAYOLA® CRAYON COLORS

Year columns (left to right): 1903 · 1949–57 · 1958–71 · 1972–89 · 1990–92 · 1993 · 1998 · 2000 · 2003

Almond
Antique Brass
Apricot
Aquamarine
Asparagus
Atomic Tangerine
Banana Mania
Beaver
Bittersweet
Black
Blizzard Blue
Blue
Blue Bell
Blue Gray
Blue Green
Blue Violet
Blush
Brick Red
Brown
Burnt Orange
Burnt Sienna
Cadet Blue
Canary
Caribbean Green
Carnation Pink
Cerise
Cerulean
Chartreuse
Chestnut
Copper
Cornflower
Cotton Candy
Dandelion
Denim
Desert Sand
Eggplant
Electric Lime
Fern

Flesh [a]
Forest Green
Fuchsia
Fuzzy Wuzzy Brown
Gold
Goldenrod
Granny Smith Apple
Gray
Green
Green Blue
Green Yellow
Hot Magenta
Inch Worm
Indian Red [b]
Indigo
Jazzberry Jam
Jungle Green
Laser Lemon
Lavender
Lemon Yellow
Macaroni & Cheese
Magenta
Magic Mint
Mahogany
Maize
Manatee
Mango Tango
Maroon
Mauvelous
Melon
Midnight Blue
Mountain Meadow
Mulberry
Navy Blue
Neon Carrot
Olive Green
Orange
Orange Red

Orange Yellow
Orchid
Outer Space
Outrageous Orange
Pacific Blue
Peach
Periwinkle
Piggy Pink
Pine Green
Pink Flamingo
Pink Sherbet
Plum
Prussian Blue [c]
Purple Heart
Purple Mountain's Majesty
Purple Pizzazz
Radical Red
Raw Sienna
Raw Umber
Razzle Dazzle Rose
Razzmatazz
Red
Red Orange
Red Violet
Robin's Egg Blue
Royal Purple
Salmon
Scarlet
Screamin' Green
Sea Green
Sepia
Shadow
Shamrock
Shocking Pink
Silver
Sky Blue
Spring Green
Sunglow

Sunset Orange
Tan
Teal Blue
Thistle
Tickle Me Pink
Timber Wolf
Torch Red
Tropical Rain Forest
Tumbleweed
Turquoise Blue
Ultra Blue
Ultra Green
Ultra Orange
Ultra Pink
Ultra Red
Ultra Yellow
Unmellow Yellow
Violet
Violet (Purple)
Violet Blue
Violet Red
Vivid Tangerine
Vivid Violet
White
Wild Blue Yonder
Wild Strawberry
Wild Watermelon
Wisteria
Yellow
Yellow Green
Yellow Orange

[a] Became 'Peach' in 1962, partially as a result of the US Civil Rights Movement. [b] Became 'Chestnut' in 1999 to avoid confusion with skin color – although the name derived from an Indian pigment. [c] Changed to 'Midnight Blue' in 1958 after requests from teachers. [Source: Crayola®]

SIGN-WRITING BRUSH SIZES

Sign-writing brushes are traditionally constructed from the quills of birds. The feathers are removed (often set aside for other purposes, such as marbling), and the hard barrel is cut and boiled. Then a knot of hair, usually sable or ox hair, is carefully shaped and placed inside the barrel. The diameter of the brush depends on the size of the quill. Small birds (such as the lark) have smaller quills and are used for more intricate work; larger birds (such as the swan) are used for broader coverage. Below are just some of the standard names of sign-writing brushes. Readers should note that not all manufacturers offer all the sizes, and that in addition to natural discrepancies in quill diameter, brush sizes tend to vary across brands.

Brush name	*diameter (mm)*
Condor (now obsolete) ..... }	8
Large Swan	
Middle.	
Small Swan	} 4–7
Extra Goose	
Goose.	
Small Goose.	
Large Duck.	} 2–4
Duck	
Small Duck.	
Crow	} 0–2
Lark.	

SMALL LARK   LARK   CROW   SWAN

EIGHT RULES FOR CHILDREN

WORK *quickly*, SING *sweetly*, STEP *lightly*, WRITE *neatly*,
SING *softly*, WALK *sprightly*, SPEAK *gently*, and *politely*.

FEMALE BEAUTY

The Arabians categorized Female Beauty into the following nine quartets:

Four BLACK	Hair	Eyebrows	Eyelashes	Eyes
Four WHITE	Skin	Whites of eyes	Teeth	Legs
Four RED	Tongue	Lips	Cheeks	Gums
Four ROUND	Head	Neck	Forearms	Ankles
Four LONG	Back	Fingers	Arms	Legs
Four WIDE	Forehead	Eyes	Seat	Lips
Four FINE	Eyebrows	Nose	Lips	Fingers
Four THICK	Buttocks	Thighs	Calves	Knees
Four SMALL	Breasts	Ears	Hands	Feet

– W. WYNN WESTCOTT, *Numbers, Their Occult Power & Mystic Virtue*, 1890

ON RECEIVING A FAVOR

Pride combined with feeling + a favor ....smarts under it
Senseless arrogance + a favor .... takes it as a due
Stupidity + a favor .... does not perceive it
Levity + a favor..forgets it
A broken spirit + a favor.................... is surprised and humbled by it
Suspicion + a favor.....................................misinterprets it
Crafty selfishness + a favor ....seeks for more
A generous spirit + a favor..................... feels it without humiliation

– RICHARD WHATELY, Archbishop of Dublin (1787–1863)

THE CURIOUSNESS OF THE WORD 'HEROINE'

Male + Female + Brave man + Opiate = HEROINE ☞ ([{⟨he⟩r}o]in)e

ON PASSING THE TIME

What makes the time pass quickly? ....ACTIVITY
What long and heavy both? .... WHAT ELSE BUT SLOTH?
What doth debts create?................................. TO BEAR AND WAIT
What brings rich gains along?......................... NOT TO THINK LONG
What doth honors collect?....................................SELF-RESPECT

– GEORGE HENRY CALVERT (1803–89)

TELEGRAPHY & TWITTER

The 140-character limit of Twitter posts was guided by the 160-character limit established by the developers of text messaging. Yet, there is nothing new about new technology imposing restrictions on articulation. During the c19th telegraphy boom, some carriers charged extra for words of >15 characters and for messages of >10 words. Thus, the cheapest telegram was often limited to 150 characters. ❦ Concerns for economy and desires for secrecy fueled a boom in codebooks that reduced common and complex phrases into single words. Dozens of different codes were published; many catered to specific occupations and all promised efficiency. ❦ The phrases below are from *The Anglo-American Telegraphic Code* (1891, 3RD EDITION):

ACESCET	Has met with a trifling accident	EDUCT	A large amount has been embezzled
ACUATE	You will accomplish but little	EMICATION	The epidemic has broken out again
ADFLUXION	The account is full of errors	EMPLOY	Take every precaution against escape
ADJUTORY	Accumulate no debts	ENRINGED	The news causes great excitement
ALAND	Advertise liberally but economically	EVIDENTIAL	A gunpowder explosion occurred
ALOOFNESS	Agent is dead	EXPEDITE	You can go to any extreme
AMPHIMACER	You must send my allowance immediately	FLANK	A fire is raging here. Please send engine
		GEYSER	Do not pay in gold
ANDALUSITE	You seem to be annoyed	HABERDASH	A writ of habeas corpus cannot be issued
ANTALGIC	Application was received, acted upon, and rejected	HEMSTICH	Hindered by ill health
ARBORIST	A libelous article	HORTYARD	There is little hope
BABYLONITE	Please provide bail immediately	HUB	Can you recommend to me (us) a competent housemaid?
BALLOTER	Returned from the bank 'no good'		
BANISHER	Forced into bankruptcy	HURST	The hunting expedition will not set out
BARRACAN	A battle is reported to have begun	ILLITERAL	A panic is thought to be imminent
BLACKTAIL	You have made a blunder	INSIDIATOR	How much is your life insured for?
BLOCKISH	Allow for a liberal bonus	KAVASS	A large number were killed
BLOWZED	Borrow as little as possible	MAHOGANY	Malaria prevails extensively
BOUTADE	Business is declining	MANNITE	The market should be manipulated
CAPRIPED	Cattle are scarce	MESSET	Energetic means must be adopted
CASSOCKED	His character as to honesty, bad	ORANGEMAN	What is the opinion on the street?
CAUSSON	Give liberally for charitable purposes	ORGANISM	Taxation is oppressive
CELLAR	The cheaper the better	PANEL	Stocks have reached panic prices
COGWARE	Compliments of the season	PHANTASTIC	Physician gives very little hope
COMMITTER	Compulsion must be used if necessary	PORY	It would establish a bad precedent
		RELEASER	The mistake cannot be rectified
CONFORMER	Condemn the entire thing	ROLLABLE	Your request is unreasonable
CONFUTER	The prisoner(s) will probably be condemned	ROSELITE	Resistance is useless
		RUSSET	Bank just robbed
CRISP	Can you recommend to me a good female cook?	SCHOTTISH	The wet season now prevails
		SLANK	Sick of the entire matter
CUISH	A crisis seems to be approaching	SLOKE	Snow impedes operations
DECEMVIR	Has been dead a long time	TITMOUSE	I (we) accept with pleasure your invitation for the theater tomorrow evening
DESERTLESS	Denial is useless		
DEWS	Destroyed by a cyclone	WASTAGE	War is inevitable

— TRADITIONAL BESTIARY OF ITALIAN WOMEN —

MAGPIES................ at the door	SAINTS .... in church
SIRENS .... at the window	DEVILS .... in the house

—— COMMON WALL-COVERING SYMBOLS ——

→|0	No match / free match	～～	Spongeable
→|←	Straight match	≈≈	Washable
→|←	Half drop / offset match	≋≋	Super-washable
$\frac{60}{30}$	Distance between repeat / Distance offset	～／	Scrubbable
↑	Direction of hanging	≋／	Extra-scrubbable
↕	Reverse alternate lengths	↗	Strippable
Colorfastness to light		↗	Peelable
☼ ☼ ☼ ☼ ○		↗	Dry peelable
moderate .... good ....excellent		＼	Wet removal
♨	Pre-pasted	)))	Duplex
▐▦	Paste the wall	↖	Impact-resistant
▥⎫	Paste the paper	≋≋≋	Coordinated fabric available

[Sources differ slightly in their wording, and include: John Lewis, Dulux, &c.]

—— ON NAIL CUTTING & DAYS OF THE WEEK ——

Cut them on MONDAY, cut them for *Health*;
Cut them on TUESDAY, cut them for *Wealth*;
Cut them on WEDNESDAY, cut them for *News*;
Cut them on THURSDAY, for a pair of new *Shoes*;
Cut them on FRIDAY, cut them for *Sorrow*;
Cut them on SATURDAY, *See Your Sweetheart Tomorrow*.
A man had better *Ne'er Been Born*, than have his nails on a SUNDAY shorn.

PANHELLENIC GAMES

Location	name	deity honored	wreath
Olympia	Olympic Games	Zeus	wild olive leaf
Delphi	Pythian Games	Apollo	laurel
Isthmia	Isthmian Games	Poseidon	pine
Nemea	Nemean Games	Zeus	wild celery

RECYCLING SYMBOLS

A bewildering array of recycling symbols exists across the world, and the confusion they cause is exacerbated by a lack of international agreement. Below are some common symbols and, underneath, those used for plastics:

some recycling costs were paid	*recyclable glass*	*is recyclable or contains recycled material – often indicated by a percentage*		*recyclable aluminium*	*European Ecolabel participant*

I	2	3	4	5	6	7
PETE	HDPE	V	LDPE	PP	PS	
polyethylene terephthalate	*high-density polyethylene*	*PVC*	*low-density polyethylene*	*polypropylene*	*polystyrene*	*other/hybrid materials*

ANON'S ALPHABETICAL WOOING

Let others talk of L N's eyes, And K T's figure, light and free,
Say L R too is beautiful — I heed them not while U I C.
U need not N V them, for U X L them all, my M L E.
I have no words when I would tell how much in love with U I B.
So sweet U R, my D R E, I love your very F E G;
And when you speak or sing, your voice I like a winsome L O D,
When U R I-C, hope D K's, I am a mere non-N T T.
Such F E K C has your smile, it shields me from N E N M E.
For love so deep as mine, I fear, there is no other M E D,
But that you love me back again — O, thought of heavenly X T C!
So, lest my M T heart and I should sing for love an L E G,
T's me no more — B Y's, B kind, O, M L E, U R, I C!

A HANDY TABLE OF DATES

The tabulation below shows the number of days from any date in one month to the same date in any other month.

E.g., How many days from May 26 to September 26? Find May in the left column and September at the top: 123 days. ☞ In a leap year, add 1 day if February is included.

From To	Jan	Feb	Mar	Apr	May	June	July	Aug	Sep	Oct	Nov	Dec
January	365	31	59	90	120	151	181	212	243	273	304	334
February	334	365	28	59	89	120	150	181	212	242	273	303
March	306	337	365	31	61	92	122	153	184	214	245	275
April	275	306	334	365	30	61	91	122	153	183	214	244
May	245	276	304	335	365	31	61	92	123	153	184	214
June	214	245	273	304	334	365	30	61	92	122	153	183
July	184	215	243	274	304	335	365	31	62	92	123	153
August	153	184	212	243	273	304	334	365	31	61	92	122
September	122	153	181	212	242	273	303	334	365	30	61	91
October	92	123	151	182	212	243	273	304	335	365	31	61
November	61	92	120	151	181	212	242	273	304	334	365	30
December	31	62	90	121	151	182	212	243	274	304	335	365

NICK'S NAMES

The Prince of Darkness · Old Nick · Old Gooseberry · Beelzebub (the Lord of the Flies) · His Satanic Majesty · Old Harry · Satan
Old Uncle · Mr Scratch · Old Horny · Lucifer · The Tempter · The Prince of Devils · Old Adam · Mephistopheles · Satanel · Deuce
The Old Gentleman · Belial · Dickon · Gentleman Jack · Abbatôn · Black Bogey · Asmodeus · Tryphôn · The Archfiend · Samiel

DECEPTIONS

A Welsh proverb has it that in *three things may a man be deceived*:

In A MAN *till known*;
A TREE *till down*; A DAY *till done*.

5 Ds OF DODGEBALL

DODGE, DUCK, DIP, DIVE, DODGE

RAIN DISMISSALS

Rain, rain, go away,
come again another day.

Rain, rain, go to Spain,
And never come back here again.

Rain on the green grass,
And rain on the tree,
And rain on the housetop,
But not on me.
[see also pp.50–51]

ON ASKING FAVORS

Before you ask a man a favor consult the weather. The same person that is as UGLY AS SIN when *cold rain* is rattling against the windowpanes will no sooner feel the gladdening influence of a little *quiet sunshine* than his heart will EXPAND LIKE A ROSEBUD.   – ANON

PARADOX OF BEDS

What a PARADOX is a bed! It is a thing that we *dislike* to be OBLIGED to keep, yet we are *unwilling* to be WITHOUT. We *go to it* with RELUCTANCE, yet *quit it* with REGRET. We *make up our minds* every night to leave it EARLY, and *make up our bodies* every morning to keep it LATE.   – ANON, *c.*1826

ON ANGER

The eight causes of anger are:

Deprivation of Riches
Ingratitude
Betraying a Secret
Neglecting a Faithful Servant
Abusive Language
Unjust Suspicion
Murder
Censoriousness

From *Ayeen Akbery; or, The Institutes of the Emperor Akber* [Translated by Francis Gladwin, 1800]

An ancient Sanskrit proverb on ANGER notes: In a GOOD MAN, wrath lasts for a moment; in a MIDDLE MAN, for two hours; in a BASE MAN, for a day and a night; in a GREAT SINNER, until death.

ON THE PROGRESS OF FRIENDSHIP

2 Glances ☞ 1 Bow ☞ 2 Bows ☞ 1 How d'ye do ☞ 6 How d'ye do's
☞ 1 Conversation ☞ 4 Conversations ☞ 1 Acquaintance

'D-DAY' & ZULU TIME

Although we tend to associate 'D-Day' with June 6, 1944[†], the 'D-Day' of any operation is simply the day on which it starts. The time an operation commences is known as its 'H-Hour', and a logical code of + and – times apply. To coordinate operations across time zones, soldiers employ 'Zulu time', which is simply Greenwich Mean Time (GMT) or Coordinated Universal Time (UTC). 'Zulu time' is indicated by appending the letter Z to the standard 24-hour clock, e.g., 2100Z. To indicate time zones on either side of GMT, the NATO alphabet is used, as this table demonstrates:

Phonetic	example city	GMT ±			
Alpha	Paris	GMT+1 (2200A)	Zulu	Greenwich	GMT (2100Z)
Bravo	Athens	GMT+2 (2300B)	November	Azores	GMT–1 (2000N)
Charlie	Moscow	GMT+3 (0000C)	Oscar	Rio de Janiero	GMT–2 (1900O)
Delta	Kabul	GMT+4 (0100D)	Papa	Buenos Aires	GMT–3 (1800P)
Echo	New Delhi	GMT+5 (0200E)	Quebec	Halifax	GMT–4 (1700Q)
Foxtrot	Rangoon	GMT+6 (0300F)	Rome	New York	GMT–5 (1600R)
Golf	Bangkok	GMT+7 (0400G)	Sierra	Chicago	GMT–6 (1500S)
Hotel	Beijing	GMT+8 (0500H)	Tango	Denver	GMT–7 (1400T)
India	Tokyo	GMT+9 (0600I)	Uniform	San Francisco	GMT–8 (1300U)
Kilo	Brisbane	GMT+10 (0700K)	Victor	Anchorage	GMT–9 (1200V)
Lima	Sydney	GMT+11 (0800L)	Whiskey	Hawaii	GMT–10 (1100W)
Mike	Kamchatka	GMT+12 (0900M)	X-ray	Wellington	GMT–11 (1000X)
			Yankee	Fiji	GMT–12 (0900Y)

The suffix J represents 'Juliet time', which is not included in this nomenclature since it describes the current local time of an observer, wherever they may be. In addition to this system, the American military employs a complex code of day and hour prefixes to organize its troops across the world:

C-Day . . . . *day deployment operations commence*
D-Day . . . . *day on which an operation commences*
I-Day . . . . *day on which intelligence indicators are recognized*
M-Day . . . . *day on which full mobilization is declared*
N-Day . . . . *day an active-duty unit is notified about (re)deployment*
R-Day . . . . *day hostile forces are first prepared to attack* or *redeployment day*
S-Day . . . . *day the President authorizes certain reservists to be called up*
T-Day . . . . *day coincident with the presidential declaration of national emergency*
W-Day . . . . *day the President decides a hostile government has initiated hostilities*
F-Hour . . . . *time of announcement by the Sec. of Defense to the military*
H-Hour . . . . *hour on D-Day at which a particular operation commences*
L-Hour . . . . *hour on C-Day at which a particular operation commences*
N-Hour . . . . *time between alert notification and first unit departure*
X-Hour . . . . *time when units plan deployment after receiving the warning order*

[Sources vary.] † Operation Overlord was postponed from June 5 by one day due to inclement weather; thus, it is conceivable that we should more properly commemorate 'D+1 Day'.

———— ALFRED HITCHCOCK'S CAMEOS ————

Alfred Hitchcock's fleeting cameos are an integral part of his filmography and personal mythology. However he said that his first such appearance, in *The Lodger*, was 'strictly utilitarian; we had to fill the screen. Later on it became a superstition and eventually a gag. But by now it's rather a troublesome gag, and I'm very careful to show up in the first five minutes so as to let the people look at the rest of the movie with no further distraction'†.

1926	THE LODGER	*AH appears twice: first seated in a newsroom; then as a bystander when the lodger is lynched by a crowd.*
1927	EASY VIRTUE	*Walking past the heroine, Larita, as he leaves a tennis court.*
1929	BLACKMAIL	*Being pestered by a small boy as he tries to read on a train.*
1930	MURDER	*Walking past the house where the murder was committed.*
1935	THE 39 STEPS	*Passing by in the street with scriptwriter Charles Bennett as protagonists Richard Hannay and Annabella Smith alight from the No. 25 London bus‡.*
1937	YOUNG AND INNOCENT	*AH appears outside a courthouse as a photographer with a tiny camera.*
1938	THE LADY VANISHES	*Walking along the platform at Victoria Station at the end of the film.*
1940	REBECCA	*Walking by in the background as character Jack Favell talks to a policeman.*
1940	FOREIGN CORRESPONDENT	*Reading a newspaper in the street; AH passes character Johnny Jones/Huntley Haverstock.*
1941	MR AND MRS SMITH	*Passing Mr Smith in the street.*
1941	SUSPICION	*Posting a letter in a village postbox.*
1942	SABOTEUR	*Standing in front of a shop selling 'cut-rate drugs'.*
1943	SHADOW OF A DOUBT	*Playing cards on a train.*
1944	LIFEBOAT	*In 'before' and 'after' pictures in a newspaper advertisement for* Reducto – Obesity Slayer.
1945	SPELLBOUND	*Leaving a crowded elevator smoking a cigar and carrying a violin case.*
1946	NOTORIOUS	*Drinking Champagne at a party.*
1947	THE PARADINE CASE	*Leaving a train station carrying a cello case, behind character Anthony Keane.*
1948	ROPE	*AH appears twice: walking along the street after the main titles; and his profile drawing is seen as a flashing neon sign advertising* Reducto.
1949	UNDER CAPRICORN	*AH appears twice: at the governor's reception, and then on the steps of Government House.*
1950	STAGE FRIGHT	*Turning in the street to look at character Eve Gill as she is practicing being her alter ego, Doris Tinsdale.*
1951	STRANGERS ON A TRAIN	*Boarding a train carrying a double bass.*
1953	I CONFESS	*Walking across the top of a long flight of steps at the beginning of the film.*

———— ALFRED HITCHCOCK'S CAMEOS cont. ————

1954	DIAL M FOR MURDER	*Seated at a table in a photograph of a class reunion.*
1954	REAR WINDOW	*Winding a clock in the songwriter's apartment.*
1955	TO CATCH A THIEF	*Sitting on a bus next to character John Robie (Cary Grant), who looks at him.*
1955	THE TROUBLE WITH HARRY	*Walking past a parked car at an outdoor art exhibition.*
1956	THE MAN WHO KNEW TOO MUCH	*In a crowd watching acrobats.*
1956	THE WRONG MAN	*AH appears in silhouette, introducing the film.*
1958	VERTIGO	*Walking past character Gavin Elster's shipyard carrying a horn case.*
1959	NORTH BY NORTHWEST	*Seen just missing a bus; the doors close in his face.*
1960	PSYCHO	*Standing in a street wearing a hat.*
1963	THE BIRDS	*Exiting a pet shop with two small dogs.*
1964	MARNIE	*Stepping out into a hotel corridor, where Marnie is staying.*
1966	TORN CURTAIN	*Holding a child in a lobby of a hotel; AH switches the infant from one knee to the other.*
1969	TOPAZ	*In an airport, standing up and shaking a man's hand after being wheeled in a wheelchair by a nurse (Peggy Robertson, his assistant).*
1972	FRENZY	*Listening to a speech being delivered beside the Thames when a body is found in the water. AH, wearing a bowler hat, is seen twice.*
1976	FAMILY PLOT	*Silhouetted in the glass-paned door of the Registrar of Births & Deaths – he is talking to another man and gesticulating.*

† As recounted in François Truffaut's *Hitchcock* (1985). Sources include Paul Duncan's *Alfred Hitchcock: Architect of Anxiety* (2003). ‡ H. Mark Glancy, in *The 39 Steps* (2003), noted that the No. 25 ran from East London – where Hitchcock grew up – to the West End.

———— NOMS DE ... ————

Nom de Dieu ..... a French oath of exasperation (literally, 'name of God')
Nom de guerre†‡ .... a fictitious name assumed during war or espionage
Nom de paix .... a euphemistic or deliberately innocent appellation
Nom d'une pipe ..... a euphemistic French oath, similar to 'for Pete's sake'
Nom de plume§ .... a pseudonymous name assumed by authors
Nom de théâtre .... a stage name assumed by actors
Nom de vente ...... an assumed name under which one bids at an auction

† According to Brewer's *Dictionary of Phrase & Fable*, it was the custom of those entering the French army to assume a *nom de guerre*; indeed, in the age of chivalry, knights were often known only by the devices on their shields. Infamous contemporary *noms de guerre* include: 'Carlos (the Jackal)' used by Ilich Ramírez Sánchez; 'Abu Abdullah', said to have been used by Osama bin Laden; and 'P. O'Neill', the name used to sign many statements issued by the Provisional Irish Republican Army. ‡ Also, *nom d'épée*. § Also, *nom littéraire*.

—— MALAGASY & 8s ——

In a fascinating 1946 article on Malagasy numerology, Arthur Leib noted that Madagascans traditionally believed that 'the number eight hides an evil, punishing power', and that '*eighth* actually means *enemy*'. Leib said that it was 'taboo to erect a heap of anything in eight shovelfuls or to wear the hair in eight strands', and that, 'In the south the natives try to prove the guilt of an accused by making him lick eight times a glowing iron. Should one or more of the wounds bleed, his guilt is proven.' Leib also reported that, 'For centuries it has been the tradition among the Hova to carry a dead man home to his native village. But it is only necessary to transport eight bones (humerus, radius, tibia of arms and legs). Evidently there is some unexplained mystical idea behind this. One sees often in Sakalava villages natives carrying eight bottles, containing honey, to the graves of the kings. Eight guardians watch day and night over the tomb. Eight persons had to carry the royal coffin to the grave, generally four men and four women.'

—— ON ADVERSITY ——

Adversity *exasperates* FOOLS, *dejects* COWARDS, *draws out the faculties* of the WISE and INDUSTRIOUS, puts the MODEST to the necessity of *trying their skill*, *awes* the OPULENT, and makes the IDLE *industrious*.

– ANON

— SPANISH PROVERB —

It is a Spanish maxim that he who *loseth wealth*, LOSETH MUCH; he who *loseth a friend*, LOSETH MORE; but he who *loseth his spirits*, LOSETH ALL.

– THE PRESS: A TOAST –

The Press: It *Ex-presses* TRUTH, *Re-presses* ERROR, *Im-presses* KNOWLEDGE, *De-presses* TYRANNY, and *Op-presses* NONE.

– ANON

—— ON COURTSHIP ——

Two or three *dears*
and two or three *sweets*,
Two or three *balls*
and two or three *treats*;
Two or three *serenades*
giv'n as a lure,
Two or three *oaths*
how much they endure;
Two or three *messages*
sent in one day,
Two or three times *led out*
from the play,
Two or three *soft speeches*
made by the way;
Two or three *tickets*
for two or three times,
Two or three *love letters*
writ all in rhymes;
Two or three *months*
keeping strict to these *rules*,
Can never fail of making
a couple of *fools*.

– JONATHAN SWIFT (1667–1745)

SOME NOTABLE FLIGHTS

Flight No. or craft name	date	from–to	significance
Unnamed	11/21/1783	Paris–Paris	said to be world's first human flight, in hot-air balloon devised by the Montgolfier brothers
Unnamed	9/24/1852	Paris–(a field near) Elancourt, France	first steerable & powered flight, in dirigible flown by Henri Giffard
Unnamed	12/17/1903	Kitty Hawk, NC–vicinity	first powered & sustained flight of a heavier-than-air craft, by the Wright brothers
Vickers-Vimy Atlantic	6/14/1919	St John's, NL–Clifden, Ireland	first nonstop transatlantic flight, by John Alcock & Arthur Brown
Spirit of St Louis	5/20/1927	New York–Paris	first nonstop solo transatlantic flight, by Charles Lindbergh
Southern Cross	5/31/1928	Oakland, CA–Brisbane, Australia	first transpacific flight, by Charles Kingsford Smith and Charles Ulm
Unnamed	20/5/1932	Harbour Grace, NL–Culmore, N. Ireland	first solo flight by a woman across the Atlantic, by Amelia Earhart
Hindenburg	5/3/1937	Frankfurt–Lakehurst, NJ	fiery disaster in NJ that killed 36 and signaled the end of dirigible travel
US Navy Flight 19	12/5/1945	Ft Lauderdale, 3-stop practice run	5 planes disappeared, fueling speculation about the Bermuda Triangle
Lucky Lady II	2/26/1949	Carswell USAF Base, TX–Carswell again	first nonstop flight around the world, by Capt. James Gallagher and crew
Pan Am 2	1/21/1970	JFK–LHR	first commercial flight of a Boeing 747, ushering in the age of the jumbo jet
Air France 085	1/21/1976	CDG–GIG	first commercial Concorde flight (one of two simultaneously)
Trans American 209†	1980?	LAX–ORD (probably)	after food poisoning hits the crew, passenger Ted Striker is forced to fly plane
Gossamer Albatross	6/12/1979	Folkestone, UK–Cap Gris-Nez, France	first human (pedal)-powered flight across the Channel
Pan Am 103	12/21/1988	LHR–JFK	Libyan terrorist bomb caused plane to explode over Lockerbie, Scotland, killing 270
Air France 8969	12/24/1994	ALG–ORY	3 killed during hijacking by Algerian terrorists; the rest were saved by a French commando raid
Oceanic 815†	9/22/2004	SYD–LAX	crashed on a mysterious island; a number of telegenic survivors struggle amid various perils
American Airlines 11	9/11/2001	BOS–LAX	hijacked by Islamic terrorists and crashed into the North Tower of the World Trade Center in NYC‡
United Airlines 175	9/11/2001	BOS–LAX	hijacked by Islamic terrorists and crashed into the South Tower of the World Trade Center in NYC‡
American Airlines 77	9/11/2001	IAD–LAX	hijacked by Islamic terrorists and crashed into the southwest side of the Pentagon‡
United Airlines 93	9/11/2001	EWR–SFO	hijacked by Islamic terrorists in Stonycreek Township, PA‡
US Airways 1549	1/15/2009	LGA–CLT	'Miracle on the Hudson'; landed safely on the Hudson River after losing power in both engines

Dates are of the flight's departure. † Fictional: *Airplane!* (1980) and *Lost* (2004–10). ‡ According to the US DoD, the 9/11 attacks killed 2,972 people.

―――――――― ON INTRODUCTIONS ――――――――

With the notable exception of reigning sovereigns, popes, presidents, and cardinals, introductions made between strangers should obey these rules:

YOUTH *is introduced to* AGE
'Strom Thurmond, may I present Doogie Howser?'

MEN *are introduced to* WOMEN
'Dame Edna, this is Count Victor Grezhinski.'

LOWER RANKS *are introduced to* HIGHER
'Colonel Sanders, this is Sergeant Bilko.'

INDIVIDUALS *are introduced to* GROUPS
'Mickey Mouse Club, this is Britney Spears.'

―――――――― MANIAS OF NOTE ――――――――

	mania for
Anthomania	*flowers*
Arithmomania	*counting; sums*
Balletomania	*ballet*
Cytheromania	*sex*
Dipsomania	*alcohol*
Dromomania	*running; roaming*
Eleutheromania	*freedom*
Empleomania	*holding public office*
Epomania	*writing epics*
Eulogomania	*eulogies*
Flagellomania	*flogging; beating*
Gamomania	*marriage; proposing*
Hexametromania	*hexameters*
Hippomania	*horses*
Islomania	*islands*
Jumbomania	*vast proportions*
Klopemania†	*theft*
Lypemania	*mournfulness*
Melomania	*music*
Metromania	*writing poetry*
Nostomania	*nostalgia*
Nugaemania	*trifling things*
Oenomania	*wine*
Onomatomania	*words; neologism*
Polkamania‡	*dancing polkas*
Pteridomania	*ferns*
Rhinotillexomania	*nose-picking*
Rinkomania	*ice-skating*
Sonnettomania	*sonnets*
Squandermania	*reckless spending*
Timbromania	*postage stamps*
Uranomania	*celestial power*
Whitmania	*Walt Whitman*
Xenomania	*things foreign*
Zoomania	*animals*

† An unusual spelling of kleptomania.
‡ *Punch*, 1845: 'The polkamania is said to have originated in Bohemia'.

― LEWIS CARROLL'S BRANCHES OF ARITHMETIC ―

AMBITION · DISTRACTION · UGLIFICATION · DERISION

BEAUTY SPOT NOMENCLATURE

'A word may follow here on the mouche, patch, or beauty spot, a fashion to the full as ridiculous as the peruke. Everyone knows that the patch was a morsel of black silk gummed on the face, but not everyone is aware of its origin. It was the custom in the C16th, says a modern commentator, to cure toothache by applying to the temples little plaisters spread on silk or velvet; and he argues the coquette would be quick to observe the effect of the black patch in enhancing the whiteness of the skin. Whatever the result of the raging tooth, there could be no doubt about the success of the plaister as an aid to the toilet; and in this manner, it seems likely enough, the mode may have arisen. It overran the whole of French society in an astonishingly short time, the clergy not excepted, for a mazarinade of 1649 threatens with the wrath of

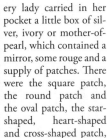

heaven the 'curled and powdered abbés, whose faces are covered with patches'. Under Louis xv, every lady carried in her pocket a little box of silver, ivory or mother-of-pearl, which contained a mirror, some rouge and a supply of patches. There were the square patch, the round patch and the oval patch, the star-shaped, heart-shaped and cross-shaped patch, and even the patch in the form of a bird or animal. Each had, moreover, its proper name. Placed near the eye, it was the *passionate* [1]; on the forehead, the *majestic* [2]; on the lips, the *coquette* [3]; at the corner of the mouth, the *kiss* [4]; on the nose, the *impertinent* [5]; in the center of the cheek, the *galante* [6], on the lower lip, the *discreet* [7].'

– TIGHE HOPKINS, *An Idler in Old France*, 1899. [Illustrated with a portrait of Louis xv's mistress, Madame de Pompadour.]

TRADITIONAL WOOL MEASURES

7 POUNDS (7lb)....... I CLOVE (cl.)	6½ TODS..................... I WEY
2 CLOVES (14lb) ...... I STONE (st.)	2 WEYS................ I SACK (sa.)
2 STONES (28lb) .... I TOD	12 SACKS...............I LAST (la.)

POUND	CLOVE					
7	I	STONE				
14	2	I	TOD			
28	4	2	I	WEY		
182	26	13	6½	I	SACK	
364	52	26	13	2	I	LAST
4,368	624	312	156	24	12	I

FIVE THINGS TO OBSERVE

If you your lips, Would keep from slips, Five things observe with care:
Of whom you speak, To whom you speak, And how, and when, and where.
If you your ears, Would save from jeers, These things keep mildly hid:
MYSELF and I, and MINE and MY, and how I DO or DID. – ANON

TRADITIONAL APOTHECARY SYMBOLS &c.

R The origin of the prescription symbol is unknown; it may derive from the Egyptian god Horus or from the Roman symbol for Jupiter, or it may be a contraction of *recipe* – the Latin for 'take'.

℔ *Libra* 1 POUND 12 OUNCES	℥ *Uncia* 1 OUNCE 8 DRACHMA	ʒ *Drachma* 1 DRACHM 3 SCRUPLES	℈ *Scrupulus* 1 SCRUPLE 20 GRAINS

℔	℥	ʒ	℈	grains
1	12	96	288	5,760
	1	8	24	480
		1	3	60
			1	20

CONGIUS 1 gallon 8 pints	℺ OCTARIUS 1 pint 16 fluid ounces	f℥ FLUIDUNCIA 1 fluid ounce 8 fluid drachms	fʒ FLUIDRACHMA 8 fluid drachms 60 minims	♏ MINIMUM 1 minim

C	O	f℥	fʒ	♏
1	8	128	1,024	61,440
	1	16	128	7,680
		1	8	480
			1	60

1 TEASPOON. . *contains c.* 1 FL. DRACHM	1 TABLESPOON . . . . . . 4 FL. DRACHMS
1 DESSERTSPOON . . . 2 FL. DRACHMS	1 WINEGLASS. . . . . 2 FL. OUNCES

TO BECOME THIN

The following may be said to be one of the most successful prescriptions in producing leanness: Take of ANXIETY as much as you can carry; of LABOR twelve hours; of SLEEP five hours [see pp.84–85]; of FOOD one meal; of DISAPPOINTED LOVE one season; of BLIGHTED FRIENDSHIP half a dozen instances. Let these ingredients be mixed carefully with a considerable weight of DEBT in a mind from which all RELIGIOUS REMEDIES have been excluded and *excessive leanness* will be produced. — ANON

—— BIG NUMBERS ——

British	number of zeroes	American
Million	6	Million
Milliard	9	Billion
Billion	12	Trillion
1,000 billion	15	Quadrillion
Trillion	18	Quintillion
1,000 trillion	21	Sextillion
Quadrillion	24	Septillion
1,000 quadrillion	27	Octillion
Quintillion	30	Nonillion
1,000 quintillion	33	Decillion
Googol	100	Googol
Googolplex	GOOGOL	Googolplex

—— THE SEASONS OF INDOLENCE ——

WINTER is too cold fer work; Freezin' weather makes me shirk.
SPRING comes on an' finds me wishin', I could end my days a-fishin'.
Then in SUMMER, when it's hot, I say work kin go to pot.
AUTUMN days, so calm an' hazy, Sorter make me kinder lazy.
That's the way the seasons run. Seems I can't git nothin' done.

– SAM S. STINSON, *Lippincott's Magazine*, c.1902

—— RULING TITLES OF NOTE ——

Abimelech	*Philistine prince*
Archon	*Athenian magistrate*
Brenhin	*Druidic ruler*
Caesar	*Roman emperor*
Cyrus	*Persian king*
Dewan	*Indian financial minister*
Doge	*Ruler of Venetian Republic*
Exarch	*Byzantine Emperor's viceroy*
Gauleiter	*Nazi ruler of a district*
Inca	*Peruvian sovereign pre-1532*
Kabaka	*King of Buganda*
Kaiser	*Germanic form of 'Caesar'*
Khan	*Mongolian ruler*
Margrave	*Provincial border governor or German Holy Roman Empire prince*
Mikado	*Japanese emperor*
Mpret	*Albanian ruler*
Negus	*Sovereign of Abyssinia*
Nizam	*Ruler of Hyderabad*
Padisha	*Sultan of Turkey*
Ptolemy	*Egyptian king*
Satrap	*Persian provincial governor*
Shah	*Persian & Iranian ruler*
Shogun	*Japanese commander*
Sindhia	*Maharajah of Gwalior*
Stadtholder	*Chief magistrate of the Dutch republic or a regional viceroy*
Tuan Muda	*The heir presumptive to the Rajah of Sarawak*
Vali	*Egyptian governor pre-1867*

ON VISITING CARDS

In the C19th an elaborate taxonomy developed regarding how visiting (or calling) cards should be left, folded, and inscribed:

Nature of call	*style of fold*
Visit	*right-hand upper corner folded down*
Felicitation	*left-hand upper corner folded down*
Condolence	*left-hand lower corner folded down*
PPC, PDA†	*right-hand lower corner folded down*
Made on all members of a family	*the lady's card folded in the middle*
Delivered in person	*right-hand side folded down*

† When individuals were going abroad, or were to be absent for a long period, if they had not the time or inclination to take leave of their friends by making formal calls, they would send cards folded in this manner, or inscribed PPC, which stood for *pour prendre congé* [to take leave] (although many assumed the initials to stand for 'presents parting compliments'), or PDA, which stood for *pour dire adieu* [to say goodbye]. Other card inscriptions included: PC – *pour condoler* [to condole]; PF – *pour féliciter* [to congratulate]; PR – *pour remercier* [to thank]; and PP – *pour présenter* [to present]. In each case, these inscriptions would be made in ink, in uppercase letters, in the lower left-hand corner.

Grose's Classical Dictionary of the Vulgar Tongue (1823) observed that PPC 'has of late been ridiculed by cards inscribed DIO, i.e., *Damn, I'm off*'. ❦ On the Continent, it was the fashion to inscribe one's cards *en personne* when they had been delivered in person. ❦ Those in mourning would present cards with the appropriate weight of black border. ❦ If a card was enclosed in an envelope, it indicated that communication between the two parties was at an end. The exceptions to this rule were: [i] when they were sent to a newly married couple; [ii] when they were in reply to a wedding invitation and sent by someone absent from their usual home; [iii] when they were PPC or PDA cards. ❦ In 1857, the Duke of Parma started the custom of leaving Cartes de Visite with his portrait for the albums of friends. ❦ Visiting cards were sometimes nicknamed Paste Boards. So, to 'shoot a PB' was to leave one's card. ❦ In 1865, the *Eclectic Magazine* noted: 'As a card may be substituted for a call, calling resolves itself into three degrees of comparison: the SUPERLATIVE – when you call, enter the house, and pay your compliments personally; the COMPARATIVE – when you drive to your friend's door, and leave your card without quitting your carriage; the POSITIVE – when you simply send your card by the hands of a servant. A card is thus a *homeopathic* call, a call administered in its mildest form; it is the *infinitesimal element of calling*.'

—— ON VISITING CARDS cont. ——

The celebrated royal and society printer Smythson of Bond Street still manufactures visiting cards in the following traditional sizes:

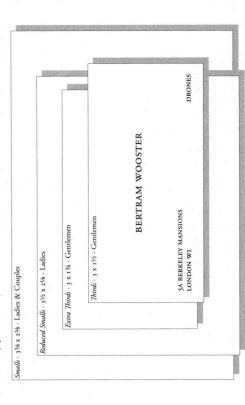

Smalls · 3⅜ x 2⅜ · Ladies & Couples

Reduced Smalls · 3½ x 2⅛ · Ladies

Extra Thirds · 3 x 1¾ · Gentlemen

Thirds · 3 x 1½ · Gentlemen

BERTRAM WOOSTER

3A BERKELEY MANSIONS
LONDON W1

DRONES

It is said that ladies of dubious repute would have their cards made up in male *Thirds* or *Extra Thirds*. This meant that if one of their married 'friends' chanced to take out his wallet in front of his wife, all of his cards would resemble those of gentlemen – thus averting suspicion and unwanted interrogation.

ON SLEEP & DIVIDING THE DAY

Nature requires 5, *Custom* gives 7,
Laziness takes 9, & *Wickedness* 11.

❦

ONE HOUR's sleep *before midnight*
is worth TWO HOURS after.

❦

He that WOULD THRIVE
must rise at 5, He that HATH
THRIVEN may lie till 7.
(He that will NEVER THRIVE
may lie till 11.)

❦

To *Rise* at five, and *Dine* at nine,
To *Sup* at five, and *Bed* at nine,
Will make a man *Live* ninety-nine.
Lever à cinque, diner à neuf,
Souper à cinque, coucher à neuf,
Fait vivre ans nonante et neuf.

❦

8 hours *Work*, 8 hours *Play*,
8 hours *Sleep*, 8 *Shillings* a day.

❦

Go to bed with the LAMB,
Rise with the LARK.

❦

He that too much *Loved* his BED,
Will surely *Scratch* a POOR MAN'S
HEAD; But he that EARLY doth *Rise*,
Is on his way to *Win* the prize.

❦

6 hours for a MAN,
7 hours for a WOMAN,
8 hours for a CHILD,
9 hours for a PIG.
– REV. JOHN WESLEY

❦

The 'Immortal Alfred' of England
divided the day into three por-
tions of 8 hours each – assigning
one for *Refreshment and the Health
of the Body by Sleep, Diet, and
Exercise*, another for *Business*, and
the third for *Study and Devotion*.

AGE can *Doze*, YOUTH must *Sleep*.

❦

Early to BED, Early to RISE
[& moderate EXERCISE] makes a
man *Healthy*, *Wealthy*, and *Wise*.

❦

The Russian physician Marie de
Manacéine advised the following
amount of sleep by age:

Age	hours' sleep
4–6 weeks	22
1–2 years	18–16
2–3 years	17–15
3–4 years	16–14
4–6 years	15–13
6–9 years	12–10
9–13 years	10–8
Increase hours at the critical age of puberty.	
19–20 years	6–8
Adults	*on average* 8

(In 1894, Marie de Manacéine discovered
that puppies died after having been kept
awake for 4–6 days, or some 92–143 hours.)

❦

The US National Sleep Foundation
cautions that there is no 'magic
number' as to how much sleep one
needs, but offers this rule of thumb:

	hours
Newborns (1–2 months)	10.5–18
Infants (3–11 months)	
9–12 at night and 30-min–2-hour naps, 1–4 times a day	
Toddlers (1–3 years)	12–14
Preschoolers (3–5)	11–13
School-aged (5–12)	10–11
Teens (11–17)	8.5–9.25
Adults	7–9
Older adults	7–9

6 hours to *Sleep*,
In law's grave *Study* 6,
4 spend in *Prayer*,
The rest to *Nature* fix.

– LORD COKE

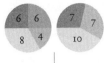

7 hours to *Law*,
To soothing *Slumber* 7,
10 to the *World* allot,
And all to *Heaven*.

– SIR WILLIAM JONES

❦

SLEEP DEPRIVATION (and its euphemistic cousin, SLEEP ADJUSTMENT) is used to 'break' detainees and make them compliant during interrogation. In Guantánamo Bay, the shuttling of prisoners from cell to cell to hinder sleep is standard procedure, and is known as the FREQUENT FLIER PROGRAM. Below are the cell transfers of Mohammed Jawad on May 11, 2004 – just one of the 14 consecutive days he was subjected to this cruel treatment.

DATE	TIME	CELL	DURATION
5/10	21:41	L48 → L40	2h:47m
5/11	00:20	L40 → L48	2h:39m
5/11	01:13	L48 → L40	53m
5/11	04:06	L40 → L48	2h:53m
5/11	07:03	L48 → L40	2h:57m
5/11	10:16	L40 → L48	3h:13m
5/11	13:05	L48 → L40	2h:49m
5/11	15:57	L40 → L48	2h:52m
5/11	19:08	L48 → L40	3h:11m
5/11	21:03	L40 → L48	2h:55m
5/12	00:02	L48 → L40	2h:59m

[Source: Court exhibit submitted by Lt. Col. David Frakt, Mr Jawad's military defense lawyer, based on the official Guantánamo Bay prison logs]

❦

In *The Madness of George III*, Alan Bennett has the king wake his servants at dawn, saying: 'Six hours' sleep is enough for a MAN, seven for a WOMAN and eight for a FOOL!'

Saint Ambrose divided every day into three *Tertia* of employment: 8 hours he spent in the *Necessities* of *Nature* and *Recreation*; 8 hours in *Charity* and *Business*; and 8 hours he spent in *Study* and *Prayer*.

❦

The difference between rising every morning at 6 instead of 8 o'clock in the course of 40 years amounts to 29,500 hours, or 3 years, 121 days, and 16 hours; which is 8 hours a day for exactly 9 years; so that rising at 6 it will be the same as if 9 years of life were added, wherein we may command 8 hours every day for the cultivation of our minds and the dispatch of business. – ANON

❦

If *Late* a man's in, and *Late* out of bed, he'll GET THIN, SHORT OF TIN, and THICK IN THE HEAD.

– *Punch*, 1866

❦

Six heures dort l'escholier, [student]
Sept le voyageur, [traveler]
Huit le vigneron, [winegrower]
Et neuf le poltron. [coward]

❦

Slothfulness is but a waking sleep and sleep is but a drowsy slothfulness; and, as sleep is the bed of slothfulness, so slothfulness is the bed of sleep. It is natural for sleep to cause slothfulness and it is natural for slothfulness to cause sleep.

– MICHAEL JERMIN (1591–1659)

ANCESTRAL LINEAGE

Below is the ascending line of lineal ancestry, used in some legal papers:

Pater ☞ *Avus* ☞ *Proavus* ☞ *Abavus* ☞ *Atavus* ☞ *Tritavus* ☞ *Tritavi-pater*
Father   Grandfather   …   …   …   …   Great-great-great-great-great-grandfather

LONGFELLOW ON ANGELS

Longfellow bestowed on the celestial bodies the angelic governors below:

Celestial body	angelic governor		
☉ .. Sun	Raphael	♃ .. Jupiter	Zobiachel
☽ ... Moon	Gabriel	☿ ... Mercury	Michael
♀ ... Venus	Anael	♂ .. Mars	Uriel
		♄ ... Saturn	Orifel

BESPOKE TAILOR JACKET-FITTING STAGES

SHELL

The shell baste[1], in its most effective form, has shoulders manipulated; shrunk canvas, or Syddo[2], through fronts; wadding or domett[3], if any is to be used, in place, all seems basted[4], under collar pressed into form and either basted on or left unattached for pinning into positions.

FORWARD

At the forward stage all pockets are in; lapels padded; facings and fourpart linings basted in; back seam sewn and pressed; front edges and facings turned together; shoulder and side seams basted; sleeves completed, except for holes, buttons, and cuff fellings[5], collar padded and basted to neck.

ADVANCE

The advance baste has all seams, except sleeve heads, sewn; edges made up but not holed or buttoned; collar completed and most of the pressing done.

[1] The skeleton jacket, loosely sewn. [2] A kind of interlining. [3] Flannel wadding. [4] Loosely sewn. [5] A hemming stitch.

– A. S. BRIDGLAND, *The Modern Tailor Outfitter & Clothier*, VOL. I, 1928

These three stages (the shell, the forward, the advance) are disturbingly reminiscent of a WW1 infantry attack. Incidentally, some modern tailors still use the traditional expression ROCK OF EYE to describe the process of cutting cloth using instinct as well as measurement.

ON HIDING FROM STORMS UNDER TREES

Beware of OAK, it *draws the stroke*; Avoid an ASH, it *courts the flash*;
Creep under the THORN, it can *save you from harm.* – TRADITIONAL *(and nonsense)*

COMMON BRICK BONDS

Bonding is the arrangement of bricks in regular, overlapping patterns to provide strength and visual appeal. Below are some of the common bonds:

Stretcher Bond

a simple pattern of repeating stretchers

Header Bond

a simple pattern of repeating headers

English Bond or *Ancient Bond*

alternating courses (i.e., rows) of stretchers and headers

English Garden Wall Bond

a course of headers followed by three courses of stretchers

Flemish Bond or *Dutch Bond*

headers and stretchers are laid alternately along each course

Flemish Garden Wall Bond

three stretchers are laid to every header, with courses overlapping

[S]TRETCHER – *a brick laid flat, with its long face exposed.*
[H]EADER – *a brick laid flat, with its short face exposed.*
[C]LOSER – *a brick to close up or equalize space (e.g., ¼ of a* STRETCHER*).*

– 87 –

────── (S+N)OSE ──────

The curious link between words that begin with the letters 'SN' and the nose has been commented upon by a number of writers – including the great lexicographer Samuel Johnson. Below are some of the many terms in the inestimable *Oxford English Dictionary* that start with these two letters and are associated with the proboscoid protuberance:

SNAFFLE · *to utter through the nose; to make a snuffling noise (also snaffler, snaffling, snuffling, &c.).* ❦ SNAFFLES · *a form of catarrh affecting respiration; the snuffles.* ❦ SNARF · *to take (a powdered drug) nasally.* ❦ SNARFLE · *to sniff or snort; or to eat greedily.* ❦ SNARK · *to snore or snort.* ❦ SNAT-NOSED · *snub-nosed.* ❦ SNATTED · *snub (also sneb, sneap, snib, &c.).* ❦ SNAVEL · *to snuffle.* ❦ SNEAP · *a snub or check; a rebuke.* ❦ SNEAP-NOSE · *one who has a pinched nose (also snub-nosed, &c.).* ❦ SNEB · *to snub.* ❦ SNEER · *a snort (of a horse) or a twitch of the nose.* ❦ SNEESH · *(a pinch of) snuff (also sneesher, sneeshing, &c.).* ❦ SNEEZE · *a sudden and involuntary expiration of breath through the nose and mouth, accompanied by a characteristic sound (also, sneeze-box, -horn, -lurker, sneeze gas, sneezer, sneezy, &c.).* ❦ SNEKE · *a head-cold.* ❦ SNEVE · *to smell (also sneving, &c.).* ❦ SNIB · *a snub.* ❦ SNICKER · *of horses: to neigh, nicker.* ❦ SNICK-UP · *a sneeze or sneezing fit.* ❦ SNIFF · *a single inhalation through the nose in order to smell something or clear the nose; the sound made in so doing (also, sniffable, sniffer, sniffing, &c.).* ❦ SNIFFLE · *the act of sniffling, or clearing one's nose in grief or low spirits (also sniffler, sniffling, &c).* ❦ SNIFFY · *showing scorn or contempt, as if smelling a bad odor (also sniffily, &c.).* ❦ SNIFT · *to sniff.* ❦ SNIFTER · *a head cold, or a blockage of the nostrils; also, a disease of poultry.* ❦ SNIFTING · *the action of sniffing.* ❦ SNIFTY · *having an agreeable smell.* ❦ SNIPY · *having a nose like a snipe's bill.* ❦ SNITCH · *the nose, hence snitch-rag as slang for handkerchief.* ❦ SNITE · *to wipe the nose (also sniter, sniting, &c.).* ❦ SNIVEL · *nasal mucus; a sniff indicating suppressed emotion.* ❦ SNIVELARD · *one who snivels (also sniveler, sniveling, &c.).* ❦ SNIVELDOM · *a slight cold causing one to snivel.* ❦ SNOACH · *to breathe or speak through the nose.* ❦ SNOKE · *to snuff or smell.* ❦ SNOOT · *a snout.* ❦ SNORE · *a harsh or noisy respiration through the mouth and/or nose during sleep (hence, snoreless, snorer, snoring, &c.).* ❦ SNORK · *a noisy sniff; to breathe nasally noisily.* ❦ SNORT · *a nasal exclamation of contempt; a measure of snortable drugs (also snorter, snorting, &c.).* ❦ SNORTER · *a blow on the nose, or the nose itself.* ❦ SNORTLE · *to snort.* ❦ SNORY · *inclined to snore; sleepy, drowsy.* ❦ SNOT · *nasal mucus (also snotter, snottery, snottiness, snotty, snotty-nosed, &c.).* ❦ SNOTTINGER · *slang for a pocket handkerchief.* ❦ SNOUCH · *to snub; to treat scornfully.* ❦ SNOUT · *the nose (also, snouted, snoutish, snoutless, snouty, &c.).* ❦ SNOZZLE · *version of schnozzle.* ❦ SNUB · *to repress or rebuke; turning up or looking down one's nose at someone (also, snubbed, snubbee, snubber, snubbiness, snubbing, snubbish, &c.).* ❦ SNUFF · *a smell; a persistent snuffling; a nasally inhaled powdered tobacco; the act of drawing in through the nose, or clearing the nose (also snuffy).* ❦ SNUFFER · *the finger and thumb as used to clear or wipe the nose; one who takes snuff.* ❦ SNUFFLE · *a nasal blockage causing a snuffling sound in the act of respiration; to exhibit disdain by sniffing in contempt; to smell; to speak through the nose (also snuffler, snuffliness, snuffling, &c.).* ❦ SNUR · *to snort.* ❦ SNURL · *a head cold; a nostril; to turn up the nose disdainfully.* ❦ SNURT · *to sneer or snort.* ❦ SNUSH · *to sniff snuff.* ❦ SNUVE · *to snuff or sniff.* ❦ SNUZZLE · *to nuzzle or snuggle.*

——— TYPES OF CUT———

THE CUT · To ignore the existence, or avoid the presence, of a person.

THE CUT DIRECT · To look an old friend in the face, and affect not to recollect him.

THE CUT MODEST OF CUT INDIRECT · To look anywhere but at him.

THE CUT COURTEOUS · To forget names with a good grace; as, instead of Tom, Dick, or Harry, to address an old friend with 'Sir,' or 'Mister ... What's your name?'

THE CUT OBTUSE · If slightly known as a fellow traveler, the cutter insists he never was at the place, nor sailed in the vessel mentioned; and finally denies his own name.

THE CUT CELESTIAL · To be intentionally engaged on the phenomena of the heavenly bodies when an old friend passes. *Also* the CUT CUMULONIMBUS.

THE CUT CIRCUMBENDIBUS · To dart up an alley, across the street, or into a shop to avoid the trouble of nodding to someone.

[From various sources] ❦ 'A GENTLEMAN must never cut a LADY under any circumstances. An UNMARRIED lady should never cut a MARRIED one. A SERVANT of whatever class (for there are servants up to royalty itself) should never cut his MASTER; NEAR RELATIONS should never cut one another at all; and a CLERGYMAN should never cut anybody, because it is at best an unchristian action.' – 'JANE ASTER', *The Habits of Good Society*, 1867

—GESTICULATIONS—

In *A Traveller in Rome* (1957), H.V. Morton wrote: 'I fancy it must be almost impossible to speak Italian without gesticulation. It is a language that demands an accompaniment either of music or gesture; and in the national art of opera, there are both. Rome is thus a city of gesticulation.' To illustrate his point, Morton proposed a hierarchy of Roman hand movements:

PIANISSIMO ☞ ANDANTE
☞ ROBUSTO ☞ FORTISSIMO
☞ FURIOSO

——— US CODE NAMES———

The US Secret Service bestows code names on the senior politicians (and their families) it protects. In 2007 it was reported that Barack Obama had been given the name *Renegade*; his wife Michelle, the name *Renaissance*; and his daughters, Malia and Sasha, *Radiance* and *Rosebud*, respectively. Below are a few other Secret Service code names – real and fictional:

Hillary Clinton	*Evergreen*
John Kerry	*Minuteman*
Al Gore	*Sawhorse/Sundance*
George W. Bush	*Tumbler*
Bill Clinton	*Eagle*
Jimmy Carter	*Deacon*
George H.W. Bush	*Timberwolf*
Ronald Reagan	*Rawhide*
Dick Cheney	*Backseat/Angler*
(Josiah Bartlet	*Eagle; Liberty*)
(Zoey Bartlet	*Bookbag*)
('C.J.' Cregg	*Flamingo*)

—— COMMON PROOF CORRECTION MARKS ——

Instruction	mark in margin	mark in text
Delete	ℒ	I ~~don't~~ have a dream
Close up; delete space	⌒	I have a d⌒ream
Delete & close up	ℒ	I hav⌢e a dream
Insert text	have	∧ a dream
Spell out	(sp)	I have ②dreams
Leave unchanged (stet)	(stet)	I have a dream
New paragraph	¶ or ⌐	I have. ⌐A dream
Transpose	(TR) or ⌐	I a have dream
Reduce space	⌒ or ∧	I have a ⌒ dream
Align	‖	‖ I have a dream ‖ I have a dream
Insert space	(#)	I have a dream
Equalize spaces	(eq #)	I have a dream
Set in capitals	(CAP)	I HAVE A dream
Set in lowercase	(lc)	I HAVE a dream
Set in small caps	(sc)	I HAVE A dream
Initial cap & small caps	(CAP+sc)	i have a dream
Set in italic	(ital)	I have a dream
Remove italic	(rom)	I have a dream
Set in bold	(bf)	I have **a dream**
Remove bold	(rom)	I have a dream

—— COMMON PROOF CORRECTION MARKS cont. ——

Set in bold italics	(bf + ital)	I have **_a dream_**
Remove bold italics	(rom)	I have a _**dream**_
Insert underline	⊂⊃	I have a dream
Remove underline	(rom)	I have a dream
Run in	⌒	I have a dream
Center text	(ctr)	] I have a dream [
Take over (to next line)		I have a dre- -am
Take back (to previous line)		I have a dre- -am
Close up line spacing		I have a dream I have a dream
Insert line space	(line #)	I have a dream I have a dream
Type to superior		πr^2
Type to inferior		H_2O
Wrong font	(wf)	I have a dream
Insert		∧ where required
Substitute	see sample symbols below	⧸ through character

⊙	∧̇	∧̇ or ;|	∧̈ or :|	≠	|◌|◌|◌|
period	comma	semicolon	colon	slash	ellipsis

=	$\frac{1}{N}$ or ℕ	$\frac{1}{M}$ or ℳ	∨̇	∨̇ ∨̇	∨̈ ∨̈
hyphen	en dash	em dash	apostrophe	single quote	double quote

Marks by SIR HAROLD EVANS, editor of the *Sunday Times* (1967–81) and the *Times* (1981–82).

——— THEATRICAL SUPERSTITIONS OF NOTE ———

Many actors and stagehands think WHISTLING or CLAPPING in a theater is unlucky. This may date from the time when the scenery was operated by sailors, since they were happy with heights and handy with ropes. The sailors communicated with one another by a system of whistles and claps that, if inadvertently used by an actor, might result in heavy weights falling on his bonce. ❦ Wishing an actor GOOD LUCK is unlucky, since folklore tells that to fool evil spirits, actors should request the very opposite of what they want – hence the phrase BREAK A LEG. Some actors wish one another luck by saying TOI, TOI, TOI – the verbal equivalent of spitting three times. ❦ DRESSING ROOMS should be exited LEFT FOOT FIRST. ❦ Never utter the word MACBETH in a theater (instead say THE SCOTTISH PLAY or HARRY LAUDER), since *Macbeth* is associated with numerous mishaps and tragedies – as well as the weird sisters. If you do happen to utter 'Macbeth', there are several cures for the curse: turn around thrice; spit over your left shoulder; say the rudest word you can imagine (yes, that one); or declaim a line from *A Midsummer Night's Dream*. ❦ WEARING GREEN is considered unwise, since green is the fairies' favorite color, and to sport it will provoke their ire. (Some similarly fear yellow.) ❦ PEACOCK FEATHERS, OSTRICHES, REAL FLOWERS, and MIRRORS are all considered unlucky – as is KNITTING, SPILLING MAKEUP, OPENING UMBRELLAS onstage, or HANGING PICTURES on a dressing-room door. ❦ CATS are considered unlucky only if they stray onstage during a performance. ❦ The PROMPT SIDE of the stage [see below] is considered unlucky by some (perhaps those apt to 'dry'). ❦ Some believe it is unlucky to perform the LAST LINE of a play until the opening night. ❦ A BAD DRESS REHEARSAL is said to presage a GOOD FIRST NIGHT – and vice versa – usually by those who have just experienced a bad dress rehearsal. ❦ Many believe in leaving a GHOST LIGHT lit on an empty stage to keep alive the theater's spirit (and to prevent stagehands from tripping over in the dark).

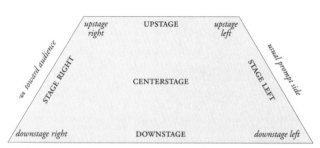

— RULE OF THE ROAD —

The RULE OF THE ROAD is a paradox quite; In riding or driving along, If you keep to the left, you are sure to go right, If you keep to the right, you are wrong.

⇌

The RULE OF THE FOOTPATH is clear as the light, and none can its reason withstand: Each side of the way you must keep to the right, and give those you meet the left hand.

⇋

The RULE OF THE RAIL is – soon come or soon go, admitting of little delay; If you go, get in quick – you're left if you're slow; Get out – and get out of the way.

—— ON THE WEEK ——

Wash on MONDAY,
Iron on TUESDAY,
Bake on WEDNESDAY,
Brew on THURSDAY,
Churn on FRIDAY,
Mend on SATURDAY,
Church on SUNDAY.

— FASHION ABBREVS —

BCBG	*Bon Chic, Bon Genre*†
LBD	Little Black Dress
NFFP	Not For Fashion People
OTK	Over The Knee
OTT	Over The Top
RTW	Ready To Wear
TFFF	Too Fat For Fashion
VBL	Visible Bra Line
VBS	Visible Bra Strap
VPL	Visible Panty Line

† Good Style, Good Attitude

— VULGAR WHISKERS —

Of all things avoid a VULGAR WHISKER. This is of various kinds. A *short, scrubby, indomitable red whisker* is a VULGAR WHISKER; a *weak, fuzzy, white, moth-eaten, moldy whisker* is a VULGAR WHISKER; a *twisting, twining, serpentine, sentimental, corkscrew of a whisker* is a VULGAR WHISKER; a *big, black, bluff, brutal-looking whisker* is a VULGAR WHISKER; a *mathematical, methodical, master-of-artsical diagram of a whisker* is a VULGAR WHISKER. Whatever is not any of these – WILL DO.

– *Dublin University Magazine*

– LAVATORY FLUSHING –

If it's YELLOW, *let it mellow*;
If it's BROWN, *flush it down*;
If it's GREEN, *nurse, fetch the screen!*

— REASONS TO DRINK —

The theologian and philosopher Dr Henry Aldrich (1647–1710) gave the following reasons for drinking:

Si bene quid memini, causae sunt quinque bibendi; Hospitis adventus, praesens sitis atque futura, Aut vini bonitas, aut quaelibet altera causa.

or, translated:

If on my theme I rightly think, There are five reasons why men drink: Good wine; a friend; because I'm dry; Or lest I should be by and by; Or, any other reason why.

MOON PHASES

new moon · waxing crescent · first quarter · waxing gibbous · full moon · waning gibbous · last quarter · waning crescent · new moon

ANIMAL CRIES

Apes	*gibber*
Asses	*bray*
Bears	*growl*
Beetles	*drone*
Bitterns	*boom, cry*
Bulls	*bellow*
Calves	*bleat, blear*
Cats	*meow, purr, hiss, caterwaul*
Chaffinches	*chirp, pink*
Crows	*caw*
Cuckoos	*call 'cuckoo'*
Deer	*bell*
Dogs	*bark, bay, howl, speak, yelp*
Dolphins	*click*
Doves	*coo*
Eagles	*scream*
Elephants	*barr, trumpet*
Elk	*bugle*
Falcons	*chant*
Foxes	*bark, yelp*
Geese	*cackle, claik, hiss, honk*
Goldfinches	*twinkle*
Grasshoppers	*chirp, pitter, click*
Grouse	*drum*
Guineafowls	*cry 'come back'*
Hares	*squeak*
Hawks	*scream*
Hens	*cackle, cluck*
Horses	*neigh, wehee, whinny, snort*
Hyenas	*haunk-haunk, laugh*
Jackdaws	*chaack, cackle*
Jays	*chatter*
Larks	*sing*
Leopards	*growl*

Linnets	*chuckle in their call*
Magpies	*chatter*
Mastodons†	*bellow*
Monkeys	*chatter and gibber*
Nightingales	*sing, pipe, 'jug-jug'*
Owls	*hoot, tu-whit, tu-whoo, &c.*
Oxen	*low and bellow*
Peacocks	*scream*
Peewits	*cry 'pee-wit'*
Pigeons	*coo*
Pigs	*grunt, squeak, and squeal*
Ravens	*croak*
Redstarts	*whistle*
Rhinos	*snort*
Rooks	*caw*
Sparrows	*chirp, yelp*
Squirrels	*chatter*
Stags	*bellow and call*
Swallows	*twitter*
Swans	*cry, bombilate, trumpet*
Swine	*squeak*
Thrushes	*whistle*
Tortoises	*grunt*
Turkeys	*gobble*
Vultures	*scream*
Whitethroats	*chirr*
Wolves	*howl, bay*
Woodpeckers	*blatter, ratatat*

† Seemingly coined by P.G. WODEHOUSE in *The Inimitable Jeeves*: '...when Aunt is calling to Aunt like mastodons bellowing across primeval swamps.' [Sources include *Brewer's Dictionary of Phrase & Fable*.]

──────── SOME NOTABLE WINDS ────────

Bise . . . . *cold northerly Alpine wind*
Bora . . . . *violent and bitter winter wind on the Adriatic Sea*
Brickfielder . . . . *hot, dry wind in southern Australia*
Chinook . . . . . . *dry, warm westerly wind of the N American Rocky Mountains*
Elephanta . . . . *strong wind from the south or southwest that*
marks the end of the monsoon in southwest India
Etesian . . . . *annual breezes in the Mediterranean Sea, lasting 40 days*
Harmattan . . . . *dry winter wind of the African interior*
Helm . . . . *cold, northeasterly wind in the Vale of Eden*
Khamsin . . . . *Egyptian wind that lasts c. 50 days from the end of February*
Levanter . . . . *strong easterly wind of the Mediterranean*
Mistral . . . . *violent northwesterly wind that hits the Gulf of Lyon*
Pampero . . . . *cold southwesterly wind of Brazil, Argentina, and Uruguay*
Puna . . . . *violent wind of the Peruvian Puna district that last four months*
Samiel . . . . *suffocating, sand-laden wind of the Sahara and Arabian deserts*
Samoor . . . . *southerly wind of Persia, which 'softens the strings of lutes'*
Shamal . . . . *hot, dry, mostly summer wind in the Persian Gulf states*
Sirocco† . . . . *soporific North African wind that blows over Italy*
Solano . . . . *hot and dusty Spanish southeasterly wind*
Sukhovey . . . . . . *hot summer wind affecting central Asia and southern Siberia*
Tehuantepecer . . . . *violent northerly wind in the Gulf of Tehuantepec, Mexico*
Tramontane . . . . *cold northerly Mediterranean wind*
Vardar . . . . *strong, northeasterly ravine wind affecting Greece in the winter*
Williwaw . . *violent cold seaward wind associated with the Straits of Magellan*

† There is an old Italian saying about a dull or foolish book: 'Era scritto in tempo
del Scirocco' – which translates as 'It was written during the Sirocco'.

──── AN ABECEDARY OF FEMALE REQUISITES ────

Amiable · Affectionate · Agreeable · Artless · Affable · Accomplished
Amorous · Beautiful · Benign · Benevolent · Chaste · Charming
Candid · Cheerful · Complacent · Careful · Charitable · Clean · Civil
Coy · Constant · Dutiful · Dignified · Elegant · Easy · Engaging
Even-tempered · Entertaining · Faithful · Fond · Free · Faultless · Good
Graceful · Generous · Governable · Good-humored · Handsome
Humane · Harmless · Healthy · Intelligent · Interesting · Industrious
Ingenuous · Just · Kind · Lively · Liberal · Lovely · Modest · Merciful
Neat · Noble · Open · Obliging · Pretty · Prudent · Polite · Pleasing
Pure · Peaceable · Religious · Sociable · Submissive · Sprightly · Sensible
Tall · Temperate · True · Unreserved · Virtuous · Well-formed · Witty
Wealthy · Young – 'AN OLD BACHELOR', *Saturday Night*, 1824

—————————— ON MODESTY IN DRESS ——————————

In thy apparel avoid *profuseness*, *singularity*, and *gaudiness*.
Let it be *decent*, and suited to the *quality* of thy *place* and purse.
Too much *punctuality*, and too much *morosity*, are the extremes of *pride*.
Be neither *too early in the fashion*, nor *too long out of it*, nor *too precisely in it*.
What *custom hath civilized* hath become *decent*; until then it was *ridiculous*.
Where the eye is the *jury*, thy apparel is the *evidence*:
The body is the *shell of the soul*, apparel is the *husk of that shell*;
and the husk will often tell you what the *kernel* is.
Seldom doth *solid wisdom* dwell under *fantastic apparel*;
neither will the *pantaloon fancy* be immured within the walls of *grave habit*.

· THE FOOL IS KNOWN BY HIS PIED COAT ·

– JOHN HALL, Bishop of Norwich (1574–*c*.1659)

—————————— RULES OF LIVING ——————————

'Whosoever would live long and blessedly, let him observe these rules —'

Let thy	be		
Thoughts ....*divine, awful, godly*	Will........ *confident, obedient, ready*
Talk................ *little, honest, true*	Sleep...... *moderate, quiet, seasonable*
Works .....*profitable, holy, charitable*	Prayers... *short, devout, often, fervent*
Manners....*grave, courteous, cheerful*	Recreation...... *lawful, brief, seldom*
Diet.....*temperate, convenient, frugal*	Memory.. *of death, punishment, glory*
Apparel ....*sober, neat, comely*	
	– *attrib.* REV. HUGH PETERS, London, 1660

—————————— FOOTE'S PANJANDRUM ——————————

Charles Macklin (*c*.1699–1797), the renowned actor and mimic, boasted he could repeat perfectly any text having heard it only once. To test this claim, the dramatist Samuel Foote (1720–77) devised a random and vexatious verse – reproduced below – in which he neologized the word 'panjandrum'. (The authorship of the text has also been credited to James Quin, John Curran, and others.)

THE GREAT PANJANDRUM HIMSELF · *So she went into the garden to cut a cabbage-leaf to make an apple-pie; and at the same time a great she-bear, coming down the street, pops its head into the shop. What! no soap? So he died, and she very imprudently married the Barber: and there were present the Picninnies, and the Joblillies, and the Garyulies, and the great Panjandrum himself, with the little round button at top; and they all fell to playing the game of catch-as-catch-can, till the gunpowder ran out at the heels of their boots.*

—— TRADITIONAL RABBINICAL HIERARCHY ——

Rab (master) · *Rabbi* (my master) · *Rabban* (great master) · *Rabboni* (my great master)

—————— LEGISLATIVE CALL SYSTEM ——————

As Senators cannot always be present in the chamber, a system of electronic bells and lights was installed in *c.*1891 to inform them of developments on the floor. This 'legislative call system' is transmitted from a console in the Senate Chamber to *c.*3,000 clocks in the Senate wing of the Capitol Building and the three Senate offices. The system is explained below:

1 long ring	*sounds at the hour of convening*	4 rings	*adjournment or recess*
1 ring	*yeas and nays*	5 rings	*7½ minutes remain to vote*
2 rings	*quorum call*	6 rings, lights off	*morning business ended*
3 rings	*call of absentees*	6 rings, lights on	*temporary recess*

Many Senate clocks also display lights, which are lit to correspond with the number of rings. A red light is lit whenever the Senate is in session. Splendidly, the House employs an even more complicated call system:

1 long ring, pause, 3 rings, 3 lights on left	*notice or short quorum call in Committee of the Whole*
1 long ring, 3 lights on left extinguished	*notice or short quorum call vacated*
2 rings, 2 lights on left	*recorded vote, yea and nay vote, or automatic roll call vote by electronic device*
2 rings, 2 lights, pause & 2 rings	*automatic roll call vote, or yea and nay vote by roll call in the House*
2 rings, pause, 5 rings	*first vote under Suspension of the Rules or on clustered votes*
3 rings, 3 lights on left	*regular quorum call by electronic device or clerks*
3 rings, pause, 3 rings	*regular quorum call by call of the roll*
3 rings, pause, 5 rings	*quorum call in Committee of the Whole, 5-minute recorded vote may follow*
4 rings, 4 lights on left	*adjournment*
5 rings, 5 lights on left	*any 5-minute vote*
6 rings, 6 lights on left	*recess*
12 rings at 2 second intervals, 6 lights on left	*civil defense warning*
7th light	*lit whenever the House is in session*

When tired of proceedings, Barry Goldwater would stroll past the console that controlled the bells and lights and press the adjournment button. Eventually a Plexiglas 'Goldwater Shield' was installed.

—— ANON'S ADVICE ON DEALING WITH OTHERS ——

Our SUPERFLUITIES should be given up for the *convenience of others,*
Our CONVENIENCES should give place to the *necessities of others,*
And even our NECESSITIES should give way to the *extremities of the poor.*

—— JUDGES & JURIES ——

Tell a JUDGE *twice* whatever you want him to hear; tell a SPECIAL JURY *thrice*; and a COMMON JURY *half a dozen times*, the view of the case you wish them to entertain.

– attrib. AUGUSTINE BIRRELL (1850–1933)

— CHOOSING FRIENDS —

To be truly charitable to all men, but singularly affected to a few particulars; to throw away intimate love too lavishly, is to affect no man sincerely, for love is composed of a jealous substance, and neither holds fair quarter with generality nor plurality; therefore in the election of his intimates let him choose those which are:

⁘

RELIGIOUS towards *God*,
HONEST towards *Men*, &
PROFITABLE to *Themselves*
& *Others.*

– adapted from
GERVASE MARKHAM
The English Husbandman, 1613

—— NO RECALL ——

*Four things for which
there can be no recall —*

The Spoken Word
The March of Fate
The Arrow Sped from the Bow
The Time that is Past

– ARABIAN PROVERB

—— ON INTELLECT ——

The UK poet William Shenstone (1714–63), perhaps best known for *The Schoolmistress* (1742), once claimed that if the general public were divided into one hundred parts, the relative distribution of intellect might be estimated thus:

Fools...........................15%
Persons of common sense.....40%
Wits 15%
Pedants........................15%
Persons of wild taste 10%
Persons of improved taste......5%

—— SOUND ADVICE ——

Do not all that you can DO,
Spend not all that you HAVE,
Believe not all that you HEAR,
& *Tell not* all that you KNOW.

— STAGES OF BRANDY —

1st	Brandy and water!
2nd	Branny and warrer!
3rd.....................	Bran warr!
4th.........................	Brraorr!
5th.........................	*Collapse!*

—— ON GENTLEMEN ——

A GENTLEMAN WITH FOUR OUTS IS:
Without *wit*, Without *money*,
Without *credit*, Without *manners.*

A GENTLEMAN OF THREE INS IS:
In *debt*, In *danger*, and In *poverty.*

– J. C. HOTTEN, *The Slang Dictionary,* 1865

THE VARIOUS TYPES OF SHAVER

shaves…

The BARBER..... *with polished blade*
The MERCER.......*with ladies' trade*
The BROKER ....*at 12 percent*
The LANDLORD ...... *by raising rent*
The DOCTOR...*in draughts and pills*
The TAPSTER.......*in pints and gills*

The FARMER .... *in hay and oats*
The BANKER .... *in his own notes*
The LAWYER ...*both friends and foes*
The PEDDLER ....*where'er he goes*
The WILY MERCHANT....*his brother*
All the PEOPLE..........*one another*

– ANON

RED CROSS, CRESCENT, & CRYSTAL

The Red Cross, Crescent, and Crystal are globally recognized emblems that, during war and peace, safeguard medical services and religious personnel. Their use is governed and protected by the Geneva Conventions.

The Red Cross, a reversal of the Swiss Flag, was designed in 1864, and given official international status of battlefield neutrality by the Geneva Convention.

The Red Crescent was adopted c.1877 as a rejection of the Red Cross, which had associations with the Christian Crusades. It is currently used by 32 countries.

The religiously neutral Red Crystal was adopted in 2005–06, and can be used alone, or in combination with the Cross, Crescent, or other symbols – such as the Star of David.

AGAINST SUICIDE

The razor is dull, and the water too cold,
The rope's so curs'd rotten, my weight it won't hold;
The pistol is rusty, the powder is damp,
I can't jump the Monument now for the cramp;
Blown out brains and cut throats make a great deal of spatter.
So I think I'd best quietly give up the matter;
I am nervous beside, with a weak constitution,
And to sum up the whole, have not resolution.

– EDWARD MACKEY, in *The Casket*, 1827 (*cf.* DOROTHY PARKER, *Résumé*, 1926)

─────── LORD BYRON'S PROGRESS OF A PARTY ───────

SILENT ☞ TALKY ☞ ARGUMENTATIVE ☞ DISPUTATIOUS ☞
UNINTELLIGIBLE ☞ ALTOGETHERY ☞ INARTICULATE ☞ DRUNK

– from a letter dated October 31, 1815. Byron noted: 'When we had reached the last
step of this glorious ladder, it was difficult to get down again without stumbling.'

─────────────── SAINTS' RELICS ───────────────

Relics have been an important part of the Catholic faith since its
inception. One of the first recorded cases of relic veneration was of St
Polycarp (AD 69–155), who was burnt to death by the Romans. His charred
remains were salvaged from the pyre and secretly worshipped in Rome's
catacombs. During the Second Council of Nicea (AD 787) it was decreed
that every church should have a relic at its altar. This order was officially
rescinded in 1969, yet many churches continue the tradition nevertheless.
Relics are generally split into three classifications, as tabulated below:

1st class....................................*part of a saint (bones, hair, teeth, &c.)*
2nd class..........*an item owned by the saint or the instrument of his or her martyrdom*
3rd class ....*an object that has touched a first- or second-class relic*

The locations of some of the most venerated first-class relics are below:

Relic	location
Skull of St Elizabeth of Hungary	Convent of St Elizabeth, Vienna, Austria
The Venerable Bede	Durham Cathedral, Great Britain
St Edward the Confessor†	Westminster Abbey, Great Britain
St John Southworth (within a silver effigy)	Westminster Cathedral, Great Britain
St Bernadette†	Convent of St Gildard, Nevers, France
Crown of Thorns and a piece of the True Cross	Notre Dame, Paris, France
St Vincent de Paul†	Church of St Vincent de Paul, Paris, France
The Three Magi	Cathedral of Cologne, Germany
St Walburga‡	Church of St Walburga, Eichstätt, Germany
The right hand of King St Stephen	Szent Istvan's Basilica, Budapest, Hungary
St Francis Xavier†	Basilica Bom Jesus, Goa, India
St Valentine	Carmelite Whitefriar Church, Dublin, Ireland
St Francis of Assisi	Lower Church of the Basilica of St Francis, Assisi, Italy
The hearts of all the popes from Sixtus V to Pius IX	Piazza di Trevi, Rome, Italy

† Indicates a saint who is 'incorrupt' – a phenomenon whereby the body of the saint has not
decomposed. ‡ St Walburga's relics excrete an 'oil of saints' that is said to have healing properties. For some reason this oil appears only between October 12 and February 25 each year.

BIBLIO–

This taxonomy of book lovers has been attributed to the Abbé Rive, librarian to the Duke de la Vallière, a celebrated book collector.

A BIBLIOGNOSTE is one knowing in title-pages and colophons, and in editions; when and where printed; the presses whence issued; and all the minutiae of a book.

A BIBLIOMANE is an indiscriminate accumulator, who blunders faster than he buys, cock-brained and purse-heavy.

A BIBLIOGRAPHE is a describer of books and other literary arrangements.

A BIBLIOPHILE, the lover of books, is the only one in the class who appears to read them for his own pleasure.

A BIBLIOTAPHE buries his books, by keeping them under lock, or framing them in glass cases.

– c. c. BOMBAUGH, *Gleanings From the Harvest-fields of Literature*, 1860

ON WELL & ILL

It is WELL to follow the law: It is ILL when the law follows us!
It is WELL to be notable: It is ILL to be not able.
It is WELL to pursue a wild beast: It is ILL when a wild beast pursuest us.
It is WELL to be in firm health: It is ILL to be in infirm health.

– ANON, *The Economist & General Adviser*, 1824

ANTI-NAZI POETRY HOAX

In April 1941, *Paris Soir* (then under Nazi control) published a poem in praise of Adolf Hitler submitted by an anonymous reader. However, a few days later the Free French paper *France* revealed that *Paris-Soir* had been elegantly duped since, when the poem is divided longitudinally into two verses [marked below with '|'], its meaning is quite different:

Aimons et admirons | Le Chancelier Hitler	*Let us love and praise | The Chancellor Hitler*
L'etenelle Angleterre: | Est indigne de vivre.	*Everlasting England: | Is unworthy of life*
Maudissons, écrasons | Le peuple d'outre mer	*Let's curse and crush | The people overseas*
Le Nazi sur la terre. | Sera seul à survivre,	*The Nazi on earth. | Will be the sole survivor*
Soyons done le soutien | Du Führer allemand	*Let's give our support | for the German Führer*
Des boys navigateurs: | Finira l'odyssée:	*For the navy boys: | The journey will end*
À cux seuls appartent | Un juste châtiment	*Only to them belongs | A fair punishment*
La palme du vainqueur. | Attend la Croix Gammée	*The conqueror's palm | Will meet the Swastika*

————— 'WITHNAIL & I' IMBIBING GUIDE —————

Below are the foods, drinks, 'rare herbs and prescribed chemicals' that pass the lips of Withnail, Marwood (*aka* 'I'), and Uncle Monty during the course of Bruce Robinson's 1987 cult film *Withnail & I* – tabulated for those foolhardy enough even to *consider* imbibing along with the cast:

TIME	CHARACTER	EAT, DRINK, &c.
00:20	I	*smoking a cigarette*
02:28	I	*sip of wine from bottle?*
03:30	I	*cup of tea (undrunk)*
04:21	W	*small tumbler of red wine*
04:44	W	*lights a cigarette*
06:08	I	*coffee (in a soup bowl)*
08:38	W	*smoking a cigarette*
10:17	W	*spits phlegm*
10:36	W	*smoking a cigarette*
12:39	W	*lighter fluid*
13:01	W	*vomits on I's boots*
13:35	W·I	*2 large gins; 2 pints of cider,*
		ice in the cider ('a couple more'†, 14:26)
13:50	W	*lights a cigarette*
15:21	W	*pork pie?*
17:18	W·I	*fish? and chips*
		(saveloy, later given as a gift to Danny)
18:38	W	*smoking a cigarette*
24:12	W	*lights a cigarette*
24:28	W	*glass of sherry*
24:34	I·M	*sip of sherry*
25:02	W	*2 large swigs of sherry from bottle*
25:49	M	*Bloody Mary (undrunk)*
		('top-up' offered, 27:10)
25:58	W	*sip of sherry*
26:39	W	*sip of sherry*
26:43	I·W	*sip of sherry*
27:30	W	*glass of whiskey?*
27:58	W	*sip of whiskey?*
29:18	I	*smoking a cigarette*
29:22	W	*smoking a cigarette*
29:55	W	*swig of whiskey from bottle*
30:05	I	*swig of whiskey from bottle*
30:24	W	*swig of whiskey from bottle*
30:40	W	*swig of whiskey from bottle*
30:44	W	*smoking a cigarette*
30:46	I	*swig of whiskey from bottle*
31:10	W	*smoking a cigarette*
31:47	W	*swig of whiskey from bottle*
36:35	W	*smoking a cigarette*
40:30	W	*smoking a cigarette*
40:45	I	*swig of whiskey from bottle*
41:03	W	*whiskey (in a teacup)*
41:16	W	*lights a cigarette*
41:21	I	*apple*
43:19	W	*smoking a cigarette*
44:00	I	*sip of red wine*
(46:32	I	*places chicken in oven)*
46:46	I	*smoking a cigarette*
49:35	W	*lights a cigarette*
50:35	W·I	*Scotch (I's glass already empty)*
50:39	I	*lights a cigarette*
50:40	W·I	*'another pair of large Scotches'†*
51:35	W	*lights a cigarette*
51:38	W·I	*'another pair of large Scotches'†*
52:36	W	*sip of Scotch*
52:39	W	*smoking a cigarette*
52:52	I	*smoking a cigarette*
52:53	I	*Scotch (undrunk)*
55:25	W·I	*vegetable stew with black pud-*
		ding; 2 half glasses of red wine (undrunk)
56:29	W	*smoking a cigarette*
57:11	I	*throws cigarette stub in fire*
1:02:20	W·I·M	*'breakfast in 15 minutes'*
		(bacon & tomatoes)
1:02:21	W	*smoking a cigarette*
1:02:23	I	*grapes*
1:02:35	M	*lights a cigarette*
1:06:18	W·I·M	*sip of sherry*
1:07:48	W·I	*smoking cigarettes; drinking*
		pints; 2 empty tumblers on bar
1:08:09	W·I	*'pair of quadruple whiskies*
		and another pair of pints'†
1:08:57	I	*pastry/biscuit*
1:09:33	I	*large bite of a scone*

———— 'WITHNAIL & I' IMBIBING GUIDE cont. ————

1:09:47	W	*lights a cigarette*
1:10:16	I	*large bite of a scone*
1:10:29	I	*leaves café with a scone*
1:10:46	W	*sip of red; cigarette in hand*
1:11:18	M	*sip of sherry*
1:11:24	M	*sip of sherry*
1:11:49	W	*smoking a cigarette;*
		half glass of red wine in hand
1:12:13	W	*swig of sherry*
1:12:16	W·I·M	*eating lunch (lamb? & veg);*
		3 glasses of red wine on table
1:12:46	W	*small glass of red wine*
1:13:17	W·M	*sip of red wine*
1:14:04	W	*raises wineglass to drink*
1:14:10	W	*sip of red wine*
1:14:29	W	*smoking a cigarette*
1:17:22	M	*smoking a cigarette;*
		glass of Pernod (undrunk)
1:17:27	W	*sip of Pernod*
1:17:28	I	*smoking a cigarette;*
		glass of red wine (undrunk)
1:18:18	I	*smoking a cigarette*
1:25:44	W	*lights a cigarette*

1:26:20	W·I	*smoking a cigarette*
1:26:20	W	*eating lunch (leftovers?)*
1:26:54	W	*sip of red wine*
1:27:16	W	*sip of red wine*
1:28:19	W	*fish? & chips*
1:28:19	I	*smoking a cigarette*
1:28:46	W	*swig of wine from bottle*
1:28:52	W	*swig of wine from bottle*
1:31:07	W	*smoking a cigarette*
1:31:49	W	*tells policeman, 'I've only had a*
		few ales'; bottles can be seen beside him
1:32:19	I	*cigarette (unlit)*
1:33:58	W	*smoking a cigarette*
1:34:41	W	*sip of red wine*
1:35:03	W	*small tumbler of red wine*
1:35:47	W	*toke of Camberwell Carrot*
1:36:13	I	*toke of Camberwell Carrot*
1:36:30	W	*toke of Camberwell Carrot*
1:37:11	I	*toke of Camberwell Carrot*
1:41:30	W	*smoking a cigarette*
1:42:27	W	*swig of '53 Margaux*
1:42:55	W	*swig of '53 Margaux*
1:43:31	W	*swig of '53 Margaux*

W takes a few more swigs of 'the best of the century' Château Margaux as the credits roll. (1953 was indeed one of the greatest years for Margaux – helped by a hot and dry August.) † Ordered but not consumed on-screen. ❦ Readers are urged to emulate neither Withnail nor I; their mechanisms have gone … they've had more drugs than you've had hot dinners.

———— ARABIC PROVERB ————

He who knows not, and knows not he knows not, is *a fool* ..... SHUN HIM
He who knows not, and knows he knows not, is *simple* .... TEACH HIM
He who knows, and knows not he knows, is *asleep* .... WAKE HIM
He who knows, and knows he knows, is *wise* .... FOLLOW HIM

This saying can be interestingly compared with the (in)famous 2002 quote by the then US Defense Secretary, Donald Rumsfeld, who, commenting on the situation in Iraq, said: 'Reports that say that something hasn't happened are always interesting to me, because as we know, there are KNOWN KNOWNS; there are things we know we know. We also know there are KNOWN UNKNOWNS; that is to say we know there are some things we do not know. But there are also UNKNOWN UNKNOWNS – the ones we don't know we don't know.'

REQUISITION FOR A LADY'S TOILET

A fine eye-water.. BENEVOLENCE
Best white paint..INNOCENCE
A mixture giving sweetness to the voice............... MILDNESS & TRUTH
A wash to prevent wrinkles....................................CONTENTMENT
Best rouge... MODESTY
A pair of the most valuable earrings............................. ATTENTION
A universal beautifier .... GOOD HUMOR
A lip salve .... CHEERFULNESS

– widely quoted, including by ANNA FERGURSON, *The Young Lady*, 1852

THE ANATOMY OF A KNIFE

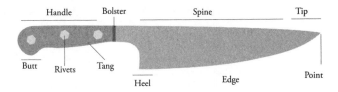

Handle   Bolster   Spine   Tip

Butt   Rivets   Tang   Heel   Edge   Point

TO MAKE A MAN OF CONSEQUENCE

A BROW *austere*, a CIRCUMSPECTIVE *eye*,
A FREQUENT SHRUG of the *os humeri*.
A NOD *significant*, a stately GAIT,
A *blustering* MANNER, and a TONE of *weight*,
A SMILE *sarcastic*, an *expressive* STARE –
Adopt all these, as time and place will bear:
Then rest assured that those of little sense
Will deem you, sure, A MAN OF CONSEQUENCE.

– quoted variously, including in *The Shrubs of Parnassus*, 1760

COMMERCIAL ARTICLES

12 Articles	Dozen	5 Score	Common Hundred
13 Articles	Long Dozen	6 Score	Great Hundred
12 Dozen	Gross	30 Deals	Quarter
20 Articles	Score	4 Quarters	Hundred

———————— CURIOUS ECONOMIC INDICATORS ————————

The global financial crisis has encouraged journalists and economists to explore unusual measures of economic activity. Some of these are anecdotal (e.g., how easily one can hail a taxi, or the length of a coffee shop's queue). Others were hitherto used by insiders (e.g., the Baltic Dry Index, which tracks global shipping prices). Below are some of the more curious measures:

THE TUNNEL INDEX · according to the *LA Times*, the city's 2nd St Tunnel is so popular a location for car ads that the number of location permits granted acts as a barometer of auto-industry confidence.

THE BIG MAC INDEX · the *Economist*'s index tracks the price of a McDonald's Big Mac (available in *c.*120 countries) as a way of assessing the purchasing-power parity of various currencies.

THE SHOE SHINE INDEX · legend has it that Joseph P. Kennedy (father of JFK &c.) said that it was time to quit the market when the shoe-shine boy started discussing stocks and shares.

THE HOT WAITRESS INDEX · Hugo Lindgren observed: 'The hotter the waitresses, the weaker the economy. In flush times, there is a robust market for hotness. Selling everything from condos to premium vodka is enhanced by proximity to pretty young people … That leaves more-punishing work, like waiting tables, to those with less striking genetic gifts.'

THE R-WORD INDEX · the *Economist*'s informal tool for predicting downturns: counting how many times the *New York Times* and the *Washington Post* use the word 'recession'.

THE HEMLINE INDEX · the economist George Taylor is credited with the idea that skirts get longer as the economy declines.

LATVIAN HOOKER INDEX · the economist John Hempton posited a link between the price of prostitutes in Latvia and the country's economic well-being: 'Well, I want a reasonable cross-border comparison of labor costs of labor of roughly equal skill. I guess I could use the price of an electrician – but I don't know how to find that. So instead I use the price of prostitutes.'

LUGGAGE SALES · Merrill Lynch proposed that sales of luggage might indicate consumer confidence.

THE COUPON REDEMPTION INDEX · when times are tough, more people clip coupons and redeem them for discounts. The *New York Times* reported that coupon redemption had increased by 23% in the first six months of 2009.

PLAYMATE INDEX · 2004 research by Pettijohn and Jungeberg suggested when times were tough, *Playboy* used 'older, heavier, taller Playmates of the Year with larger waists, smaller eyes, larger waist-to-hip ratios, smaller bust-to-waist ratios, and smaller Body Mass Index values'.

—————————— CLASSICAL MUSIC CATALOGS ——————————

The work of some composers, especially those prolific in the c18th–c19th, has been organized and cataloged – often by a dedicated scholar – to aid the identification of each piece. To take a famous example, the work of Mozart was chronologically ordered by the Austrian naturalist Ludwig von Köchel (1800–77), who gave each piece a number prefixed with his initial, 'K'. So, Mozart's *Eine Kleine Nachtmusik* (1787) is generally referred to as K525. Some other notable thematic catalogs are tabulated below:

Code	composer	cataloger
BWV	Johann Sebastian Bach	Wolfgang Schmieder
BB	Béla Bartók	László Somfai
BuxWV	Dietrich Buxtehude	Georg Karstadt
HWV	George Frideric Handel	Bernd Bäselt
Hob.	Franz Joseph Haydn	Anthony van Hoboken
S	Franz Liszt	Humphrey Searle
D	Franz Schubert	Otto Erich Deutsch
TrV	Richard Strauss	Franz Trenner
RV	Antonio Vivaldi	Peter Ryom
WWV	Richard Wagner	J. Deathridge, M. Geck, & E. Voss

—————————————— ECONOMY COLORS ——————————————

Economy color	relates to
Black	*trade in illegal goods or through illegal channels*
Blue	*ocean and waterway industries, including fishing and tourism*
Brown	*the pre-green (i.e., polluting, wasteful, &c.) economy*
Green	*sustainable, eco-friendly, recyclable goods and services*
Gray	*trade in legal commodities through unofficial channels*
Pink	*goods and services sold to (or provided by) homosexuals*
Purple	*the subsidy of religious organizations via tax breaks†*
Red	*the South Korean economy after the 2002 World Cup‡*
Silver	*goods and services sold to (or provided by) the elderly*
White	*the 'legitimate' economy; homemaking*
Yellow	*that which relates to illegal sex-related activities (e.g., prostitution)§*

† Max Wallace, of the Australian National Secular Association, defined the purple economy as 'the wealth generated by the eternal mass-exemption from taxation of religious organizations, their subsidiaries, and their charitable arms'. ‡ South Koreans were exuberant after co-hosting the 2002 soccer World Cup, which saw an unprecedented showing by their Red Devils. After supporters thronged the streets wearing red, the press dubbed the euphoria 'red fever'. The term 'red economy' was used to describe the related rise in commercial activity, as interest rates fell and sales soared. § In China, according to the economist Yang Fan.

——— ON BUYING ———

He that buys LAND
buys *many stones*,
He that buys FLESH
buys *many bones*,
He that buys EGGS
buys *many shells*,
He that buys GOOD ALE
buys *nothing else.*
He that buys ...
must have *a hundred eyes.*

——— ON JOURNEYS ———

It helpeth to make a journey pleasant:
To go upon a good errand. ❧ To
have strength and ability for it. ❧
To have daylight. ❧ To have a good
guide. ❧ To be under good guard, or
convoy. ❧ To have the way tracked
by those who have gone before on
the same road, and on the same
errand. ❧ To have good company.
❧ To have the way lie through
green pastures. ❧ To have it fair
overhead. ❧ To be furnished with
needful accommodations for traveling. ❧ To sing on the way. ❧ And
lastly, it helpeth to make a journey
pleasant to have a good prospect.

– The Pulpit Assistant, Vol. 2, 1826

——— COLOR LORE ———

BLUE is *true,* YELLOW's *jealous,*
GREEN's *forsaken,* RED's *brazen,*
WHITE is *love,*
And BLACK is *death!*

– ANON

– ANIMAL LIFE-SPANS –

Flemish folklore gave this estimate
of animal life-spans, premised
upon the belief that a town (or
enclosure) lasted just three years:

A TOWN lives three YEARS,
A DOG lives three TOWNS,
A HORSE lives three DOGS,
A MAN lives three HORSES,
An ASS lives three MEN,
A WILD GOOSE lives three ASSES,
A CROW lives three WILD GEESE,
A STAG lives three CROWS,
A RAVEN lives three STAGS,
& the PHOENIX lives three RAVENS.

A German equivalent has it:

A FENCE lasts three YEARS;
A DOG lasts three FENCES;
A HORSE lasts three DOGS;
And a MAN three HORSES.

Hesiod (*fl.*c8th BC) wrote:

The NOISY CROW lives nine genera-
tions of MEN who die in the bloom
of years; the STAG attains the age of
four CROWS; the RAVEN, in its turn,
equals three STAGS in length of
days; while the PHOENIX lives nine
RAVENS. *We nymphs, fair-of-tresses,
daughters of Jove the aegis-bearer,* at-
tain to the age of ten PHOENIXES.

And, Italian folklore maintained:

A DOG lasts 9 years;
A HORSE lasts 3 DOGS: 27 years;
A MAN lasts 3 HORSES: 81 years;
A CROW lasts 3 MEN: 243 years;
A DEER lasts 3 CROWS: 729 years;
An OAK lasts 3 DEER: 2,187 years.

—————————— DEMONIC HIERARCHY ——————————

The Demonic Hierarchy has been debated by a host of demonologists over the centuries. Peter Binsfeld (*c.*1590) created a heptad of devils, each with the power to incite a particular deadly sin (Lucifer, pride; Mammon, avarice; Satan, anger; &c.). Alphonsus de Spina (*c.*1480) proposed a decadic hierarchy, including Clean Demons (who tormented only holy men). And, according to Rossell Robbins in his *Encyclopedia of Witchcraft & Demonology* (1959), Father Sebastien Michaëlis, in 1612, claimed that a possessed nun had described to him a Demonic Hierarchy to rival the Hierarchy of Angels:

TEMPTATION TO MAN	FIRST HIERARCHY	HEAVENLY ADVERSARY
Pride	BEELZEBUB	Francis
Sins repugnant to faith	LEVIATHAN	Peter the Apostle
Luxury, wantonness	ASMODEUS	John the Baptist
Blasphemy, murder	BALBERITH	Barnabas
Idleness, sloth	ASTAROTH	Bartholomew
Impatience	VERRINE	Dominic
Impurity	GRESSIL	Bernard
Hatred against enemies	SONNEILLON	Stephen

TEMPTATION TO MAN	SECOND HIERARCHY	HEAVENLY ADVERSARY
Heartlessness	CARREAU	Vincent
Obscenity, shamelessness	CARNIVEAN	John the Evangelist
Abandonment of poverty	OEILLET	Martin
Love	ROSIER	Basil

TEMPTATION TO MAN	THIRD HIERARCHY	HEAVENLY ADVERSARY
Arrogance, ostentation	BELIAS	Francis de Paul
Cruelty, mercilessness	OLIVIER	Lawrence
Prince of fallen angels	IUVART	*unknown*

—————————— HAIR-CLIPPER SPECIFICATIONS ——————————

The electric hair-clippers used by barbers can be fitted with a variety of numbered combs, each number indicating the final length the hair is left:

Comb	*length* (mm)				
No. 1	3	No. 4	14	No. 8	25
No. 2	6	No. 5	16	No. 10	32
No. 3	9	No. 6	19	No. 12	32·5
		No. 7	22	[1 mm = 0·0393700787"]	

—— RARE DELUSIONAL CONDITIONS ——

A delusion is an irrational belief, unshakably held even in the face of evidence to the contrary. Delusions are often out of keeping with an individual's social and cultural background, and may be seen in psychiatric disorders (such as schizophrenia or severe depression) and in those suffering from dementia. Some specific – though rare – delusions are given below:

CAPGRAS SYNDROME · the delusion that a close relative or friend has been replaced by an exact double.

OTHELLO SYNDROME · the delusion of infidelity of the spouse, which can occur in a pure form or as part of a psychotic illness.

ANTON'S SYNDROME · a delusion affecting blind people who become convinced that they can see.

FOLIE À DEUX & FOLIE À PLUSIEURS · states in which delusional ideas are transmitted to one or more persons who come to share them.

KORO · the delusion of genital shrinking and retraction where sufferers anticipate impotence, sterility and, in extremis, death. The delusion is accompanied by acute anxiety and vegetative symptoms. Koro is usually associated with Chinese, African, and SE Asian cultures.

FREGOLI SYNDROME · the delusion that familiar individuals have disguised themselves to appear as others. [Named after the Italian quick-change artist and mimic Leopoldo Fregoli (1867–1936).]

POOR MOUTH · the delusion, often seen in older people, that one is on the brink of impoverishment, despite sufficient wealth.

COTARD'S SYNDROME · where the sufferer believes that people or objects do not exist. In extreme cases, sufferers may become convinced that they are dead.

CINDERELLA SYNDROME · when a child believes it has been rejected or neglected by its parents.

DON JUAN SYNDROME · in men, characterized by excessive sexual philandering and conquest.

PSEUDOCOMMUNITY · the delusion that a group of people is conspiring against one.

DELUSIONAL PARASITOSIS · the belief that insects are swarming over one's body – especially the skin and eyes.

COUVADE SYNDROME · when the male partner of a pregnant woman claims sympathetic symptoms.

DE CLÉRAMBAULT'S SYNDROME · the delusion, most commonly seen in women, where the sufferer becomes convinced that a particular man is in love with her. The man, often a casual acquaintance, tends to be older and of higher social status.

GANSER'S SYNDROME · characterized by giving nonsensical answers to elementary questions.

———————— A FORMULA FOR 'SAVAGE' LOVE ————————

In his bizarre 1887 book, *Romantic Love and Personal Beauty*, Henry Theophilus Finck presents an 'approximate list of the ingredients in the Love of savage and semi-civilized people'. Curiously, the author, whose views on race and definition of 'savagedom' leave a great deal to be desired, seems to find nothing odd in parsing love to four decimal places, as below:

Selfishness	25·6784%	Monopoly	0–7·3024%
Inconstancy	20·3701%	Pride of possession	4·5082%
Jealousy	0–20·7904%	Sympathy	[sic] 0·0000%
Coyness	0–10·5523%	Gallantry	0·0006%
Individual preference	0–5·0073%	Self-sacrifice	traces
		Ecstatic adoration	traces
Personal beauty	0–5·7002%	Mixed emotions	traces

———————— HOLLYWOOD'S FORMULA FOR LOVE ————————

According to Rob Wagner's 1918 book *Film Folk*, Hollywood's 'regular formula for love at first sight' then consisted of: 'Enlarging the eyes, to indicate *wonder*; then a smile, suffusing the face, to register *satisfaction*; ending, however, in the pointed brows, the sign by which one *interrogates*. The next spasm is the heaving chest, to indicate that the heart has been *stirred to its nethermost depths*. Now, "*determination to have her at any cost*" must be shown. This is accomplished by a toss of the head, a forward thrust of the chin and a tense clenching of the fists.'

———————— COURTLY LOVE ————————

Below are the rules of courtly love given by Andreas Capellanus in his noted c12th Latin treatise on the subject, *The Art of Honorable Loving*:

Thou shalt avoid avarice – embrace prodigality. ♥ Thou shalt keep thyself chaste for thy beloved. ♥ Thou shalt not knowingly break up a correct love affair of others. ♥ Thou shalt not love whom thou cannot marry. ♥ Be mindful completely to avoid falsehood. ♥ Thou shalt not have many who know of thy love affair. ♥ Be obedient to ladies' commands and strive to ally thyself in the service of love. ♥ In giving and receiving love's solaces let modesty be ever present. ♥ Thou shalt speak no evil. ♥ Thou shalt not be a revealer of love affairs. ♥ Thou shalt be in all things polite and courteous. ♥ In practicing the solaces of love thou shalt not exceed the desires of thy lover.

[Adapted by R. J. Schoeck from a translation by John Jay Parry from the Latin]

———————— AN ALPHABET OF LOVE ————————

In *Don Quixote*, the novelist Miguel de Cervantes (1547–1616) gave the four S's of true lovers, and mooted an abecedarium of the qualities of lovers:

Sabio ♡ **S**olo ♡ **S**olicito ♡ **S**ecreto
apience *olitary* *olicitous* *ecret*

Agradecido · Bueno · Caballero · Dadivoso · Enamorado
Firme · Gallardo · Honrado · Ilustre · Leal · Mozo · Noble
Onesto · Principal · Quantioso · Rico · y las SS que dicen
Y Luego Tácito · Verdadero · La X no le quadra, porque es letra
áspera · La Y ya está dicha · La Z Zelador de tu honra.

The translation of the S's is taken from Ulick Ralph Burke's 1877 book, *Spanish Salt*. Various translators have attempted to fashion an English version of this alphabet including, in 1749, Charles Jarvis: 'Amiable, Bountiful, Constant, Daring, Enamoured, Faithful, Gallant, Honourable, Illustrious, Kind, Loyal, Mild, Noble, Obliging, Prudent, Quiet, Rich, and the S's, as they say [i.e., as above]; lastly, True, Valiant, and Wise: the X suits him not, because it is a harsh letter; the Y, he is Young; the Z, Zealous of your honour.'

———————— C. S. LEWIS'S FOUR LOVES ————————

AGAPE (*altruism*) · AFFECTION (*attachment*)
PHILIAS (*friendship*) · EROS (*romantic love*)

———————— THE ENGINE OF LOVE ————————

From SMILES to the STATION AT KISSES is 500 SIGHS,
From KISSES to POP-THE-QUESTION is 1,500 SIGHS,
And from thence to the TERMINUS OF PA'S-CONSENT, is 2,500 SIGHS,
Making a grand total of 4,500 SIGHS.

To arrive at Pa's-Consent, however, the engine of LOVE has to ascend a steep incline, the gradients of which are enormous – 2 in 3 – causing a vast number of SIGHS to be heavily drawn in reaching it. Some sentimental Surveyors have therefore proposed to facilitate the communication between POP-THE-QUESTION and the TERMINUS OF PA'S-CONSENT (which may easily be done if they can raise sufficient capital), or failing that, to form a LOOP-LINE TO MA'S. Being personally interested in the undertaking, we wish it success with all our heart. The estimated saving is not far short of A THOUSAND SIGHS!

– from *Punch, or The London Charivari*, 1858

────────── A PHILOSOPHY OF LOVE ──────────

Love, taken in its most extensive signification, may be considered as the principle of morality … We might comprise the whole moral philosophy in the single word *love*, and in the sentiment which it expresses, and deduce from this new mode of viewing morality the following subdivisions:

1. Love of a man's self, when rightly understood and properly directed;
   the principle of all other legitimate and salutary species of love, and of all the actions.
2. Love of his parents; *filial affection, piety, respect.*
3. Love of his brothers and sisters; *fraternal affection.*
4. Love of the sex (properly directed and restrained within due bounds);
   an imperious instinct, implanted in man for the perpetuation of the species,
   and which is the bond and charm of society.
5. Love of his wife; *conjugal affection.*
6. Love of his children; *paternal affection.*
7. Love of his friends; *friendship.*
8. Love of his country and its government; *patriotism, public spirit.*
9. Love of mankind; *humanity, enlightened philanthropy, genuine philosophy.*
10. Love of the unfortunate; *beneficence.*
11. Love of glory (rightly understood and properly directed); *heroism.*
12. Love of justice, of virtue, *of all that is good and useful.*
13. Love of the beautiful, *in the productions of nature and the arts, the principle of taste.*
14. Love of God; *piety, admiration of, or gratitude to the supreme ruler of the universe.*

– *The Art of Employing Time to the Greatest Advantage*, Henry Colburn [publisher], 1822

────────── STAGES OF LOVESICKNESS ──────────

Prof. Albrecht Weber listed the following ten stages of Hindu lovesickness:

LOVE OF THE EYES ☞ ATTRACTION OF THE MIND ☞ BIRTH OF DESIRE
☞ LOSS OF SLEEP ☞ INDIFFERENCE TO OBJECTS OF SENSE
☞ LOSS OF FLESH ☞ LOSS OF SHAME ☞ DISTRACTION OF THOUGHT
☞ LOSS OF CONSCIOUSNESS ☞ † DEATH †

────────── DIVISIONS OF LOVE ──────────

Devised by Peter Clark in 1972:

1 ......Selfish love & unselfish love
2 ....The love of men & women
3 ....The Christ love of fellow men
4 ...... Buddhist love for all beings
5 .... Union, the love of unity,
   embracing the universe
6 ....The love of the Father,
   the divine impulse of creation

—————————— ON THE DEGREES OF LOVE ——————————

The five degrees of love, according to Heinrich Kornmann (1579–1627), are:

VISUS (sight) · COLLOQUIUM (conversation)
CONVICTUS (a tête-a-tête) · OSCULA (a kiss) · TACTUS (a touch)

In *The Life Primer* (1906), Charles Richard Tuttle delineates ten degrees:

PHYSICAL LOVE · ANIMAL LOVE · HUMAN LOVE · MENTAL LOVE
CELESTIAL LOVE · ANGELIC LOVE · DIVINE LOVE · SPIRITUAL LOVE
the love of PERFECT HARMONY · and, *above all these*, the LOVE OF GOD

The Andalusian-Arab writer Ibn Hazm (994–1064) enumerated five degrees:

1. THE APPROVAL: when after seeing a person, our imagination represents that person to us as a beautiful thing or reminds us of his or her moral qualities as good: this first-degree love has in common with friendship.

2. ADMIRATION: when one finds pleasure in looking at the person beloved and being near him or her.

3. FALLING IN LOVE: which is to feel sadness when the beloved is absent.

4. OBSESSION: when the lover is dominated by the preoccupation or fixed idea of the beloved: in sexual love this is called passion.

5. AMOROUS MADNESS: which means loss of sleep and appetite for food and drink or becoming ill or coming into ecstasy, speaking to one's self like a madman or even dying of love. Beyond this degree there is none.

(Translated by A. R. Nykl, 1923)

In his 1832 novel, *Swallow Barn*, John Pendleton Kennedy lists five degrees of love: The MANNERLY DEGREE *'when a man first begins to discover that a lady has an air, a voice, and a person more agreeable than others'*. The POETI-CAL DEGREE *'when he was singing out your name so musically'*. QUIXOTIC LOVE which *'carries a gentleman in pursuit of stray hawks, and sets him to breaking the heads of saucy bullies'*. SENTIMENTAL LOVE *'when out comes all his learning, and he fills his mistress's head with unimaginable conceits'*. And finally, the HORRIBLE, distinguished by *'a yellow cheek, a wild eye, a long beard, an unbrushed coat, and a most woe-begone, lackadaisical style of conversation'*.

♥ ♥ ♥

'In the following love couplet, there is great paucity of words, but as much meaning as there are in many most moving love songs.' – ANON
I look'd and lov'd, and lov'd and look'd, and look'd and lov'd again,
But look'd and lov'd, and lov'd and look'd, and look'd and lov'd in vain.

--------- CURIOUS BIBLES OF NOTE ---------

Typos, mistranslations, and gender confusions have bespoiled numerous editions of the Bible – not surprisingly, perhaps, given the 'good book's' status as one of the most widely and diversely printed texts in history. A 1682 edition contained the alarming phrase 'if the latter husband ate her', instead of 'hate her' [Deuteronomy 24:3]; and a 1923 edition solemnly declared in the table of affinities: 'A man may not marry his grandmother's wife'. Tabulated below are some other (in)famous Bibles of note:

Breeches Bible	A Bible printed in 1560 by Whittingham, Gilby, and Sampson rather unusually stated that Adam and Eve 'sowed figge-tree leaves together, and made themselves breeches' [Genesis 3:7].
Bug Bible	Also known as Matthew's Bible, the Bug Bible was published in London in 1561 and translated Psalms 91:5 thus: 'So thou shalt not need to be afraid of any bugges by night.'
Camels Bible	An 1823 Bible stated: 'And Rebekah arose, and her camels' – instead of 'damsels' [Genesis 24:61].
Ears to Ear Bible	A Bible printed in 1810 declared: 'Who hath ears to ear [hear], let him hear' [Matthew 13:43].
Fool Bible	A 1763 edition of the Bible said: 'The fool hath said in his heart there is a God' where it ought to have said 'there is no God' [Psalms 14:1].
He Bible	A 1611 King James Bible is known as the He Bible because Ruth 3:15 read: 'And he went into the city', rather than 'she', as is usual in newer editions. This edition also used the word 'hoopes' instead of 'hookes' in Exodus 38:11.
Idle Shepherd Bible	In an 1809 King James Bible the 'idol shepherd' became the 'idle shepherd' [Zechariah 11:17].
Landscape Painters Bible	Ferrar Fenton's 1903 Bible identified Paul and Apollos as 'landscape painters' rather than 'tent makers', as is usual [Acts 18:3].
Lions Bible	I Kings 8:19, in a Bible printed in 1804, stated: 'But thy son that shall come forth out of thy lions' instead of 'loins'. Meanwhile, Galatians 5:17 said – 'for the flesh lusteth after the spirit' instead of 'against the spirit'.
Murderers Bible	A Bible issued in 1795 by Thomas Bensley declared 'Let the children first be killed' instead of 'filled' [Mark 7:27]. ❦ An 1801 Bible is also known as The Murderers Bible because of a misprint which rendered 'murmurers', 'murderers' [Jude 1:16].

———————— CURIOUS BIBLES OF NOTE cont. ————————

Placemakers Bible	An error in a 1562 Bible named 'placemakers' blessed, rather than 'peacemakers' [Matthew 5:9].
Printers Bible	In a 1702 edition of the Bible, King David said: 'Printers have persecuted me without a cause'. The persecutors were in fact 'princes' [Psalms 119:161].
Religious Bible	A Bible printed in Edinburgh in 1637 declared: 'She hath been religious against me', rather than 'rebellious' [Jeremiah 4:17].
Sin On Bible	8,000 Bibles printed and bound in Ireland in 1716 enjoined readers to 'Go and sin on more' – rather than 'no more' [John 8:11].
Standing Fishes Bible	The Standing Fishes Bible of 1806 read: 'And it shall come to pass that the fishes shall stand upon it' – instead of 'fishers' [Ezekiel 47:10].
To Remain Bible	In Bible Society editions from 1805, 1806, & 1819, an editor's note in the margin instructing that a comma should be kept ('to remain') was included in Galatians 4:29: 'Persecuted him that was born after the spirit to remain, even so it is now.'
Treacle Bible	Beck's Bible of 1549 asked, 'Is there no treacle in Gilead?', rather than, 'Is there no balm'. A 1609 Douay (Roman Catholic) edition used the word 'rosin' instead of 'balm' or 'treacle' [Jeremiah 8:22].
Unrighteous Bible	A Cambridge Press edition printed in 1652 mistakenly asked: 'Know ye not that the unrighteous shall inherit the Kingdom of God?' It should have read, 'shall not inherit' [I Corinthians 6:9].
Vinegar Bible	Luke 20 was titled 'The Parable of the Vinegar' not 'vineyard' in a 1717 Clarendon Press edition.
Wicked Bible†	The seventh commandment of a Bible printed in 1631 in London instructed: 'Thou shalt commit adultery' [Exodus 20:14].
Wife-Hater Bible	An 1810 Bible read: 'If any [man] come to me, and hate not his father … yea, and his own wife also', instead of 'life' [Luke 14:26].

† For this embarrassing error, the printers, Robert Barker and Martin Lucas, were fined £300 by Archbishop Laud, and all copies were suppressed. In 1878, Henry Stevens wrote, in *The Bibles in the Caxton Exhibition*, that four copies of the Wicked Bible were known to have escaped suppression: one in Glasgow; one in the British Museum; one at the Bodleian in Oxford; and one at the Lenox Library in New York. ❦ Sources include: Erin McKean's *Verbatim* (2001); *The (Wordsworth) Dictionary of Phrase and Fable* by Ebenezer Cobham Brewer; and *American Notes & Queries*, Vol. 5, No. 25 (1890), edited by Samuel R. Harris.

TO CURE VARIOUS FITS

FOR A FIT OF PASSION · walk out in the open air; you may speak your mind to the winds, without hurting anyone, or proclaiming yourself to be a simpleton.

FOR A FIT OF IDLENESS · count the tickings of a clock. Do this for one hour, and you will be glad to pull off your coat the next, and work like a dervish.

FOR A FIT OF EXTRAVAGANCE OR FOLLY · go to the workhouse, or speak with the ragged and wretched inmates of a jail, and you will be convinced *Who makes his bed of brier and thorn, must be content to lie forlorn.*

FOR A FIT OF AMBITION · go into the churchyard, and read the gravestones. They will tell you the end of man at his best estate.

FOR A FIT OF REPINING · look about for the halt and the blind, and visit the bedridden, the afflicted, and the deranged, and they will make you ashamed of complaining of your lighter afflictions.

FOR A FIT OF ENVY · go to Brighton, Cheltenham, or some other place of the kind, and see how many who keep their carriages are afflicted with rheumatism, gout, and dropsy; how many walk abroad on crutches, or stay at home wrapped up in flannel; and how many are subject to epilepsy and apoplexy.

FOR A FIT OF DESPONDENCY · look on the good things which God has given you in this world, and at those which he has promised to his followers in the next. He who goes into his garden to look for cobwebs and spiders, no doubt will find them; while he who looks for a flower, may return into his house with one blooming in his bosom.

FOR ALL FITS OF DOUBT, FEAR, AND PERPLEXITY · whether they respect the body or the mind, whether they are a load to the shoulders, the head, or the heart, the following is a radical cure which may be relied on, for I had it from the Great Physician: *Cast thy burden upon the Lord, and he shall sustain thee.*

(Psalms 4:22)

– widely quoted, including by GEORGE MOGRIDGE, *Old Humphrey's Observations,* 1841

THE BENEFITS OF DRINK

He which DRINKETH well SLEEPETH well;
He which SLEEPETH well THINKETH no harm;
He which THINKETH no harm is a GOOD MAN;
Therefore the DRUNKARD is a *good man.*

– quoted by G. BEAUMONT, Minister of the Gospel, in *'Fixed Stars,'* 1814

——————ST JOHN'S LADDER OF PARADISE——————

St John Climacus (*c.* 570–649) was a Greek ascetic whose treatise on monastic virtue – *Klimax tou paradeisou* – enumerated these thirty steps to Paradise:

· PARADISE ·

FAITH, HOPE, CHARITY

PEACE OF GOD

PRAYER *without ceasing*

SOLITUDE

INNER LIGHT

Death of the NATURAL MAN

SINGLE-MINDEDNESS, or ONLY ONE AFFECTION, and that FOR GOD

Abandonment of FALSE HUMILITY and DOUBT

PRIDE *utterly crushed out*

SELF-GLORIFICATION *cast out*

Conquest of FEAR

WATCHFULNESS; the ETERNAL LAMP *burning*

PSALMODY

Death of the CARNAL MIND

POVERTY, or *loss* of the LOVE OF ACCUMULATING

CHASTITY

TEMPERANCE

Conquest of INDOLENCE of MIND and BODY

Restraint of EXAGGERATION and FALSE REPRESENTATION

SILENCE

Shunning SLANDER and IDLE TALK

Forgiveness of INJURIES

EQUANIMITY

SORROW, *the seed of joy*

Constant thought of DEATH

PENITENCE

OBEDIENCE

Giving up FATHER and MOTHER

Giving up all EARTHLY GOOD and HOPE

Renouncement of THE WORLD

· THE WORLD ·

OCCUPATIONS OF NOTE

Accipitrary.... *a bird-of-prey catcher*
Agistor. *an official of the royal forests*
Amanuensis ..... *secretary or copyist*
Belly builder. *piano-interior builder*
Bowyer ...... *maker of archery bows*
Brachygrapher...*a shorthand writer*
Chandler ...... *candlemaker; grocer*
Colporteur ..*door-to-door bookseller*
Coteler ....*knife maker*
Delver ....*a digger of ditches*
Ecdysiast†............*striptease artist*
Eggler.......... *egg or poultry dealer*
Eyer..............*a needle-eye maker*
Funambulist....... *tightrope walker*
Girdler.................*girdle maker*
Hoggard.................*a pig herder*
Idleman..... *one who is unemployed*
Jerquer...... *customs officer for ships*
Kempster..............*wool comber*
Knockknobbler ....*dog catcher*
Lum-sweeper...... *a chimney sweep*
Milliner......... *women's hat maker*

Nim-gimmer...............*a doctor*
Ocularist ....*false-eye manufacturer*
Ostler.......... *stableman at an inn*
Petrifactioner.......... *stone worker*
Quiller........ *one who quills fabric*
Quister . *one who bleaches cloth &c.*
Rattoner................ *a rat catcher*
Sawyer.........*one who saws timber*
Scrivener . *writer of legal documents*
Stevedore .... *one who unloads ships*
Tinker ....*a mender of pots &c.*
Tranqueter..............*hoop maker*
Ulnager.......*one who examines the*
            quality of woolen goods
Victualler..*a food and drink vendor*
Vintner.................*a wine merchant*
Whitesmith ..*polisher of metalwork*
Xylographer ...... *a wood engraver*
Yawler ....*a person who sails a yawl*
Zitherist .... *a player of strings*

† Coined by the satirist H. L. Mencken.

A number of children's counting rhymes are said to divine the profession of a future spouse:

Tinker ☞ Tailor ☞ Soldier ☞ Sailor ☞ Rich Man ☞ Poor Man ☞ Beggar Man ☞ Thief [see p.61]
Tinker ☞ Tailor ☞ Soldier ☞ Sailor ☞ Gentleman ☞ Apothecary ☞ Plough-boy ☞ Thief
Soldier Brave ☞ Sailor True ☞ Skilled Physician ☞ Oxford Blue ☞ Gouty Nobleman ☞
Squire so Hale ☞ Dashing Airman ☞ Curate Pale (*or* Remain a Spinster ☞ Take the Veil)
A Laird ☞ A Lord ☞ A Rich Man ☞ A Thief ☞ A Tailor ☞ A Drummer ☞ A Stealer o' Beef
Rich Man ☞ Poor Man ☞ Beggar Man ☞ Thief ☞ Doctor ☞ Lawyer ☞ Merchant ☞ Chief

Other ditties also foretold: the wedding dress material (Silk, Satin, Muslin, Rags); the bride's footwear (Boots, Shoes, Slippers, Clogs); transport to the church (Coach, Carriage, Wheelbarrow, Trindle [trolley]); the couple's abode (Big House, Small House, Pigsty, Barn) [see p.14]; and the timing of the union (This Year, Next Year, Three Years, Never).

A BESTIARY OF THE TRAVELING MAN

To travel safely through the world, a man must have –
a FALCON'S *Eye*, an ASS'S *Ears*, an APE'S *Face*, a MERCHANT'S *Words*,
a CAMEL'S *Back*, a HOG'S *Mouth*, and a HART'S *Legs*.

─────────── APRIL FOOL'S DAY ───────────

The origins of April Fool's Day are almost as disputed as the placement of its apostrophe. Some suggest a Biblical etymology, citing as the first fool's errand Noah's fruitless dispatch of a ship-to-shore dove [see p.59]. Some look to the joyous Hindu festival of Holi – a five-day celebration of fertility that culminates in a frenzy of hoaxes and pranks. Others suggest that April Fool's Day is an outlet for liminal exuberance as winter gives way to spring (just as Halloween is an outlet as autumn gives way to winter), citing Roman, Celtic, or Druidic precedents. Those with an almanacist's turn of mind note that the adoption of the Gregorian calendar shifted the New Year from March 25 to January 1, creating a parcel† of April fools who either objected to this change or simply forgot about it. Whichever of these theories is correct (all may be erroneous), April Fool's Day is now celebrated by misrule in many countries – notably in France, where the tradition of the *poisson d'Avril* involves sticking cut-out paper fish onto the backs of hapless victims, and eating ichthyoid confectionery. ❦ Although Robert Steele described April 1 as 'the merriest day in the year', not everyone shares the joke. Laurence Hutton wrote that 'April Fooling is the most asinine of all the performances of silly man; and its prosperity lies in the conduct of him who makes it, never in the action of him who is made its victim'. Similarly, *Poor Robin's Almanac* cautioned:

> *It is a thing to be disputed, Which is the greatest fool reputed,*
> *The man who innocently went, Or he that him designedly sent?*

Most agree that fools cannot be made after midday April 1, and that the joke rebounds on those who attempt any post-meridial high jinks. *Notes & Queries* cited the following rhyme, said to come from Hampshire:

> *April fool's gone past, You're the biggest fool at last;*
> *When April fool comes again, You'll be the biggest fool then.*

Some proverbs and quotations of note: Fools chew the chaff while cunning eats the bread. ❦ Fools rush in where angels fear to tread. [POPE] ❦ A fool is often as dangerous to deal with as a knave. ❦ A fool walks with his mouth open and his eyes shut. ❦ A fool must now and then be right, by chance. [COWPER] ❦ He who discovers that he is a fool has found the right road to wisdom. ❦ Even a wise man may sometimes make a fool of himself. ❦ There is no cure for a fool. ❦ The fool finds a stone wall in his way by bumping his head against it. ❦ Every fool has a goose that lays a golden egg tomorrow. ❦ A fool blames others for his faults; a wise man blames himself. ❦ The land of fools is the paradise of knaves. ❦ He is a fool who gets two black eyes to blacken one of his enemy. ❦ The fool doth think he is wise, but the wise man knows himself to be a fool. [SHAKESPEARE] ❦ A fool may ask questions that a wise man cannot answer. ❦ Fools, bairns, and drunks tell all that is in their minds. † This seems to be the collective noun. ❧ In Cockney rhyming slang, April Fools = tools.

—————— LOCAL IDIOSYNCRASIES ——————

Arkansas toothpick.. *a large knife*
Boston marriage.................... *long-term, same-sex romantic friendship*
Brazilian wax... *linear pubic topiary*
Bronx cheer .... *jeers of derision*
Canadian tuxedo.... *'double denim' – i.e., denim jacket with denim trousers*
China syndrome .... *a sequence of catastrophic events*
Chinese burn.............................. *twisting skin around wrists*
Chinese compliment.................. *a pretense of deference and agreement*
Chinese fire drill .. *when, at a red light, all the passengers in a car swap seats*
Chinese walls................ *metaphorical walls of (business) confidentiality*
Chinese whispers *or* Russian scandal................. *misheard overhearings*
Cornish hug.. *a wrestling match*
Egyptian darkness.......... *'darkness so thick that it can be felt' (Exodus 10:22)*
English disease .... *homosexuality; syphilis*
English rule .... *that guests of a common host need not wait to be introduced*
French inhale.. *exhaling cigarette smoke orally before drawing it back nasally*
French leave/exit .... *going off without asking permission/saying goodbye*
Full Cleveland.. *white shoes, white belt*
Glasgow kiss.. *a head-butt*
Greek gift................................. *one that hides an act of treachery*
Indian summer.................... *an autumnal recurrence of warm weather*
Irish confetti .... *bricks, stones, &c., used as weapons*
Irish exit .... *to leave drunk*
London particular... *a dense fog*
Maine lawman .... *one who advocates prohibition*
Manchurian candidate...................... *a brainwashed agent of another*
Maryland parson.................. *one adept at fitting in with any company*
Mexican holster (*or* Mexican carry) .... *stuffing a handgun into one's belt*
Mexican stand-off...................... *a stalemate; a massacre in cold blood*
Michigan bankroll .....*where a high-value bill conceals others of lower value*
New York minute ....*a few seconds*
Ohio fever...*a yearning to move west*
Oklahoma rain...*a dust storm*
Pennsylvania caps................ *recapped tires with an unbroken tread line*
Philadelphia lawyer ...... *a highly skilled (and perhaps unscrupulous) lawyer*
Portuguese parliament...............................*where all speak at once*
Roman holiday.............................*enjoyment at the expense of others*
Russian roulette............................ *suicidal gambling with firearms*
Sheffield finish ..*when a (club) singer goes to town on the final note of a song*
Spanish practices...................*tolerated graft, corruption, and indolence*
Texas hankie...............................*blowing one's nose into one's hand*
Texas stop .... *slowing down but not halting at a Stop sign*
Virginia vapor...*tobacco smoke*

——————— THE BESTIARY OF A GOOD HOST ———————

The GOOD HOST must have the *Forehead* of an OX; the *Ears* of an ASS;
the *Back* of a NAG; the *Belly* of a SWINE; the *Subtlety* of a FOX;
Skip Up and Down like a FROG; and *Fawn and Lie* like a DOG.

——————————— NIMBUS SYMBOLISM ———————————

Nimbuses are the haloes that surround the heads of holy figures in
Christian art, the colors of which (sometimes†) have symbolic meaning:

Apostles, martyrs, and confessors............................ *yellow nimbus*
Penitents.. *yellow nimbus*
Prophets and patriarchs.............................. *white or silver nimbus*
Living saints... *square nimbus*
Married saints...*green nimbus*
Saints who have struggled with temptation......................*red nimbus*
Christ.. *more or less cruciform nimbus*
Angels .... *rays of light surrounded by a circle of quatrefoils, like roses*
God the Father.........*triangular nimbus; or a circle surrounding His hand*
The Virgin Mary......................................*a nimbus of small stars*

It seems that in the C19th another, albeit similar, taxonomy was popular:

Square nimbus .... *indicates that the person was living*
Circular nimbus................. *indicates that the person had gone to heaven*
Green nimbus........................... *indicates that the person was married*
Red nimbus .... *indicates those who fought against sin*
Black nimbus... *awarded to Judas*
Gold nimbus...........................*awarded to saints of the highest order*
Silver nimbus.............................. *next in honor to the gold nimbus*
Yellow nimbus ... *indicates sinners who become saints by prayer and penance*

† However, in his 1851 text *Christian Iconography*, Adolphe Napoléon Didron cautioned,
'It will not indeed be correct, constantly to seek a meaning in the color; nor must we form
an exaggerated idea of the importance to be attached to it; for, in numerous instances,
[nimbus color] may easily be proved to be without signification.' ❦ Sources include
EBENEZER COBHAM BREWER, *The Historic Note-Book: With an Appendix of Battles*, 1891.

—— SAMUEL TAYLOR COLERIDGE ON SPEECH ——

The object of RHETORIC is *persuasion* ☞ of LOGIC, *conviction* ☞ of GRAMMAR,
significancy. A fourth term is wanting, the RHEMATIC, or logic of sentences.

─────────────── NINE RULES FOR READING ───────────────

[1] Don't try to read everything.
[2] Read two books on the same subject, one solid and one for pleasure.
[3] Don't read a book for the sake of saying you have read it.
[4] Review what you have read. [5] Read with pencil in hand.
[6] Use your blank book. [7] Condense what you copy.
[8] Read less and try to remember more. [9] Read regularly.

– DR EDWARD EVERETT HALE (1822–1909)

─────────────── PARABLES OF ACCUMULATION ───────────────

[This is] the kid that my father bought for two zuzim
[This is] the cat that ate...
[This is] the dog that bit...
[This is] the stick that beat...
[This is] the fire that burnt...
[This is] the water that quenched...
[This is] the ox that drank...
[This is] the butcher that killed...
[This is] the Angel, the Angel of Death, that slew...

⁂

[This is] the house that Jack built
[This is] the malt that lay in...
[This is] the rat that ate...
[This is] the cat that killed...
[This is] the dog that scared...
[This is] the cow with the crumpled horn that tossed...
[This is] the maiden, all forlorn, that milked...
[This is] the priest, all shaven and shorn, that married...

─────────────── ARCHAIC MILES ───────────────

Country mile	*yards*		
Swiss mile	9,153	Arabian mile	2,140
Vienna mile	8,296	Roman mile	2,025
German mile	8,106	Scotch mile	1,984
Swedish mile	7,341	Turkish mile	1,826
Flemish mile	6,869	Tuscan mile	1,808
Dutch & Prussian mile	6,480	Italian mile	1,766
Irish mile	2,240	English & American mile	1,760
		MODERN MILE	1,760

—————————— CREDIT RATINGS ——————————

Countries, like individuals and corporations, have credit ratings. These ratings offer forward-looking opinions about risk, helping to answer the question, Will a country be able to pay back its debts in full and on time? Lenders pay close attention to nations' credit scores. Indeed, some banks and investment organizations are prohibited from lending to countries with all but the best ratings. The creditworthiness of entire countries has become increasingly thorny as governments around the world face tough choices about how much money to borrow (or print) to secure their economies. ❦ Credit ratings are offered by various agencies, each of which employs different methods to calculate and define risk, usually using an alphabetical scale. Below are the credit rating definitions used by the Standard & Poor's:

Rating	opinion
AAA	*Extremely strong capacity to meet debts*
AA	*Very strong capacity to meet debts*
A	*Strong capacity to meet debts but somewhat more susceptible to adverse changes in economic conditions*
BBB	*Adequate capacity to meet debts, but adverse economic conditions or changing circumstances are more likely to lead to a weakened capacity*
BB	*Faces major ongoing uncertainties – exposure to adverse business, financial, or economic conditions could lead to an inadequate capacity to meet debts*
B	*Currently has the capacity to meet its debts, but adverse business, financial, or economic conditions will be likely to impair its capacity or willingness to do so*
CCC	*Currently vulnerable, and dependent upon favorable business, financial, and economic conditions to meet debts*
CC	*Currently highly vulnerable*
SD/D	*Selective [i.e., partial] default / Default*
+/–	*The ratings AA to CCC may be modified with plus or minus signs to indicate relative standing within the categories*

—————————— ITCHING SIGNIFICANCE ——————————

Body part	itching signifies
Ear	longing to hear news or gossip
Palm	the imminent receipt of money
Thumb	the approach of danger or evil[†]
Right eye	imminent laughter or jollity; arrival of a loved one
Left eye	imminent sadness or grief
Lips	imminent prospect of kissing
Nose	imminent arrival of a stranger; the risk of a fire; fighting

† 'By the pricking of my thumbs, Something wicked this way comes.' *Macbeth*, IV i

THE HAND

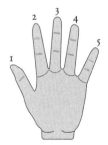

1 . . . . *Thumb; Anglo-Saxon thuma*
2 . . *Towcher or Foreman; Anglo-Saxon scite-finger*
3 . . . . *Long man; Dogon finger of death*
4 . . . . *Ring finger; Anglo-Saxon gold-finger*
5 . . . . *Little Man; Anglo-Saxon ear-finger*

The thumb, in chiromancy, we give to Venus;
The fore-finger, to Jove; the midst, to Saturn;
The ring, to Sol; the least, to Mercury.
– BEN JONSON, *The Alchemist*, 1610

There are 27 bones in the human hand: 8 carpal bones; 5 metacarpals; and 14 phalanges. ❧ The hand was considered a symbol of STRENGTH in ancient Egypt, and of FIDELITY in Rome, where a hand placed upon the head of another implied SERVITUDE, as did covering one's own hand in one's sleeve. ❧ Clasped hands represent UNITY and ENTENTE in many cultures; in Buddhism, the closed hand represents SECRECY and INSULARITY. ❧ In Christianity, the hand with the first two fingers raised is a symbol of BENEDICTION. ❧ In Weimar Germany, an open hand was the symbol of the COMMUNIST party. ❧ To have the UPPER HAND is to be superior, and to have a HEAVY HAND is to lack subtlety or be brutal. To be OFFHAND is to be dismissive, and to act HIGH-HANDEDLY is to be imperious. We LEND A HAND when helping people, and employ SLEIGHT OF HAND to deceive them. ❧ The 'secret' MASONIC HANDSHAKE involves asserting subtle pressure on the knuckles. ❧ The RED HAND OF ULSTER is said to derive from the fable of O'Neill, who won the race to touch the shore of Ireland by cutting off his hand and throwing it from his boat onto land. ❧ In medicine, MITTEN HAND is where several fingers are fused with a common nail; MIRROR HANDS occur when two hands develop from a common wrist; and PHANTOM HAND is where pseudo-sensations are felt from an amputated hand. ❧ Adam Smith, in promulgating his *laissez-faire* view of the economy, stated that the individual was 'led by an INVISIBLE HAND to promote an end which was no part of his intention'. ❧ An ancient form of servant's oath involved placing one's hand under the thigh of one's master. ❧ The Devil finds work for IDLE HANDS. ❧ God placed Jesus at his RIGHT HAND. ❧ Justice, the blindfolded statue atop London's famous Old Bailey court, holds a SWORD in her right hand and the SCALES OF JUSTICE in her left. ❧ A BIRD IN THE HAND is worth two in the bush – or, as the Germans say, *Ein Spatz in der Hand ist besser als eine Taube auf dem Dach*. ❧ In Mexican art, hands symbolize DEATH. ❧ Boudicca, Queen of the Iceni, invoked Andraste, the goddess of war, by raising her HAND TO HEAVEN. ❧ British folklore asserts that if you place a dislodged eyelash on your THUMB, you can make a wish that will come true but *only* if you avoid thinking of foxes' tails at 'the fatal moment'.

—————— THE HAND cont. ——————

Ancient Greek Hand Measures	
1 finger (or digit)	0·76 inches
4 fingers	1 palm
12 fingers	1 span
16 fingers	1 foot
24 fingers	1 cubit

Ancient Hebrew Hand Measures	
1 finger (*azba*)	0·74 inches
4 fingers	1 palm (*tefah*)
12 fingers	1 span (*zeret*)
24 fingers	1 ordinary cubit (*ammah*)
28 fingers	1 royal cubit

The ancient Romans entrusted the hand and its fingers to Minerva, patron saint of arts and trades. However, every finger joint on each hand was additionally dedicated to a saint, as below.

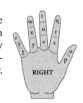

(LEWIS DAYTON BURDICK, *The Hand*, 1905)

a ....Christ	h .. James the Great	o ....God	v .... Joseph
b ....The Virgin	i ....Jude	p ....The Virgin	w ....Zaccheus
c ....James	j ..... Bartholomew	q ....Barnabas	x ....Stephen
d ....John	k ....Andrew	r................John	y ....Luke
e ....Peter	l ....Mathias	s................Paul	z ....Leatus
f............Simeon	m ....Thomas	t..Simeon Cleophas	† ....Mark
g ....Matthew	n ....Philip	u .... Tathidio	‡ ......Nicodemus

Hand type	*personality*
Great and thick	strong and stout
Little and slender	weak and timorous
Long with long fingers	mechanical artifice and liberal ingenuity
Short with short fingers	a fit-for-nothing fool
Hard and brawny	dull and rude
Soft	witty but effeminate
Hairy	luxurious
Often clapped and folded	covetousness
Much moving with speech	loquaciousness
Ambidextrous	ireful, crafty, injurious
With short, fat fingers	intemperate and silly
With long, lean fingers	witty
With fingers that crook upward/downward	liberal/niggardly
With long and crooked nails	brutish, ravenous, unchaste
With short nails, pale and sharp	false, subtle, beguiling
With round nails	libidinous
With nails broad, plain, thin, white, or reddish	with a fine wit

– adapted from JOHN BRAND, *Popular Antiquities*, 1877

GREEK ALPHABET

A	Alpha	α	I	Iota	ι	P	Rho	ρ
B	Beta	β	K	Kappa	κ	Σ	Sigma	σ
Γ	Gamma	γ	Λ	Lambda	λ	T	Tau	τ
Δ	Delta	δ	M	Mu	μ	Y	Upsilon	υ
E	Epsilon	ε	N	Nu	ν	Φ	Phi	φ
Z	Zeta	ζ	Ξ	Xi	ξ	X	Chi	χ
H	Eta	η	O	Omicron	o	Ψ	Psi	ψ
Θ	Theta	θ	Π	Pi	π	Ω	Omega	ω

'And he said unto me, It is done. I am Alpha and Omega, the beginning and the end. I will give unto him that is athirst of the fountain of the water of life freely. He that overcometh shall inherit all things; and I will be his God, and he shall be my son. But the fearful, and unbelieving, and the abominable, and murderers, and whoremongers, and sorcerers, and idolaters, and all liars, shall have their part in the lake which burneth with fire and brimstone: which is the second death.'
(Revelation 21)

THE CIRCLE OF PROGRESS

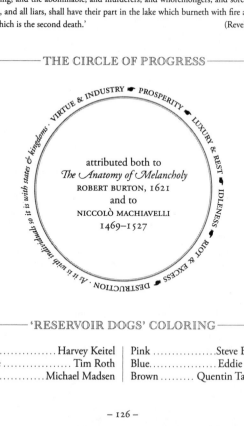

VIRTUE & INDUSTRY ➤ PROSPERITY ➤ LUXURY & REST ➤ IDLENESS ➤ RIOT & EXCESS ➤ DESTRUCTION · As it is with individuals so it is with states & kingdoms ·

attributed both to
The Anatomy of Melancholy
ROBERT BURTON, 1621
and to
NICCOLÒ MACHIAVELLI
1469–1527

'RESERVOIR DOGS' COLORING

White	Harvey Keitel	Pink	Steve Buscemi
Orange	Tim Roth	Blue	Eddie Bunker
Blonde	Michael Madsen	Brown	Quentin Tarantino

INDIA'S CASTE SYSTEM

Traditionally, Indian society has been influenced by the caste system – a method of stratifying people into classes based on birth, marriage, and occupation. The term 'caste' derives from the Portuguese *casta* (borrowed from the Latin *castus*, for 'race' or 'clan'), which the Portuguese used to describe Indian society after arriving in the c16th. While discrimination on the basis of caste has been illegal in India since 1949, the system remains embedded in some areas, and continues to affect some social interactions. ❧ The Hindu *varnas* ('colors') are an overarching division of society first mentioned in a creation myth about the first being in the sacred Sanskrit *Rig Veda*.

The 4 *varnas* correspond to the following (historically hereditary) occupations:

Brahmins . . . .*priests and teachers*	Vaishyas . . . .*farmers and merchants*
Kshatriyas . . . . . *nobles and warriors*	Shudras. . . . . . .*peasants and laborers*

A fifth class, now called the Dalit, is said to exist outside of the *varnas*. Once called the 'untouchables', this group performed the lowest forms of labor, including anything to do with 'polluting' waste, death, or violence.

Origins · Some trace the roots of the system to an Aryan invasion of N India *c.*1500 BC, when the conquerors used the caste system to legitimize their own rule while placing the region's aboriginal populations on the lowest rungs.

Colors · Traditionally, Brahmins were associated with the color white, Kshatriyas red, Vaishyas brown, and Shudras black. Some have thus proposed a racialized division, but genetic analysis has produced varying results.

While *varna* exists as a symbolic division of society, it is *jati* that today principally structures the caste system. A *jati*, literally meaning 'birth', is a kinship group that is (historically) responsible for a particular craft or occupation. There are thousands of *jati*, which vary geographically, and can each be roughly fitted into a particular *varna*. Notions of *jati* are governed by rules of ritual purity and pollution. Thus the bodily substances and secretions of each *jati* are prohibited from mixing with those of others, and to work, marry, or dine below one's *jati* is to pollute oneself. Such transgressions require participation in cleansing activities – which may include bathing, purifying rites, or the payment of fines, depending on the severity of the offense. ❧ Traditionally, movement across castes was quite limited. However, lower castes could sometimes improve their standing by adopting the practices of higher castes. Today the lower castes are the subject of affirmative action. Globalization, migration, urbanization, and the introduction of new, caste-free occupations (such as computer programming) are also responsible for weakening the hierarchy.

DRUNKEN BEAST

There are five requisites for a
PROFESSED DRUNKARD

A FACE of *brass.*
NERVES of *steel.*
LUNGS of *leather.*
HEART of *stone.*
An *incombustible* LIVER.

Without which he shall die. – ANON

CONVERSATION

When the meaning is too big for the words, the expression is QUAINT. When the words are too big for the meaning, it is BOMBASTIC. The one is pleasing, as an imperfection of growth; the other unpleasing, as that of decay. The talk of children is often QUAINT; that of worn-out men of the world often BOMBASTIC, where the error is not precluded by that of a perpetual sneer or a drivelling chatter. – *Blackwood's Magazine,* 1837

SWIFT + 'LED'

'Who is not governed by the word *led*?' asked JONATHAN SWIFT. 'Our noblemen and drunkards are *pimp-led*, physicians and pulses *fee-led*, their patients and organs *pil-led*, a new-married man and an ass are *bridle-led*, an old married man and a pack-horse *sad-led*, cats and dice are *rat-led*, swine and nobility are *sty-led*, a coquette and a tinder-box are *spark-led*, a lover and a blunderer are *grove-led*.'

ADVICE TO LADIES

If you have blue eyes you need not languish. ❦ If black eyes you need not stare. ❦ If you have pretty feet there is no occasion to wear short petticoats. ❦ If you are doubtful as to that point, there can be no harm in letting the petticoats be long. ❦ If you have good teeth, do not laugh for the purpose of showing them. ❦ If you have bad ones, do not laugh less than the occasion may justify. ❦ If you have pretty hands and arms, there can be no objection to your playing on the harp if you play well. ❦ If they are disposed to be clumsy, work tapestry. ❦ If you have a bad voice, rather speak in a low tone. ❦ If you have the finest voice in the world, never speak in a high tone. ❦ If you dance well, dance but seldom. ❦ If you dance ill, never dance at all. ❦ If you sing well, make no previous excuses. ❦ If you sing indifferently, hesitate not a moment when you are asked, for few people are judges of singing, but every one is sensible of a desire to please. ❦ If you would preserve beauty, rise early. ❦ If you would preserve esteem, be gentle. ❦ If you would obtain power, be condescending. ❦ If you would live happily, endeavor to promote the happiness of others.

– A. W. CHASE, *Dr Chase's Recipes,* 1876

TRILOGY OF WIVES

The FIRST wife is ..... *Matrimony*
The SECOND wife is ...... *Company*
The THIRD wife is .... *Heresy*

———————— HUNGER STRIKES ————————

The origins of the hunger strike have been lost to time, although the idea of fasting as a means of seeking redress is found in both ancient Ireland and India – two areas where hunger strikes became a prominent feature of c20th politics. The earliest modern hunger strikes were undertaken by suffragettes in the early 1900s, first in England and then Ireland, and the tactic was swiftly adopted by Irish nationalists [see below]. Since then, hunger strikes have become a well-known, if high-risk, strategy for the powerless to protest against an injustice. The World Health Organization differentiates between two types of hunger strikes, and details the physical effects of the latter:

DRY FASTING · refusing all solids or fluids · *death after 4–10 days*

TOTAL FASTING · accepting only water · *death after c.40–75 days*

1st week . . . . *feelings of hunger and fatigue, stomach cramps*
2nd–3rd . . . .*weakness, dizziness, hunger & thirst disappear, feeling of cold*
3rd–4th. . . . . *worsening of symptoms above, intellectual powers slow*
5th. . . . .*change in consciousness, lack of motor coordination, difficulty swallowing, uncontrollable eye movements, loss of vision and hearing*

Below are just a few of the many notable hunger strikes of the c20th:

Date	striker(s)	location	cause	duration
1909	*Marion Dunlop*	England	suffrage‡	91 hours
1912	*Lizzie Barker*	Ireland	suffrage‡	several days
1917	*Thomas Ashe*†	Ireland	Irish Republicanism‡	5 days
1920	*Terence MacSwiney*†	England	Irish Republicanism‡	74 days
1968	*Cesar Chavez*	California	migrant farmworkers	25 days
1972	*Pedro Luis Boitel*†	Cuba	anti-Castro	53 days
1981	*Bobby Sands*§	Ireland	Irish Republicanism‡	66 days
1987	*Thileepan*†	Sri Lanka	Tamil rights	12 days
1989	*c.1,000 students*	Tiananmen Sq	democratic reform	various
1996	*c.2,000 prisoners*†	Turkey	mistreatment	<69 days
2005–	*Inmates*	Guantánamo Bay	mistreatment	various
2009	*P. Subramaniam*	England	Sri Lankan war	24 days
2009	*Roxana Saberi*	Iran	prison sentence	c.2 weeks

Gandhi undertook at >17 fasts, many of which sought to obtain particular ends; however, some scholars are wary of viewing these as 'hunger strikes', because of their spiritual dimension. ❦ The Malta Declaration advises that doctors should respect the wishes of a mentally competent person to refuse food, and states that force-feeding is morally unacceptable. ❦ Some strikers above undertook multiple hunger strikes. † Strike resulted in death(s). ‡ Strike to protest detainment and seek status as a political prisoner. § Sands was one of 10 Republicans who starved themselves to death during the notorious H-Block prison protests.

--------------- PROUST QUESTIONNAIRE ---------------

In *c.*1886, a fifteen-year-old Marcel Proust responded (in French) to questions posed (in English) by a Victorian 'confessions' album belonging to
his friend Antoinette Faure (the daughter of the future French president Félix Faure).
Some five years later, in *c.*1891, Proust responded to a French confessions
questionnaire, which he titled *Marcel Proust par lui-même* ['Marcel Proust on
himself']. Although such confessional questionnaires were popular parlor
games in Britain and France during the C19th, they have since become
inextricably associated with Proust – not least because, since 1993, *Vanity
Fair* has published a 'Proust questionnaire' in which celebrities respond
to questions based on those answered by the French novelist. Below
are the answers Proust gave in Antoinette Faure's book, *Confessions: An
Album to Record Thoughts, Feelings, &c.*,† and those he gave later in *c.*1891:

CONFESSIONS · c.1886

Your Favorite: virtue	*All those that are not specific to any one sect, those universal.*
– qualities in man	*Intelligence, moral sense.*
– qualities in a woman	*Tenderness, naturalness, intelligence.*
– occupation	*Reading, daydreaming, poetry, history, theater.*
– color and flower	*I like all colors; and as for flowers, I do not know.*
– prose authors	*George Sand, Aug Thierry.*
– poets	*[Alfred de] Musset.*
– painters & composers	*[Ernest] Meissonier, Mozart, [Charles François] Gounod.*
– heroes in real life	*A combination of Socrates, Pericles, Mohammed, Musset, Pliny the Younger, Aug Thierry.*
– heroines in real life	*A woman of genius leading the life of an ordinary woman.*
– heroes in fiction	*The romantic, poetic heroes, those who represent an ideal rather than a model.*
– heroines in fiction	*Those who are more than women without betraying their sex, everything tender, poetic, pure, beautiful in every genre.*
– motto	*One that cannot be summed up because its simplest expression is in all that is beautiful, good, and grand in nature.*
Your idea of happiness	*To live near those I love, surrounded by the beauties of nature, lots of books & musical scores, & not far from a French theater.*
Your idea of misery	*To be separated from mummy.*
If not yourself, who would you be?	*Not having to ask this question, I prefer not to answer it. However, I would rather like to have been Pliny the Younger.*
Where would you like to live?	*In the realm of the ideal, or rather of my ideal.*
Your pet aversion	*People who do not sense what is good, who are ignorant of the tenderness of affection.*
Fault you most tolerate	*… The private lives of geniuses.*

Translation adapted from WILLIAM C. CARTER, *Marcel Proust: A Life* (1941). † Proust
left five questions unanswered; the original album was sold at auction in Paris in May 2003.

————— PROUST QUESTIONNAIRE cont. —————

CONFESSIONS · *c.*1891

Your Favorite: bird	*The swallow.*
– names	*I only have one at a time.*
– qualities in a man	*Feminine charm.*
– qualities in a woman	*A man's virtues, and frankness in friendship.*
– occupation	*Loving.*
– color	*Beauty lies not in colors but in their harmony.*
– flower	*Hers – but, that apart – all.*
– prose writers	*At the moment, Anatole France & Pierre Loti.*
– poets	*Baudelaire and Alfred de Vigny.*
– composers	*Beethoven, Wagner, Shuhmann* [sic].
– painters	*Leonardo da Vinci, Rembrandt.*
– heroes in real life	*Monsieur Darlu, Monsieur Boutroux.*
– heroines in history	*Cleopatra.*
– hero in fiction	*Hamlet.*
– heroines in fiction	*~~Phèdre~~, Berenice.*
What is your motto?	*I prefer not to say, in case it brings me bad luck.*
What is your dream of happiness?	*Not, I fear, a very elevated one. I really haven't the courage to say what it is, and if I did, I should probably destroy it by the mere fact of putting it into words.*
Greatest of misfortunes?	*Never to have known my mother or grandmother.*
You would like to be?	*Myself – as those whom I admire would like me to be.*
In what country would you like to live?	*One where certain things that I want would be realized – and where feelings of tenderness would always be reciprocated.*
You most dislike	*My own worst traits.*
Faults you most indulge	*Those that I understand.*
Your principal defect	*Lack of understanding; weakness of will.*
Despised historical figure	*I am not sufficiently educated to say.*
Would like to die	*A better man than I am, and much loved.*
What is your present state of mind?	*Annoyance at having to think about myself in order to answer these questions.*
Natural gift you'd like	*Willpower and irresistible charm.*
Admired military event	*My own enlistment as a volunteer!*
Your most marked characteristic?	*A craving to be loved, or, to be more precise, to be caressed and spoiled rather than to be admired.*
What do you most value in your friends?	*Tenderness – provided they possess a physical charm which makes their tenderness worth having.*
Reform you most admire	[no answer]

Adapted from ANDRÉ MAUROIS, *The Quest for Proust* (1949), translated by Gerard Hopkins. ❦ Other notable respondents to such questionnaires include Claude Debussy, who, in 1889, nominated his 'hair' as his most distinctive feature, and revealed that he most disliked 'feeling cold'. In February 1873, Prince Alfred cited as his idea of misery: 'A mother-in-law'.

--------------------------------- BORTLE SCALE ---------------------------------

In 2001, the astronomer John E. Bortle created the Bortle Dark Skies Scale as a way for astronomers to gauge the quality of their observation sites. (The scale is also used by the International Dark-Sky Association to establish 'Dark Sky Parks'.) A summary of the Bortle Scale appears below:

1 · EXCELLENT DARK-SKY SITE	*zodiacal light, gegenschein[†], zodiacal band visible; surroundings basically invisible; Triangulum Galaxy seen by naked eye*
2 · TYPICAL TRULY DARK SITE	*airglow may be visible near horizon; clouds as dark holes; Triangulum Galaxy seen with direct vision; surroundings barely visible*
3 · RURAL SKY	*some light pollution on horizon; clouds may appear illuminated; Milky Way is detailed; M4, M5, M15, and M22[‡] visible to naked eye*
4 · RURAL / SUBURBAN	*light pollution over population centers; zodiacal light doesn't extend halfway to zenith at beginning or end of twilight; Milky Way lacks detail*
5 · SUBURBAN SKY	*Milky Way very weak; light sources in most directions*
6 · BRIGHT SUBURBAN SKY	*no trace of zodiacal light; sky glows grayish white within 35° of horizon; Triangulum Galaxy impossible to see without binoculars*
7 · SUBURBAN / URBAN TRANSITION	*entire sky grayish white; strong light sources in all directions; Milky Way is (nearly) invisible*
8 · CITY SKY	*sky glows whitish-gray or orange; newspaper headlines would be visible; Andromeda Galaxy and Cancer constellation may be glimpsed on good nights*
9 · INNER-CITY SKY	*entire sky is bright, even at zenith; many familiar constellations invisible; the only pleasing telescopic objects are Moon, planets, and brightest stars*

† Literally 'counter-glow' in German, the gegenschein is a faint light seen opposite the sun at dawn or dusk under good conditions. ‡ The prefix 'M' denotes a 'Messier object' included in the catalog of deep-sky objects compiled by the French astronomer and comet-hunter Charles Messier (1730–1817). Further information on these objects may be found at messier.obspm.fr. [Source for the Bortle Scale: *Sky & Telescope* magazine]

--------------------------- THE PROGRESS OF RAINFALL ---------------------------

A MIST, which successively becomes A MIZZLE
☞ A DRIZZLE ☞ A SHOWER ☞ A RAIN ☞ A TORRENT

– JAMES BERESFORD, *The Miseries of Human life*, 1826 [see also pp.50–51]

──── HIEROGLYPHS OF TRAMPS AND THIEVES ────

In his pioneering mid-C19th exploration of working-class poverty, *London Labour & the London Poor*, Henry Mayhew noted the secret symbols chalked by tramps on the doorposts of properties that served as guides to their comrades in alms. A decade or so later, in his *Slang Dictionary*, John Hotten added further detail to Mayhew's description, warning: 'The reader may be startled to know that, in addition to a sacred language, the wandering tribes of this country have private marks and symbolic signs with which to score their successes, failures, and advice to succeeding beggars; in fact, that the country is really dotted over with beggars' fingerposts and guide-stones.' ❦ Mayhew observed that 'in almost every one of the padding kens, or low lodging-houses in the country, there is a list of walks written on a piece of paper, and pasted up over the kitchen mantel-piece. Now at St Alban's, for instance … there is a paper stuck up in each of the kitchens. This paper is headed "Walks Out of This Town", and underneath it is set down the

names of the villages in the neighbourhood at which a beggar may call when out on his walk, and they are so arranged as to allow the cadger to make a round of about six miles, each day, and return the same night.' ❦ Hotten reproduced 'a correct facsimile of one of these singular maps' – depicting an area near Maidstone, Kent – which was sketched by 'a wandering SCREEVER [pavement artist] in payment for a night's lodging'. This curious map is printed above, and the tramp's hand-scrawled hieroglyphs are decoded below:

✗	NO GOOD; too poor and know too much.
♫	STOP; if you have what they want, they will buy. They are pretty '*fly*' (knowing).
⟩	GO IN THIS DIRECTION, it is better than the other road. Nothing that way.
◇	BONE (good). Safe for 'cold tatur' [potato] if nothing else. '*Cheese your patter*' (Don't talk much) here.
▽	COOPER'D (spoilt) by too many tramps calling there.
□	GAMMY (unfavorable) likely to have taken you up. Mind the dog.
☉	FLUMMOXED (dangerous) sure of a month in '*quod*' (prison).
⊕	RELIGIOUS, but tidy on the whole.

── INTERNATIONAL WEATHER SYMBOLS ──

No cloud development *during past hour*	Clouds generally dissolving *during past hour*	State of sky unchanged *during past hour*	Clouds forming or developing *during past hour*	Visibility reduced by smoke	Haze	Widespread dust in suspension, not raised by wind	Dust or sand raised by the wind	Well-developed dust/sand whirls	Duststorm or sandstorm
Mist	Patches of shallow fog *≤6' deep on land*	Continuous shallow fog *≤6' deep on land*	Lighting visible no thunder	Precipitation in sight *not reaching ground*	Precipitation in sight *reaching ground; distant*	Precipitation in sight *reaching ground; near*	Thunder, but no precipitation at the station	Squalls within sight during past hour	Funnel clouds / tornadoes *now or in past hour*
Drizzle/snow grains not falling as shower *ended in past hour*	Rain not falling as shower *ended in past hour*	Snow not falling as shower *ended in past hour*	Rain and snow / ice pellets not falling as shower *ended in past hour*	Freezing drizzle or rain not falling as shower *ended in past hour*	Shower of rain *ended in past hour*	Shower of snow, or rain & snow *ended in past hour*	Shower of hail, or rain & hail *ended in past hour*	Fog or ice fog *ended in past hour*	Thunderstorm ± precipitation *ended in past hour*
Slight or moderate duststorm or sandstorm *decreased in preceding hour*	Slight or moderate duststorm or sandstorm *no major change in preceding hour*	Severe duststorm or sandstorm *begun/increased in preceding hour*	Severe duststorm or sandstorm *decreased in preceding hour*	Severe duststorm or sandstorm *no major change in preceding hour*	Severe duststorm or sandstorm *begun/increased in preceding hour*	Slight/moderate drifting snow *below eye level*	Heavy drifting snow *below eye level*	Slight/moderate blowing snow *above eye level*	Heavy drifting snow *above eye level*
Fog at a distance	Fog in patches	Fog sky visible *no major change in preceding hour*	Fog sky visible *no major change in preceding hour*	Fog sky obscured *no major change in preceding hour*	Fog sky obscured *no major change in preceding hour*	Fog sky obscured *no major change in preceding hour*	Fog, depositing rime ice or ice fog *sky visible*	Fog, depositing rime ice *sky visible*	Fog, depositing rime ice or ice fog *sky obscured*

Drizzle, not freezing

| *intermittent; slight at time of observation* | *continuous; slight at time of observation* | *intermittent; moderate at time of observation* | *continuous; moderate at time of observation* | *intermittent; heavy at time of observation* | *continuous; heavy at time of observation* | Drizzle, freezing, slight | Drizzle, freezing, moderate/heavy | Drizzle & rain, slight | Drizzle & rain, moderate/heavy |

Rain, not freezing

| *intermittent; slight at time of observation* | *continuous; slight at time of observation* | *intermittent; moderate at time of observation* | *continuous; moderate at time of observation* | *intermittent; heavy at time of observation* | *continuous; heavy at time of observation* | Rain, freezing, slight | Rain, freezing, moderate/heavy | Rain or drizzle & snow, slight | Rain or drizzle & snow, moderate/heavy |

Fall of snowflakes

| *intermittent; slight at time of observation* | *continuous; slight at time of observation* | *intermittent; moderate at time of observation* | *continuous; moderate at time of observation* | *intermittent; heavy at time of observation* | *continuous; heavy at time of observation* | Ice needles (± fog) | Snow grains (± fog) | Isolated star-like snow crystals (± fog) | Ice pellets (sleet) |

Rain & snow showers mixed

| *slight* | *moderate/heavy* | — | — | **Snow showers** *slight* | **Snow showers** *moderate/heavy* | Shower of snow pellets/small hail; ± rain or rain & snow mixed *slight* | Shower of snow pellets/small hail; ± rain or rain & snow mixed *moderate/heavy* | Shower of hail; ± rain or rain & snow mixed; no thunder *slight* | Shower of hail; ± rain or rain & snow mixed; no thunder *moderate/heavy* |

Rain showers *slight · moderate/heavy · violent*

Thunderstorm during preceding hour; not at time of observation

At observation: *w. slight rain* — *w. moderate or heavy rain* — *w. slight snow, or rain & snow mixed, or hail* — *w. moderate/heavy snow, or rain & snow mixed, or hail*

Thunderstorm at time of observation

slight/moderate, w. hail — *slight/moderate, w/o hail but w. rain ± snow* — *heavy without hail but w. rain ± snow* — *heavy, w. hail* — *with duststorm or sandstorm* — *heavy with hail*

[Source: NOAA, National Weather Service. The explanation of some symbols has been simplified.]

———————— ON FRAGMENTS OF TIME ————————

The Chancellor of France, Henri François d'Aguesseau (1668–1751), realized that his wife always kept him waiting a quarter of an hour after the dinner bell had rung, and resolved to devote this time to writing a book on jurisprudence. Over time, he completed this task in a work of four quarto volumes.

♣

SEVEN WAYS OF WASTING TIME
TO BE GUARDED AGAINST

1 .... *Indefinite musings*
2 ....*Anticipating needlessly*
3 ....*Needless speculations*
4 ....*Indulgence in reluctance*
                    to begin a duty
5 .... *In doubtful cases,*
                not deciding at once
6 .....*Musing needlessly on what has*
    been said or done, or what may be
7 ....*Spending time in reveries*
      which should be spent in prayer
    – MARY LYON, founder
    Mount Holyoke Female Seminary

♣

Moments are commonly used in a figurative sense; *seconds* only so applied occasionally; and *instants* always made to convey their direct, positive, and literal definition. A *prudent man* will pause a *moment*, before he undertakes any thing of importance, a *less experienced person* will not take a *second*, and a *fool* not an *instant*.
    – JOHN BRADY, *Clavis Calendaria*, 1812

♣

If time be of all things the most precious, wasting time must be the greatest prodigality.
    – BENJAMIN FRANKLIN (1706–90)

Lost wealth may be restored by INDUSTRY; the *wreck of health* regained by TEMPERANCE; *forgotten knowledge* restored by STUDY; *alienated friendship* smothered into FORGETFULNESS; even *forfeited reputation* won by PENITENCE and VIRTUE. But who ever looked upon his *vanished hours* – recalled his *slighted years* – stamped them with WISDOM – or effaced from Heaven's record the FEARFUL BLOT OF WASTED TIME?
    – ANON

♣

Time by moments, steals away,
First the hour, and then the day,
Small the daily loss appears,
Yet it soon amounts to years.
    – WATCH MOTTO (& HYMN)

♣

Time darks the sky,
Time brings the day,
Time glads the heart,
Time puffs all joys away;
Time builds a city,
and o'erthrows a nation,
Time writes a story
of their desolation.
Time hath a time
when I shall be no more,
Time makes poor men rich,
and rich men poor.
    – ANON

♣

When asked how he found the time to write books, Archbishop Michael Ramsey (1904–88) is said to have replied: 'Monday, a quarter of an hour; Tuesday, 10 minutes; Wednesday, rather better, half an hour; Thursday, not very good, but 10 minutes; Friday, a lull, an hour; Saturday, half an hour.'

TYPOGRAPHIC CONUNDRUM

	cur	*f*	*w*	*d*	*dis*	*and p*
A	SED	IEND	ROUGHT	EATH	EASE	AIN
	bles	*fr*	*b*	*br*	*and*	*ag*

THE HIPPOCRATIC OATH

The Greek physician Hippocrates (*c.*460–*c.*377 BC) – 'the father of medicine' – constructed an oath of ethics, to which his students pledged. Although the oath is now rarely sworn, the British Medical Assoc. estimates that about half of UK medical schools administer some form of ethical pledge.

I SWEAR by Apollo the physician and Æsculapius, and Hygeia, and Panacea, and all the gods and goddesses, that, according to my ability and judgment, I will keep this Oath and this stipulation – to reckon him who taught me this Art equally dear to me as my parents, to share my substance with him, and relieve his necessities if required; to look upon his offspring in the same footing as my own brothers, and to teach them this Art, if they shall wish to learn it, without fee or stipulation; and that by precept, lecture, and every other mode of instruction, I will impart a knowledge of the Art to my own sons, and those of my teachers, and to disciples bound by a stipulation and oath according to the law of medicine, but to none others. I will follow that system of regimen which, according to my ability and judgment, I consider for the benefit of my patients, and abstain from whatever is deleterious and mischievous. I will give no deadly medicine to anyone if asked, nor suggest any such counsel; and in like manner I will not give to a woman a pessary to produce abortion. With purity and with holiness I will pass my life and practice my Art. I will not cut persons laboring under the stone, but will leave this to be done by men who are practitioners of this work. Into whatever houses I enter, I will go into them for the benefit of the sick, and will abstain from every voluntary act of mischief and corruption; and, further, from the seduction of females or males, of freemen and slaves. Whatever, in connection with my professional practice, or not in connection with it, I see or hear, in the life of men, which ought not to be spoken of abroad, I will not divulge, as reckoning that all such should be kept secret. While I continue to keep this Oath unviolated, may it be granted to me to enjoy life and the practice of the Art, respected by all men, in all times. But should I trespass and violate this Oath, may the reverse be my lot.

————————— CHURCHILLIANA —————————

'Odd things, animals,' Winston Churchill is reported to have said, 'all dogs look up to you. All cats look down to you. Only a pig looks at you as an equal.' Below is a bestiary of the numerous animals Churchill owned:

1885 ....*Chloe* [dog]	1946–49 ...... 2 white kangaroos†
1895 ....*Pinky Poo* [dog]	1950s–60s .... racehorses:
1896 ... *Lily of the Valley* [polo pony]	*Colonist II, Pol Roger, Cyberine,*
1897 ....*Peas* [dog]	*Prince Arthur, Le Pretendant,*
1897 ....*Firefly* [polo pony]	*Vienna, High Hat, Canyon Kid,*
1920s .. *Jupiter* & *Juno* [white swans]	*Non Stop, Loving Cup, Gibraltar*
1920s .... various: black swans,	*III, Pigeon Vole, Pinnacle, First*
chickens, ducks, white pigs,	*Light, Planter's Punch, Holiday*
12 black pigs, cows, sheep	*Time, Sunstroke, Collusion, Tudor*
1930s ....*Punch* [Mary's pug]	*Monarch, Welsh Abbot, Halo,*
1930s .. *Trouble* [Sarah's brown spaniel]	*Galaxy, Aura, Punctuation, Release,*
1930s .. *Harvey* [Randolph's fox terrier]	*Seraph, Welsh Monk, Kemal,*
1930s ...... *Tango*, aka *Mr Cat* [cat]	*Alba, Novitiate, Why Tell, Satrap,*
1930s ....*Golden Orfe* [fish]	*Dark Issue, The Minstrel, Sunhat,*
1930s ....*Polly* [parrot]	*Aberdilla, Lupina, Honeycomb*
1934 ....bees	1951 ....robin
1935 ....*Mary* & *Sarah* [goats]	1950s ....*Jock* [ginger cat]
1935 .... 2 wallabies	1950s .. *Gabriel* [Clementine's Siamese]
1935 ....opossum	1950s–62...*Rufus* [red-brown poodle]
1940 ....*Nelson* [No. 10 cat]	1953–55 ....*Sheba*† [leopard]
1940 ..... *Smoky* [No. 10 'Annexe' cat]	1954 ....*Toby* [blue budgerigar]
Late 1940s.............tropical fish	1955–60...............*Rusty*† [lion]
1943–55 ....*Rota*† [lion]	† Animals were housed at London Zoo.

Below are some of the escapes and near misses of Churchill's charmed life:

Nearly died of pneumonia, aged 11 (1886, Brighton). ❦ Fell *c.*30' leaping off a bridge, and ruptured a kidney (1893, Branksome Dene). ❦ Came under fire, on his 21st birthday, observing Spanish forces fighting Cuban rebels (1895, Cuba). ❦ Escaped injury during fighting against Pathan tribesmen (1897, Mamund Valley, NW Frontier). ❦ Survived the British cavalry charge at the Battle of Omdurman (1898, Sudan). ❦ Captured after Boers attacked the armored train in which he was traveling as a war correspondent; he escaped from prison 3 weeks later (1899, S Africa). ❦ Narrowly missed by a German shell on the Western Front (1916, Ploegsteert, Belgium). ❦ Suffered minor injuries when his airplane crashed (1919, Croydon aerodrome). ❦ Hit by a car while looking the wrong way crossing 5th Avenue (1931, New York). ❦ Taken seriously ill with pneumonia (1943, Carthage). ❦ Almost decapitated by a concrete post as he leaned out of a train while traveling to Venice on holiday (1951, Italy).

—————————— CHURCHILLIANA cont. ——————————

Tabulated below are Winston Churchill's various addresses during his life:

48 Charles St	1874–79	16 Lower Berkeley St	1918
The Little Lodge, Dublin	1877–80	3 Tenterden St	1918
29 St James's Place	1880–82	1 Dean Trench St	1919–20
2 Connaught Place	1882–92	Templeton, Roehampton	1920
35A Great Cumberland Place		2 Sussex Square	1920–24
	1883–1900	Hosey Rigge, Westerham	1923–24
105 Mount St	1900–05	Chartwell, Westerham	1924–65
12 Bolton St	1905–09	11 Downing St	1925–29
22 Carlton House Terrace	1909	11 Morpeth Mansions	1932–39
33 Eccleston Sq.	1909–13; 1916–17	10 Downing St	1940–45; 1951–55
Admiralty House	1913–15; 1939–40	The No. 10 'Annexe'	1940–45
21 Arlington St	1915	28 Hyde Park Gate	1945–65
41 Cromwell Road	1915–16		
Lullenden, East Grinstead	1917–19	(Addresses are in London, unless noted.)	

Below are some of the many awards and decorations bestowed on Winston:

Knight Companion of the Most Noble Order of the Garter, 1953 ✻ The Order of Merit (Civil Division), 1946 ✻ The Order of the Companions of Honour, 1922 ✻ India Medal 1895–1902, with clasp ✻ Queen's Sudan Medal 1896–1898 ✻ Queen's South Africa Medal 1899–1902, with clasps ✻ 1914–1915 Star ✻ British War Medal 1914–1920 ✻ Victory Medal 1914–1919 ✻ 1939–1945 Star ✻ Africa Star, 1945 ✻ Italy Star, 1945 ✻ France and Germany Star, 1945 ✻ Defence Medal 1939–1945 ✻ War Medal 1939–1945 ✻ King George V Coronation Medal, 1911 ✻ King George V Silver Jubilee Medal, 1935 ✻ King George VI Coronation Medal, 1937 ✻ Queen Elizabeth II Coronation Medal, 1953 ✻ Territorial Decoration (King George V), 1924 ✻ Order of Military Merit, First Class, Spain, 1895 ✻ Grand Cordon of the Order of Leopold with Palm, Belgium, 1945 ✻ Knight Grand Cross, Order of the Lion of the Netherlands, 1946 ✻ Grand Cross, Order of the Oaken Crown, Luxembourg ✻ Grand Cross with Chain, Royal Norwegian Order of St Olav, 1948 ✻ Order of the Elephant, Denmark, 1950 ✻ Order of Liberation, France, 1958 ✻ Most Refulgent Order of the Star of Nepal, First Class, Nepal, 1961 ✻ Grand Sash of the High Order of Sayyid Mohammed bin Ali of Senoussi, 1962 ✻ Croix de Guerre 1939–1945, Belgium ✻ Medaille Militaire, Luxembourg, 1946 ✻ Medaille Militaire, France, 1947 ✻ Croix de Guerre 1939–1945, France ✻ Cuban Campaign Medal, Spain, 1895–1898 ✻ Khedive of Sudan's Medal, Egypt 1899, with clasp ✻ King Christian X Liberation Medal, Denmark, 1946

[Source: The Churchill Museum, in the subterranean Cabinet War Rooms, London, SW1]

──── ON GUESTS ────

A guest ought, on his *arrival*, to be CIVIL; POLITE, during the *first service*; GALLANT, in the *second*; TENDER at the *dessert*; and DISCREET, on *going away*.

– DICK HUMELBERGIUS SECUNDUS
Apician Morsels, 1829

──── TYPES OF SPIES ────

There are five kinds of spy: the LOCAL SPY, the INSIDE SPY, the REVERSE SPY, the DEAD SPY, and the LIVING SPY. ❦ When the five kinds of spies are all active, no one knows their routes. This is called organizational genius, and is valuable to the leadership. LOCAL SPIES are hired from among the people of a locality. INSIDE SPIES are hired from among enemy officials. REVERSE SPIES are hired from among enemy spies. DEAD SPIES transmit false intelligence to enemy spies. LIVING SPIES come back to report.

– SUN TZU, *The Art of War*, c6th BC

── BLASTING SIGNALS ──

1 long whistle … *3 minutes to blast*
2 short whistles.. *2 minutes to blast*
3 long whistles …………*all clear*

──── HEDGE FUN ────

The three types of hedge sold by Stephen Fry and Hugh Laurie are:
THE ROYAL, THE IMPERIAL, and THE STANDARD.

─ LOVE'S TELEGRAPH ─

If a GENTLEMAN wants a wife, he wears a ring on the first finger of the left hand; if he be engaged, he wears it on the second finger; if married, on the third; and on the fourth, if he never intends to be married. When a LADY is disengaged, she wears a hoop or diamond on the first finger; if married, on the third; and on the fourth, if she intends to die a maid. When a GENTLEMAN presents a flower, a fan, or a trinket to a lady, with the left hand, it is, on his part, an overture of regard; should she receive it with the left hand, it is considered as an acceptance of his esteem; but if with the right hand, it is a refusal of the offer. ♥ Thus by a few simple tokens, explained by rule, the passion of love is expressed; and, through the medium of the telegraph, the most diffident and timid man may, without difficulty, communicate his sentiments of regard for a LADY; and (in case his offer should be declined,) avoid experiencing the mortification of an explicit refusal.   – ANON

────── THE JUMP, THE GO, & THE FINISH ──────

The three stages of a c18th pub crawl were known as the JUMP (supper and wine), the GO (max or punch), and the FINISH (ale, grog, and coffee).

MATH TOAST

'The schoolmasters of London held a meeting in the year 1794, and after dinner the following toasts were given from the chair:'

Addition to the Whigs!
Subtraction from the Tories!
Multiplication to the
Friends of Peace!
Division to its Enemies!
Reduction to Abuses!
Rule of Three to King, Lords,
& Commons!
Practice to Reformation!
Fellowship to the Patriots!
Discount to the National Debt!
Decimal Fractions to the Clergy!

ON HOSPITALITY

Hospitality is threefold:

For one's FAMILY . . *this is of necessity*
For STRANGERS . . . . *this is of courtesy*
For the POOR . . . . *this is charity*

– THOMAS FULLER (1608–61)

WARM HOUSES

A house with a wife is often warm enough; a house with a wife and her mother is rather warmer than any spot on the known globe; a house with two mothers-in-law is so excessively hot, that it can be likened to no place on earth at all, but one must go lower for a simile.

– WILLIAM MAKEPEACE THACKERAY
A Shabby Genteel Story, 1840

TO DO AT ONCE

[1] *Shutting one's self up in a convent*, [2] *Marrying*, and [3] *Throwing one's self over a precipice* – are three things which must be done WITHOUT THINKING TOO MUCH ABOUT THEM.   – ANON

ON NOTES

A note of one page is usually an honest affair. A note of two pages is seldom frank. *It either says too much or not enough. Look out!* A note of three pages is generally weak, but may be honest. *Usually, burn it.* A note of four pages is designed to humbug. *Don't answer, but lock it up against the day when your supposed friend becomes your enemy.*
           – *Punch*, 1957

PLATO ON WISDOM

According to Plato (*c*.428–*c*.348 BC), *perfect wisdom* hath four parts, viz.:

WISDOM, the principle of doing things aright; JUSTICE, the principle of doing things equally in public and private; FORTITUDE, the principle of not flying danger, but meeting it; and TEMPERANCE, the principle of subduing desires, and living moderately.

MEN: THREE TYPES

The *Choleric* . . . . DRINKS
The *Melancholic* . . . . EATS
The *Phlegmatic* . . . . SLEEPS

TROLLOPE ON LEISURE TIME

When an *Englishman* has nothing to do, and a certain time to wait, his one resource is to walk about. A *Frenchman* sits down and lights a cigar, an *Italian* goes to sleep, a *German* meditates, an *American* invents some new position for his limbs as far as possible asunder from that intended for them by nature. – ANTHONY TROLLOPE, *The West Indies & the Spanish Main*, 1859

A TRILOGY OF SOUND ADVICE

A SOUND FAITH is the best *Divinity*; A GOOD CONSCIENCE the best *Law*;
And TEMPERANCE the best *Physic*. – ANON

THE SCULPTOR'S HOOF CODE

One of the more inexplicable and persistent pieces of modern folklore concerns a supposed 'secret code' of equestrian statues. For decades it has erroneously been claimed that the fate of the rider on such statues can be deduced from the number of hooves on the plinth:

Four hooves on the plinth ....*died of natural causes*
Three hooves on the plinth ....*died later of wounds received in battle*
Two hooves on the plinth.....................................*died in battle*

TRADITIONAL FASTING TERMS

Jejunium Generale ....a fast binding on all
Jejunium Consuetudinarium ....a local fast
Jejunium Poenitentiale..............................a fast by way of penance
Jejunium Votivum ....a fast consequent on a vow
Jejunium Voluntare ....for the better execution of an undertaking

Each of which could be observed in one of the following ways:

Jejunium Naturale.......... total abstinence (e.g., before receiving the Eucharist)
Abstinentia.....................certain food allowed, but several times a day
Jejunium cum Abstinentia ....the same food, taken once a day only
Jejunium sine Abstinentia.............all kinds of food, but only once a day

─── ROYAL COLORS ───

PURPLE · 'The royal color', purple's privileged associations stem from the ancient Mediterranean. There, a prized dye, perhaps of a deep raspberry, was created using marine mollusks of the genus *Murex* and *Purpura*. Since each mollusk produced only a few drops of ink, cloth so-colored was extremely expensive and restricted to the elite. In ancient Rome, purple was reserved (sometimes on pain of death) for the emperor, senior magistrates, military commanders, &c. Precise rules about who could wear purple varied by reign, though Nero is said to have been among its most zealous protectors. Byzantine rulers also favored the shade, and restricted its use†. Purple continued its association with royalty through the Middle Ages, and only lost its exclusivity when the first synthetic mauve dye was created in 1856.

RED · Crimson has long been the regal color of England, an association that derives from the uniforms of British soldiers and red Cross of St George. Red has also been the royal color of Korea and Malaysia.

BLUE · Blue was adopted by the kings of medieval France as a color of sacred authority, supposedly because high priests of ancient Israel wore robes of this shade. Of note is a hyacinth-blue robe dotted with gold *fleurs-de-lis* that was given to the French king as part of his coronation ceremony. George II selected blue for the Royal Navy's uniform after espying the Duchess of Bedford in a blue riding habit.

GREEN · Green was a key color for the Chinese Ming dynasty (1368–1644), who reserved it for imperial use. It is a royal color among Guatemalan weavers, because the ancient Maya (who once ruled the region) reserved the quetzal bird's blue-green feathers for royalty.

IMPERIAL YELLOW · A sunshine yellow called *ming huang* was adopted by China's imperial family in the 1650s during the Qing dynasty. The color represented the celestial nature of the royal bloodline, and its use was restricted to the imperial family. During the reign of Emperor Qianlong (1736–96), at the height of the dynasty, *ming huang* was worn only by the emperor, empress, and empress dowager, though others wore different yellows. *Jin huang*, a golden yellow, was worn by the emperor's sons and second- and third-degree consorts; *xiang se*, an incense yellow, by the two lowest degrees of consorts, the daughters of the emperor and the wives of his sons; and *xing huang*, an apricot yellow, by the crown prince and his consort.

† Children born to Byzantine emperors were said to be 'born in [or to] the purple', apparently after the porphyry lining the birthing rooms (porphyry is a purple stone). In the UK, 'purple airspace' once referred to an air exclusion zone around royal and VIP flights. ❦ Debate and speculation surround a number of these entries. [Various sources]

On The Various

STAGES

& DIVISIONS OF

~ LIFE ~

Perhaps the most famous division of life is that described by Shakespeare:

> *All the world's a stage,*
> *And all the men and women merely players:*
> *They have their exits and their entrances;*
> *And one man in his time plays many parts,*
> *His acts being seven ages. At first the* INFANT,
> *Mewling and puking in the nurse's arms.*
> *And then the whining* SCHOOLBOY, *with his satchel,*
> *And shining morning face, creeping like snail*
> *Unwillingly to school. And then the* LOVER,
> *Sighing like furnace, with a woeful ballad*
> *Made to his mistress' eyebrow. Then a* SOLDIER,
> *Full of strange oaths, and bearded like the pard,*
> *Jealous in honour, sudden and quick in quarrel,*
> *Seeking the bubble reputation*
> *Even in the cannon's mouth. And then the* JUSTICE,
> *In fair round belly with good capon lin'd,*
> *With eyes severe and beard of formal cut,*
> *Full of wise saws and modern instances;*
> *And so he plays his part. The sixth age shifts*
> *Into the lean and slipper'd* PANTALOON,
> *With spectacles on nose and pouch on side,*
> *His youthful hose, well sav'd, a world too wide*
> *For his shrunk shank; and his big manly voice,*
> *Turning again toward childish treble, pipes*
> *And whistles in his sound. Last scene of all,*
> *That ends this strange eventful history,*
> *Is* SECOND CHILDISHNESS *and mere oblivion,*
> *Sans teeth, sans eyes, sans taste, sans everything.*

– *As You Like It*, II vii [see p.145 & p.152]

———— ON THE STAGES OF LIFE cont. ————

According to Manly P. Hall's *Astrological Keywords* (1931), Shakespeare's delineation of the ages of man may be based upon the astrological divisions of Hermes Trismegistus, Claudius Ptolemy, and Proclus (AD 410–485), viz:

Age	years	governed by		keyword
Infancy	0–4	The Moon	☽	growth
Childhood	5–14	Mercury	☿	education
Youthhood or adolescence	15–22	Venus	♀	emotion
Young manhood	23–41	The Sun	☉	virility
Mature manhood	42–56	Mars	♂	ambition
Old age	57–68	Jupiter	♃	reflection
Decrepit age	69–	Saturn	♄	resignation

The Athenian statesman Solon (*c.*638–*c.*558 BC) described 10 divisions of life:

0–7	the boy, still an infant, grows and loses his milk teeth
7–14	a child; signs of maturity appear; he arrives toward puberty
14–21	his limbs develop; a beard grows upon his chin
21–28	he arrives at his full strength, and proves his manly valor
28–35	he begins to think of a wife, children, and his future prosperity
35–42	his mind is fit for all things and no longer cares for trivialities
42–49 49–56	his understanding and speech are at their zenith
56–63	some powers remain, but eloquence and wisdom are diminished
63–70	at 70, he makes preparations for a not untimely death

SPRING = *boyhood* = moist & hot = air & blood
SUMMER = *early manhood* = hot & dry = fire & red bile
AUTUMN = *manhood* = cold & dry = earth & melancholy
WINTER = *old men* = cold & moist = water & black bile
– *adapted from* BYRHTFERTH'S MANUAL, AD 1011

At 20 years of age, a man thinks contentment in money matters, as well as in all else, *a sorry thing*; at 30, he *ceases to despise* whatever he is and has; at 40, tolerably well off, he feels that he could really be satisfied with *a very little more*; at 50, he has learnt thoroughly to understand what a blessing a *contented mind* must be; at 60, continuing as wealthy as he ever was, be the amount of his worldly riches what it may, he must be a *covetous old fool* if he is not there content.
– T.C. HENLEY
A Handful of Paper Shavings, 1861

YOUTH is a *blunder* – MANHOOD a *struggle* – OLD AGE a *regret*.
– BENJAMIN DISRAELI (1804–81)

———————— ON THE STAGES OF LIFE cont. ————————

St Isidore of Seville (*c.*560–636 BC) outlined the following six stages of life:

Infantia	0–7	Iuventus	28–50
Pueritia	7–14	Auetus senioris/gravitas	50–70
Adolescentia	14–28	Senectus	70–

Hippocrates (*c.*460–377 BC) is credited (perhaps erroneously) with these seven:

Infant (*paidion*)	0–7	Man (*aner*)	29–49
Child (*pais*)	8–14	Elderly (*presbytes*)	50–56
Boy (*meirakion*)	15–21	Old (*geron*)	57–
Youth (*neaniskos*)	22–28	[see also p.137]	

Aristotle (384–322 BC) conceived of three stages of life: YOUTH (growth), MIDDLE AGE (stasis), and OLD AGE (decline). ❦ Horace (65–8 BC) described four stages – the CHILD (*puer*), the BEARDLESS YOUTH (*inberbus iuvenis*), the MAN (*aetas virilis*), the OLD MAN (*senex*) – and at least one medieval commentator asserted that he wrote different types of poems for each age: *Odes, Ars Poetica, Satires,* and *Epistles,* respectively. ❦ Seneca (*c.*4 BC–AD 65) observed, 'Life is a voyage, in the progress of which, we are perpetually changing our scenes; we first leave childhood behind us, then youth, then the years of ripened manhood, then the better and more pleasing part of old age'.

In *Observations on the Origin of the Division of Man's Life into Stages* (1861), J. W. Jones gave two examples from ancient Jewish law in the Mishna:

> *A son of 5 years of age shall be put to study the law; of 10 years to the Mishna; of 13 years to the observance of the commandments; of 15 years to the Talmud; of 18 years to be married; of 20 years to seek his living; at 30 years he comes to strength; at 40 years to wisdom; at 50 years to give counsel; at 60 years he becomes old; at 70 years he comes to a gray old age; at 80 years to a great age; at 90 years to a decrepit age. He who is 100 years old is as though he were gone by and already out of the world.*

Jones's second example compared the divisions of man's life to animals:

At 1	*he resembles a* KING *on a dais whom everyone kisses and adores*
At 2 or 3	*he resembles a* PIG *routing in dirt*
At 10	*he capers about like a* GOAT
At 20	*a neighing* HORSE, *he attires himself and looks out for a wife*
With children	*he must find food and is therefore as impudent as a* DOG
Grown old	*he gets like a* MONKEY *– but only the ignorant man: whereas of the wise man Scripture says, 'King David was old' – old but still a king*

─────── ON THE STAGES OF LIFE cont. ───────

Vedic philosophy divides our life span into four *ashrams* (literally, 'shelters'):

Brahmacharya	'celibacy'	0–25		*Vanaprastha*	'hermitage'	50–75
Grahasta	'householder'	25–50		*Sanyasa*	'renunciate'	75–100

There is a traditional German rhyme that divides man's stages of life thus:

Zehn Jahr ein Kind,	For ten years a child
Zwanzig Jahr ein Jüngling,	At twenty years, a youth
Dreißig Jahr ein Mann,	At thirty years a man
Vierzig Jahr wohlgetan,	At forty years, done well
Fünfzig Jahr stille stahn,	At fifty years, standing still
Sechzig Jahr geht's Alter an,	At sixty years, old sage starts
Siebzig Jahr ein Greis,	At seventy years, a wise old man
Achtzig Jahr nimmer weis,	At eighty years, no more wisdom
Neunzig Jahr der Kinder Spott,	At ninety years, the scorn of children
Hundert Jahre gnade Gott.	At hundred years, God have mercy

In *Il Convito*, Dante (1265–1321) listed four stages (*quatro etadi*) of a life not cut short by premature death:

Adolescenzata	'adolescence'	0–25
Gioventute	'maturity'	25–45
Senettute	'old age'	45–70
Senio	'senility'	70–*c*.80

⁂

According to the Spanish proverb:
He that is not gallant at 20,
strong at 30, rich at 40,
or experienced at 50 will NEVER
be gallant, strong, rich, or prudent.

⁂

At 20	A PEACOCK
At 30	A LION
At 40	A CAMEL
At 50	A SERPENT
At 60	A DOG
At 70	A MONKEY
At 80	NOTHING AT ALL

– ? BALTASAR GRACIÁN (1601–58)

This 'Dial of Life' was conceived
by Granville Penn, 1812

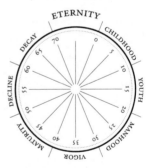

⁂

'It is a novel but a true observation...'

At 10	*we are led by* A BAUBLE
At 20	A MISTRESS
At 30	INDOLENCE
At 40	AMBITION
At 50	AVARICE

– attributed to ROUSSEAU, 1777

─────── ON THE STAGES OF LIFE cont. ───────

The following is taken from *The Youth's Miscellaneous Sketch Book* (1829):

1–7	**CHILDHOOD** *the age of accidents, griefs, wants, sensibilities*	1–7
8–14	**ADOLESCENCE** *the age of hopes, improvidence, curiosity, impatience*	8–14
15–21	**PUBERTY** *the age of triumphs, desires, self-love, independence, and vanity*	15–21
22–28	**YOUTH** *the age of pleasure, love, sensuality, inconstancy, enthusiasm*	22–28
29–35	**MANHOOD** *the age of enjoyments, ambition, and the play of the passions*	29–35
36–42	**MIDDLE AGE** *the age of consistency, desire of fortune and of glory*	36–42
43–49	**MATURE AGE** *the age of possessions, the reign of wisdom, reason, and love of property*	43–49
50–56	**DECLINE OF LIFE** *the age of reflection, love of tranquility, foresight, and prudence*	50–56
57–63	**COMMENCEMENT OF OLD AGE** *the age of regrets, cares, inquietudes, ill temper, and desire of ruling*	57–63
64–70	**OLD AGE** *the age of infirmities, exigencies, love of authority, and submission*	64–70
71–77	**DECREPITUDE** *the age of avarice, jealousy, and envy*	71–77
78–84	**CADUCITY** *the age of distrust, vain boasting, unfeelingness, suspicion*	78–84
85–91	**AGE OF FAVOR** *the age of insensibility, love of flattery, of attention, and indulgence*	85–91
92–98	**AGE OF WONDER** *the age of indifference, and love of praise*	92–98
99–105	**PHENOMENON** *the age of insensibility, hope, and the last sigh*	99–105

In 2002, the deranged then-leader of Turkmenistan, President Saparmurat Niyazov (Turkmenbashi the Great), declared that his country would return to the traditional 'clearer and more reasoned division of the ages of man':

Childhood....................0–13	White-bearded elder........72–85
Adolescence.................13–25	Old age......................85–97
Youth.......................25–37	Age of Oguz Khan‡........97–109
Age of maturity.............37–49	
Age of the prophet..........49–62	† Niyazov was 62 when he made his decree.
Age of inspiration†..........62–72	‡ A founder of the early Turkmen states.

─────── ON THE STAGES OF LIFE cont. ───────

THE ELEVEN (DIETARY) AGES OF MAN
– variously quoted, including in *The Rotarian*, 1951

Milk
Milk and bread
Milk, eggs, bread, and spinach
Oatmeal, bread and butter, green apples, all-day suckers
Ice cream sodas and hot dogs
Minute steak, fried potatoes, coffee, and apple pie
Bouillon, roast duck, scalloped potatoes, creamed broccoli,
fruit salad, divinity fudge, and demitasse
Pâté de foie gras, Wiener Schnitzel, potato Parisienne,
eggplant á L'Opera, demitasse, Roquefort cheese
Two soft-boiled eggs, toast, and milk
Crackers and milk
Milk

⁂

Anthony Powell's 12-volume *roman fleuve* ('river novel'), *A Dance to the Music of Time*, paints a picture both of the C20th, and of the divisions of life:

⁂

THE 10 SEVEN YEARS OF LIFE
– David Bepler, *Bepler's Handy Manual of Knowledge and Useful Information*, 1890

7	Seven years in childhood's sport and play	7
14	Seven years in school from day to day	14
21	Seven years at trade or college life	21
28	Seven years to find and place a wife	28
35	Seven years to pleasure's follies given	35
42	Seven years by business hardly driven	42
49	Seven years for fame, a wild-goose chase	49
56	Seven years for wealth, a bootless race	56
63	Seven years for hoarding for your heir	63
70	Seven years in weakness spent, and care	70
—	*Then die and go you know not where.*	—

——— ON THE STAGES OF LIFE cont. ———

The following schematic is attributed to Karl Friedrich Burdach (1776–1847):

Stages	*weeks*	YEARS	WEEKS	DAYS	*natural epoch*	*age*
	40	–	40	–	Lactation	} CHILDHOOD
I	400	7	34	6	Milk teeth	
2	800	15	27	3	Childhood	} YOUTH
3	1,200	23	–	–	Youth	
4	1,600	30	34	5	Maturity	} MIDDLE AGE
5	2,000	38	17	2		
6	2,400	45	52	–		
7	2,800	53	34	–		} DECLINE
8	3,200	61	17	1		
9	3,600	68	51	6		
10	4,000	76	3	3		

'If you be 20 years of age, *one third* of your life is already gone; if you be 30, *one half* of it is already behind you; and if you be 50, you have but poor 10 or 20 years to see the sun, and sojourn among the sons of men. Of the time that is gone, you cannot now call back one hour, undo one single action, nor recover so much as a moment to live it over again, though all the joys of heaven, and all the torments of hell, depended upon its return.'

– 'RIDDOCH'

∴ ∴ ∴

0–7 . . . . INFANCY
7–14 . . . . CHILDHOOD
14–22 . . . . STRIPLING AGE
22–34 . . . . YOUNG MAN
34–60 . . . . MAN'S AGE
60–74 . . . . . . FLOURISHING OLD AGE
74+ . . . . DECREPIT OLD AGE

– WILLIAM VAUGHAN

∴ ∴ ∴

There are but three ages of man:

JUVENILE ☞ VIRILE ☞ SENILE

– TRADITIONAL

1st . . . . Infancy, 7 months
2nd . . . . Childhood, 7 years
3rd . . . Boyhood to Puberty, 14 years
4th . . . . Youth, to 21 years
5th . . . . Manhood, to 42 years
6th . . . . Zenith stage, to 49 years
7th . . . . Declination, to 70 years

– the allotted Age of Man! thence, with patriarchal strength, the old man may progress, but mark, he dies! This is a remarkable fact, that at the end of every 7 years of human life, there is a radical change in the physical system, which is acknowledged by the connoisseurs of every age, and verified in the experience of mankind to the latest period of time, the secret movings of which, mysterious are to us; and ever shall remain, well known alone to Him, with whom we have to do, whose mighty workings were at first, in secret wrought; the hidden source of which, our Father still retains, to carry out His wondrous scheme of Nature, and of Grace!

– JOHN WRIGHT, 1760

———— ON THE STAGES OF LIFE cont. ————

He who DIES NOT in his 23rd year,
DROWNS NOT in his 24th,
and is SLAIN NOT in his 25th,
may boast of GOOD DAYS.
 – DUTCH PROVERB

⁘ ⁘ ⁘

'The seven ages of man have been well tabulated by someone or other on an acquisitive basis' – according to the *International Horseshoers' Monthly Magazine*, October 1918:

1st AGE	Sees the earth
2nd	Wants it
3rd	Hustles to get it
4th	Decides to be satisfied with only about half of it
5th	Becomes still more moderate
6th	Now content to be satisfied with a six-by-two strip of it
7th	Gets the strip

⁘ ⁘ ⁘

A man of 30 years of age is like a LION; a man 40 years old is like a TORN, WORN MAT; and a man 60 years of age is a FOOL.
 – Kashmiri proverb

⁘ ⁘ ⁘

At 10 a CHILD, at 20 WILD,
At 30 TAME, or NEVER,
At 40 WISE, at 50 RICH
At 60 GOOD, or NEVER.

⁘ ⁘ ⁘

The various seasons of the year,
As they successively appear
Life's stages, as they roll, display,
And much morality convey.
In SPRING we *bud*,
In SUMMER *blow*,
And in the prime of manhood glow;
In AUTUMN we in *part decay*,
And WINTER *sweeps us quite away*.
 – ANON

In 1857, Sir John Bowring, the 4th Governor of Hong Kong, wrote: 'The Chinese divisions or epochs of life are marked by decennial periods, or progress decimally' – viz:

10	Opening degree
20	Youth expired
30	Strength and marriage
40	Officially apt [sic]
50	Error knowing
60	Cycle closing
70	Rare bird of age
80	Rusty visaged
90	Delayed
100	Age's extremity

⁘ ⁘ ⁘

ACT 1	*The state of innocence*
ACT 2	*The passions*
ACT 3	*The love of study*
ACT 4	*Ambition*
ACT 5	*Devotion and quiet*

 – ANON

⁘ ⁘ ⁘

At 10 years	a wonder child
At 15	a talented youth
At 20	a common man

 – JAPANESE PROVERB

⁘ ⁘ ⁘

0–7	infancy
7–14	childhood
14–21	youth
21–35	stayed youth
35–45/49	manhood
49–62/63	green old age
63–97	decrepit old age

 – JAMES HART, 1633

⁘ ⁘ ⁘

Bowel problems seem to be universal, lending some credence to the idea that there are three ages of man – SEX, MONEY, and BOWELS – in that order. – DR L. E. LAMB, 1970

The stages of women's lives were often divided into simple triads, such as:

MAIDEN ☞ MOTHER ☞ CRONE
VIRGIN MAIDEN ☞ LOYAL WIFE ☞ GRIEVING WIDOW
PRE-MENSTRUATION ☞ MENSTRUATION ☞ POST-MENSTRUATION

George Elgar Hicks (1824–1914) painted a triptych of a *Woman's Mission*:

Guide of Childhood ☞ *Companion of Manhood* ☞ *Comfort of Old Age*

Similarly, Goldie Hawn, as Elise Elliot in *The First Wives Club* (1996), said:

'There are only three ages of women in Hollywood …
BABE, DISTRICT ATTORNEY, and DRIVING MISS DAISY.'

In her 1995 book, *Coda*, Thea Astley described the four stages of woman:

BIMBO ☞ BREEDER ☞ BABYSITTER ☞ BURDEN

And the German satirist Johann Fischart (*c.*1545–91) proposed this octad:

At 10 .... A CHILD	At 50 ....A GRANDMOTHER
At 20 ....A MAID	At 60 ....AGE-WORN
At 30 ....A WIFE	At 70 .... DEFORMED
At 40 .... A MATRON	At 80 ..... BARREN & GROWN COLD

In 1882, *Punch* published this septad by a *Cantankerous Old Curmudgeon*:

All the world's a wardrobe,
And all the girls and women merely wearers:
They have their fashions and their fantasies,
And one she in her time wears many garments
Throughout her Seven Stages. First, the baby,
Befrilled and broidered, in her nurse's arms.
And then the trim-hosed schoolgirl, with her flounces
& small-boy-scorning face, tripping, skirt-waggling,
Coquettishly to school. And then the flirt,
Ogling like Circe, with a business oeillade
Kept on her low-cut corset. Then a bride
Full of strange finery, vestured like an angel,
Veiled vaporously, yet vigilant of glance,
Seeking the Woman's heaven, Admiration,

Even at the Altar's steps. And then the matron,
In fair rich velvet with suave satin line,
With eyes severe, and skirts of youthful cut
Full of dress-saws and modish instances,
To teach her girls their part. The sixth age shifts
Into the grey yet gorgeous grandmamma
With gold pinz-nez on nose and fan at side,
Her youthful tastes still strong, and worldly wise
In sumptuary law, her quavering voice
Prosing of Fashion and Le Follet, pipes
Of robes and bargains rare. Last scene of all,
That ends the Sex's Mode-swayed history,
Is second childishness and sheer oblivion
Of youth, taste, passion, all – save love of Dress!

The poet Samuel Taylor Coleridge remarked: 'There are three classes into which all the women past seventy that ever I knew were to be divided:'

THAT DEAR OLD SOUL / THAT OLD WOMAN / THAT OLD WITCH

———————— ON THE STAGES OF LIFE cont. ————————

Lord Askwith is said to have devised this division of life at the age of 67:

At 10 ....A boy begins to think
At 20 .... He thinks he is a man
At 30 ....He thinks he ought to be married, if he is not
At 40 .... He is in the prime of life
At 50 .... He begins to think of the future
At 60 .... He is again in the prime of life
At 70 .... He thinks he will wait and see
At 80 .... Well, I don't know what he is

⁂

In the 1950s Sir John Gielgud pioneered a one-man show of Shakespeare readings – based on George Ryland's 1939 anthology, *The Ages of Man*. Below is the program listing from *The Best* [American] *Plays of 1958–59*:

I · YOUTH · *Childhood · Magic & Faery · Love · Jealousy · Lust*
As You Like It · Hamlet I ii · Sonnet 11 · *A Midsummer Night's Dream* II i · *The Tempest* III ii
Romeo & Juliet I iv & V i · *The Merchant of Venice* V i · *Much Ado About Nothing* II iii
Sonnet 18 · *Romeo & Juliet* I v · Sonnet 116 · Sonnet 130 · *Romeo & Juliet* II vi & III v
The Winter's Tale I ii · Sonnet 129 · *Measure for Measure* II ii

II · MANHOOD · *War · Civil Strife · Kingship · Government & Society · Passion & Character*
Othello I iv · *Henry IV Part 1* I iii · *Henry VI Part 3* II v
Richard II III iii & IV i · *Julius Caesar* I ii · Sonnets to Sundry · *Hamlet* II ii

III · OLD AGE · *Sickness · Man Against Himself · Old Age · Death · Time*
Sonnet 138 · Sonnet 73 · *Macbeth* II · *Henry IV Part 2* III i · *Richard III* I iv
Richard II II i · *Measure for Measure* III i · *Julius Caesar* II ii
Hamlet II ii, III i, & V ii · Sonnet 29 · *Romeo & Juliet* V iii · *King Lear* V iii
The Tempest IV i, V i, & Epilogue · *Much Ado About Nothing* V iii

⁂

Writing in the *Sunday Times*, on July 5, 2009, A. A. Gill noted, 'I've often thought that Europe is an allegory for the ages of man', and explained:

You're born ITALIAN. *They're relentlessly infantile and mother-obsessed. In childhood, we're* ENGLISH: *chronically shy, tongue-tied, cliquey, and only happy kicking balls, pulling the legs off things, or sending someone to Coventry. Teenagers are* FRENCH: *pretentiously philosophical, embarrassingly vain, ridiculously romantic and insincere. Then, in middle age, we become either* SWISS *or* IRISH. *Old age is* GERMAN: *ponderous, pompous and pedantic. Then finally we regress into being* BELGIAN, *with no idea who we are at all.*

INDEX

'Kindly look her up in my index, doctor,' murmured Holmes, without opening his eyes. For many years he had adopted a system of docketing all paragraphs concerning men and things, so that it was difficult to name a subject or a person on which he could not at once furnish information. In this case I found her biography sandwiched in between that of a Hebrew Rabbi [see p.97] and that of a staff-commander who had written a monograph upon the deep-sea fishes.

– ARTHUR CONAN DOYLE, *A Scandal in Bohemia*, 1891

& – BORTLE SCALE

BRAHMINS – EVANS, SIR HAROLD

—— 'KAMA SUTRA' – PIPE SMOKING, PERILS OF ——

❧

British journalist Keith Waterhouse (1929–2009) was a Fleet Street legend. A prolific columnist for the *Mirror* and the *Mail*, he was also a talented author, playwright, and drinker. Additionally, Waterhouse was responsible for the best (only?) joke about indexes: 'Should not the Society of Indexers be know as "Indexers, Society of, The"?'

————— AN AUTHORIAL MISCELLANY —————

Date of birth	26 v 1974
Time of birth	02:07
Star sign	Gemini · Ⅱ
Chinese zodiac animal	Tiger
Birth stone	emerald
Birth flower	lily of the valley
Patron Saint	Francis de Sales
Angelic governor	Ambriel
Belief in astrology	nil
Eye color	brown
Spectacle prescription	Sph –0.50; Cyl –0.50; Axis 85°
Height	*c.*5'8"
Weight	*c.* 10 stone 10
Fillings	none
Scars	ax wound, left hallux
Glasgow Coma Score	15
Mini Mental Score	30/30
Plantar responses	flexor
Allergies	none known
Tattoos	none
Phobias	spiders, typos
Handedness	right
Hair color	black
Collar size	15½"
Sleeve length	32½"
Hat size	7¼
Shoe size	9½
Socks	red
Spouse	1×♀ (♍)
Siblings	1×♂ (18 x 1971)
Godchildren	1½
Superstitious	very
Side of bed	left
Rock, paper, scissors?	scissors

Coffee	black, no sugar
Tea	mahogany, no sugar
Cup or mug?	cup for tea; mug for coffee
Sweet or savory	savory
Marmite	♥
Dining at Chick & Nello's?	have the roast chicken
BBC radio stations	4,7,5,6,2,3,1
Favorite color	lavender
Favorite word	crayon
Fonts	Adobe Garamond Pro & Monotype Old Style Outline
Lucky number	42
Reading room	Humanities 2
Pen or pencil?	pen
Pets	penguin, dodo
Operating system	osx 10·6·6
DTP software	InDesign cs4
Highest snooker break	16
Hockey position	left back
Handicap	28(+!)
Glass half	full
Stimulant	$C_8H_{10}N_4O_2$
Life after death	probably not
007	Sean Connery
London buses	210, 214, 268, c2
NYC subways	1/2/9; A/C/E
Tie knot	four-in-hand
Hammond	B-3
Cymbals	Zildjian
Morning or night?	morning
Muppet(s)	Statler & Waldorf
Desert island	Lo Scoglio, Nerano
Swings or roundabouts?	swings

I want to delight in the smallest of things, a bit of moss two centimeters in diameter on a little piece of rock, and I want to try here what I have been wishing for so long, namely to copy these tiniest bits of nothing as accurately as possible just to realize how great they are.

— M[AURITS] C[ORNELIS] ESCHER (1898–1972)